Exploring
Romans

A DEVOTIONAL COMMENTARY

GEORGE R. KNIGHT

REVIEW AND HERALD® PUBLISHING ASSOCIATION
Since 1861 | www.reviewandherald.com

The author assumes full responsibility for the accuracy of all facts and quotations as cited in this book.

All Bible texts quoted are the author's unless otherwise noted.

Bible texts credited to ESV are from the *English Standard Version* of the Bible, copyright © 2001, by Crossway Bibles, a division of Good News Publications. Used by permission.

Bible texts credited to Goodspeed are from Smith and Goodspeed, *The Complete Bible: An American Translation.* Copyright © 1939 by the University of Chicato Press.

Bible texts credited to Jerusalem are from *The Jerusalem Bible,* copyright © 1966 by Darton, Longman & Todd, Ltd., and Doubleday & Company, Inc. Used by permission of the publisher.

Bible texts credited to KJV are from the King James Version of the Bible.

Texts credited to Message are from *The Message.* Copyright © by Eugene H. Peterson 1993, 1994, 1995, 1996, 2000, 2001, 2002. Used by permission of NavPress Publishing Group.

Bible texts credited to Moffat are from: *The Bible: A New Translation,* by James Moffatt. Copyright by James Moffatt 1954. Used by permission of Harper & Row Publishers, Incorporated.

Scripture quotations marked NASB are from the *New American Standard Bible,* copyright © 1960, 1962, 1963, 1968, 1971, 1972, 1973, 1975, 1977, 1994. by The Lockman Foundation. Used by permission.

Texts credited to NEB are from *The New English Bible.* © The Delegates of the Oxford University Press and the Syndics of the Cambridge University Press 1961, 1970. Reprinted by permission.

Texts credited to NIV are from the *Holy Bible, New International Version.* Copyright © 1973, 1978, 1984, International Bible Society. Used by permission of Zondervan Bible Publishers.

Texts credited to NKJV are from the New King James Version. Copyright © 1979, 1980, 1982 by Thomas Nelson, Inc. Used by permission. All rights reserved.

Scripture quotations marked NLT are taken from the *Holy Bible,* New Living Translation, copyright © 1996. Used by permission of Tyndale House Publishers, Inc., Wheaton, Illinois 60189. All rights reserved.

Bible texts credited to NRSV are from the New Revised Standard Version of the Bible, copyright © 1989 by the Division of Christian Education of the National Council of the Churches of Christ in the U.S.A. Used by permission.

Bible texts credited to Phillips are from J.B. Phillips: *The New Testament in Modern English,* Revised Edition. © J. B. Phillips 1958, 1960, 1972. Used by permission of Macmillan Publishing Co.

Texts credited to REB are from *The Revised English Bible.* Copyright © Oxford University Press and Cambridge University Press, 1989. Reprinted by permission.

Bible texts credited to RSV are from the Revised Standard Version of the Bible, copyright © 1946, 1952, 1971, by the Division of Christian Education of the National Council of the Churches of Christ in the U.S.A. Used by permission.

Bible texts credited to TEV are from the *Good News Bible*—Old Testament: Copyright © American Bible Society 1976, 1992; New Testament: Copyright © American Bible Society 1966, 1971, 1976, 1992.

Texts credited to Weymouth are from Richard Francis Weymouth, *The New Testament in Modern Speech* (London: James Clarke & Co., 1903).

Texts credited to Wuest are from Kenneth S. Wuest, *The New Testament: An Expanded Translation.* Grand Rapids: Erdmans, 1961. Reprinted 1994. Originally *Wuest's Expanded Translation of the Greek New Testament,* 1956-1959.

This book was
Edited by Gerald Wheeler
Cover designed by Left Coast Design
Cover illustration by Jerry Blank
Electronic makeup by Tina M. Ivany
Typeset: 11/14 Bembo

PRINTED IN U.S.A.

14 13 12 11 10   5 4 3 2 1

Library of Congress Cataloging-in-Publication Data
Knight, George R.
 Exploring Romans : a devotional commentary / George R. Knight.
   p. cm.
 1. Bible. N.T. Romans—Commentaries. I. Title.
 BS2665.53.K55 2010
 227'.1077—dc22
                                        2009046611

ISBN 978-0-8280-2503-4

Dedicated to

Bonnie and Ray Bowman,
a much appreciated
daughter and "son"

Other books by George R. Knight (selected):

A Brief History of Seventh-day Adventists
A Search for Identity:
The Development of the Seventh-day Adventist Beliefs
A User-friendly Guide to the 1888 Message
Ellen White's World
I Used to Be Perfect (Andrews University Press)
If I Were the Devil
Joseph Bates: The Real Founder of Seventh-day Adventism
Lest We Forget
Meeting Ellen White
Millennial Fever and the End of the World (Pacific Press)
*Organizing for Mission and Growth: The Development of Adventist Church
    Structure*
Reading Ellen White
Sin and Salvation
The Apocalyptic Vision and the Neutering of Adventism
The Cross of Christ
Walking With Paul Through the Book of Romans
Walking With Ellen White

The Exploring Series
    Exploring Ecclesiastes & Song of Solomon
    Exploring Galatians & Ephesians
    Exploring Hebrews
    Exploring the Letter of John & Jude
    Exploring Mark

A study guide to *Exploring Romans* is available on adventistbookcenter.com.

Forthcoming Exploring volumes
    Exploring Daniel
    Exploring Thessalonians

To order, call 1-800-765-6955.

Visit us at www.reviewandherald.com for information on other
Review and Herald® products.

Contents

Exploring the "Exploring" Idea

Exploring Romans is the sixth volume in a series of user-friendly commentaries aimed at helping people understand the Bible better. While the books have the needs and abilities of laypeople in mind, they will also prove beneficial to pastors and other church leaders. Beyond individual readers, the "Exploring" format will be helpful for church study groups and in enriching participation in midweek meetings.

Each volume is best thought of as a devotional commentary. While the treatment of each passage seeks to develop its exegetical meaning, it does not stop there but moves on to practical application in the daily life of believers in the twenty-first century.

Rather than focusing on the details of each verse, the "Exploring" volumes seek to give readers an understanding of the themes and patterns of each biblical book as a whole and how each passage fits into its context. As a result, they do not attempt to solve all of the problems or answer all the questions related to a given portion of Scripture.

In an effort to be user-friendly these devotional commentaries on the Old and New Testaments present the entire text of each biblical book treated. The volumes divide the text into "bite-sized" portions that are included immediately before the comments on the passage. Thus readers do not have to flip back and forth between their Bibles and the commentary.

The commentary sections aim at being long enough to significantly treat a topic, but short enough for individual, family, or group readings.

The translation of each New Testament book is my own, and claims no special merit. Although I have based it on the original languages, in making it I have conferred with several English versions. While not being a "technical achievement," the translation has sought to take every significant translational problem and issue into consideration and to remain as close as possible to the original text of the Bible. In order to accomplish that goal the translation employs word-for-word translation wherever possible but utilizes thought-for-thought translation when word-for-word fails adequately to carry God's message from the original languages and cultures into modern English.

George R. Knight
Rogue River, Oregon

Foreword

Martin Luther wrote of Romans that "this Epistle is really the chief part of the New Testament and the very purest Gospel, and is worthy not only that every Christian should know it word for word, by heart, but occupy himself with it every day, as the daily bread of the soul. It can never be read or pondered too much, and the more it is dealt with the more precious it becomes, and the better it tastes" (Luther, *Commentary on Romans,* p. xiii).

Like Luther, the letter of Paul to the Romans has always been one of my favorite books in the Bible. I fulfilled a dream of mine some years ago when I wrote a daily devotional entitled *Walking With Paul Through the Book of Romans* (2002). That book took my fellow travelers through 365 days of meditation on what is not only the Bible's most complete explanation of the plan of salvation, but perhaps the most influential single document in world history.

Exploring Romans moves beyond the devotional approach to one in which I systematically unfold the progression of Paul's argument step by step throughout the letter's 16 chapters. Having spent much of my Christian life meditating and studying on the meaning and implications of Romans, I am convinced more than ever of the book's importance for the life of every person who has ever sinned. And that means all of us.

One can read this devotional commentary as a freestanding book or it can be utilized with the on-line study guide developed to accompany it. The study guide to *Exploring Romans* will provide those who use it with an opportunity to let the biblical book speak to them personally through structured questions before they turn to the commentary itself. (To download and print the free study guide, go to www.AdventistBookCenter.com, find the book *Exploring Romans*, then "Click for Details" and follow the instructions for downloading the study guide.)

I would like to express my appreciation to my wife, who typed my handwritten manuscript; and Gerald Wheeler and Jeannette R. Johnson, who shepherded the manuscript through the publication process.

I trust that *Exploring Romans* will be a blessing to each of its readers as they seek to learn more of their Lord and as they put that knowledge into practice in daily living.

Exploring
Romans

Introduction to the Book of Romans

What a book! Paul's letter to the Romans stands at the very center of Western history. Protestant James Dunn points out that it is the "first well-developed theological statement by a Christian theologian which has come down to us, and one which has had incalculable influence on the framing of Christian theology ever since—arguably the single most important work of Christian theology ever written" (in Hawthorne, p. 838). And Roman Catholic scholar Joseph Fitzmyer claims that it is probably the most important book in the New Testament. "The impact that this letter has had on the history of the Christian church is incalculable . . . In fact, one can almost write the history of Christian theology by surveying the ways in which Romans has been interpreted" (Fitzmyer, p. xiii).

He might just as well have said that the impact of Paul's letter on Western history in general has been "incalculable." Take the case of Augustine of Hippo (A.D. 354-430), for example. Struggling in the chains of lust and sin, he suddenly heard a voice "repeating over and over, 'Take up and read. Take up and read.'" In response he picked up his Bible and read the first passage his eyes fell on: "'Not in rioting and drunkenness, not in chambering and impurities, not in strife and envying; but put you on the Lord Jesus Christ, and make not provision for the flesh in its" lust (Augustine, *Confessions* 8.29). Those words from Romans 13:13, 14 led Augustine to victory over his special problems. In the book of Romans he met Jesus as Savior from sin. He went on to be the leading voice in Europe for the next 1,000 years. The writings of that Romans-converted man did more than any other person to shape Western thought.

More than a millennium afterward Martin Luther had a similar experience with the book of Romans. At one time he wrote that "if ever a man could be saved by monkery that man was I" (in Barclay, *Galatians*, p. 23). But religious practice just didn't do it. He was driven to despair until he discovered Christ's righteousness in Romans. "Thereupon," he wrote, "I felt myself to be reborn and to have gone through open doors into paradise. The whole of Scripture took on a new meaning" (in Bainton, pp. 49, 50). The result was the Protestant Reformation.

Two hundred years later John Wesley, who had struggled to be righteous for years, found himself in utter despair. In that condition on May 24, 1738, he went to a chapel on Aldersgate Street in London where he heard someone reading Luther's *Preface to . . . Romans*. "I felt," he penned, "my heart strangely warmed. I felt I did trust in Christ, Christ alone for salvation: And an assurance was given me, that he had taken away *my* sins, even *mine*, and saved *me* from the law of sin and death" (Wesley, vol. 1, p. 103). The result was the rise of the Methodist movement with its forceful impact on the modern evangelical, holiness, and Pentecostal movements. Young Ellet J. Waggoner would go through an almost identical experience in the face of God's saving grace in the early 1880s that led to the beginning of the righteousness by faith revival of 1888 (see Whidden, p. 19).

The twentieth century saw the book of Romans impact the mind and life of Karl Barth. Looking for meaning and explanations in the wake of the devastation of World War I, Barth found himself transformed by Romans. His commentary on Paul's letter fell "like a bombshell on the playground of the theologians" (in Vanhoozer, p. 700) and stimulated the rise of Neo-orthodoxy, a movement that led much of Christendom to take the Bible more seriously.

And what is the moral to all this history? Simply put: *Reading Romans changes lives.*

Founding and History of the Church at Rome

Paul composed his letters either for individuals or for congregations that he had personally organized. Romans is an exception to that rule. The apostle in fact, had never even been to Rome at the time he wrote to the church there (Rom. 1:13).

One of the interesting facts about that important Christian outpost is that "next to nothing is known about the circumstances surrounding the founding and early history of this church" (Harrison, p. 21). The best lead we have is in Luke's account of the Pentecostal outpouring in Acts 2, in which he tells us that those in the congregation visiting from Rome included both Jews and proselytes to the Jewish faith (Acts 2:10). It is probable that converts among those groups returned to Rome to become the nucleus of the church there.

We know from history that the Jewish population in Rome by the middle of the first Christian century was substantial. The Roman historian Suetonius (cir. A.D. 75-140) records one important event in their history when he wrote that the emperor Claudius "expelled" the Jews from Rome because they "constantly made disturbances at the instigation of Chrestus" (*Suetonius* 5.4). Most scholars agree that "Chrestus" is a corruption of the Greek *Christos* "and that the reference is probably to disputes within the Jewish community over the claims of Jesus to be the *Christos*, the Messiah" (Moo, *Epistle*, pp. 4, 5). That expulsion probably took place in A.D. 49 and is witnessed to in Acts 18:2, which tells us that Aquila and Priscilla had arrived in Greece "because Claudius had commanded all the Jews to leave Rome" (RSV). According to Romans 16:3 they were back in Rome when Paul sent his letter. The return of the Jews probably took place soon after the death of Claudius in A.D. 54.

Their arrival, however, set up the Roman Christian community for conflict. The probable sequence of events is that the earliest Christians had been Jewish. As a result, they dominated Roman Christianity up until the expulsion, even though Gentiles were also being baptized. But between A.D. 49 and A.D. 54 the Gentile element ran the Roman congregations. During that time it was only natural for the Christian community to move away from its Jewish origins in the direction of non-Jewish Christianity. With the return of the Jewish Christians, however, tension between the two groups inevitably arose between Jewish and Gentile Christians. Those tensions provide the background against which Paul wrote.

The writing itself took place between the return of the Jews and Jewish Christians after the death of Claudius and A.D. 64, when the emperor Nero accused the Christians of burning Rome and instigated a period of persecution against the Roman church. External evidence points to the composition of Romans between A.D. 55 to 59 (see Cranfield, *Romans*, vol. 1, pp. 12-16).

Purpose of Romans

The book of Romans has at least three purposes, all of them related in one way or another to the checkered history of the church in Rome. The first is a practical one. Paul has reached a critical juncture in his ministry. His evangelization thus far had covered the Roman provinces of Galatia, Asia, Macedonia, and Achaia (territories that roughly comprise the modern nations of Turkey, Greece, and Macedonia), and he was preparing to move the focus of his ministry to Spain.

But before going to Spain, the apostle needed to visit two other places. The first was Jerusalem, so that he could deliver the contribution for the poor among the Jewish Christians that he had collected from the Gentile churches. His second visit on the way to Spain would be Rome (Rom. 15:23-28). Those two impending visits set the stage for Paul's letter to the Christians in Rome.

Of course, he could have gone to Spain without stopping in Rome on the way. But Paul hoped that the Roman Christians would provide a base of support for him in much the same way that Antioch had done during his early evangelization of the East. Thus his appeal to have them "assist" him in his mission after he had got to know them in his forthcoming visit (Rom. 15:24, NIV).

That practical aspect set the stage for what we can call his strategic purpose—namely, that if the Roman church was to provide a solid base, its warring Gentile and Jewish factions would have to pull together. "Echoes of this controversy, in both its theological and it practical implications, may be heard rumbling throughout Romans. And Paul is seen from beginning to end as an authentic peacemaker, pouring oil on troubled waters, anxious to preserve both truth and peace without sacrificing either to the other" (Stott, p. 35). The letter's most extensive treatment of the peacemaking goal occurs in Romans 14:1-

> Purpose in Romans comes in Three flavors:
> 1. Practical
> 2. Strategic
> 3. Theological

15:13, in which he deals with their bickering and mutual judgmentalism over Jewish issues. But his climactic statement on the topic is that God will have "mercy upon all" (i.e. both Jew and Gentile) in the plan of salvation (11:32, RSV; cf. 1:16, 17: 3:22, 23).

That thought brings us to the apostle's theological purpose in Romans. Put bluntly, Paul felt the need to establish his theological credentials. As a result, he wrote a letter that set forth his view of "the inner logic of the gospel" (Cranfield, *Romans*, vol. 1, p. 23). That was a crucial task since his battles against certain Jewish Christian legalists as portrayed in the books of Galatians and 2 Corinthians had given him a reputation for being against the law and perhaps even anti-Jewish. Rumors of Paul's position on those matters had apparently reached Rome. Thus the apostle's reference to those who "slanderously" charged him with saying "let us do evil that good may result" (Rom. 3:8, NIV). Paul "is aware that he must defuse these rumors and perhaps even win over some who were already hostile toward him" (Moo, *Epistle*, p. 21).

His tactic was to write out a rather complete exposition of the gospel he had been preaching for more than 20 years so that both Jewish and Gentile Christians would understand his position before he arrived.

And while he undoubtedly aimed his gospel exposition at the Roman Christians, as indicated by its repeated reference to the tensions on the racial front, it may also have had other purposes. Jacob Jervell, for example, has suggested that Romans may have been a defense that Paul intended to present to the Jerusalem church that might also be useful in Rome (see Donfried, pp. 61-74). That possibility takes on credibility when we read of other Jewish plots against Paul's life (see, e.g., Acts 20:3) and his request that the Roman Christians pray for him that he might "be delivered from the unbelievers in Judea" (Rom. 15:31, 32, RSV). And if the apostle didn't live to preach the gospel in the West, we can view his extensive treatment of salvation in Romans as his "last will and testament, a precious deposit bequeathed to the church and through it to the community of the faithful everywhere" (Harrison, p. 25).

The possibility of several reasons for Paul's extensive treatment of salvation in Romans goes a great distance in helping us understand the letter's format. After all, unlike 1 and 2 Corinthians, Galatians, Philippians, Colossians, Philemon, 1 and 2 Thessalonians, 1 and 2 Timothy, and Titus that constantly reflect on local circumstances, Romans 1:16-11:36 presents a very general argument devoid of such issues. Rather than being responses to specific problems, Romans develops out of the inner logic of Paul's teaching. Nowhere in these chapters do we find Rome or a specific situation in Rome mentioned. As a result, Richard Longenecker identifies Romans as a "tractate" letter rather than a pastoral letter like those listed above. He claims that while tractate-type letters are "broadly pastoral," "their content and tone suggest that they were originally intended to be more than strictly pastoral responses to specific sets of issues arising in particular places." Rather, they were general theological expositions that could fit many contexts. Such letters as Hebrews and James also belong to the tractate category (in Carson, *Scripture*, pp. 104-106).

Having said that, we should not make the mistake of viewing Romans as having tractate qualities in its entirety. After all, Romans 1:1-15 and 14:1-16:27 have all the earmarks of a pastoral letter. Thus it is perhaps best to see Romans as an expression of the apostle's pastoral concern that contains a theological tractate nuanced toward the needs of the Roman community running from 1:16-11:36. A tractate format for Romans might also explain shorter versions of the letter that apparently circulated in the ancient world and that delete mentions of Rome in 1:7, 15 and do not contain chapter 16, with all of its personal greetings (see Bruce, pp. 25-30; Moo, *Epistle*, pp. 5-9).

Romans' Theological Themes

When asked to describe the contribution of the letter to Romans, the first thing that generally comes to the mind of many people is theology, especially the Christian understanding of salvation. While that is true, it is important to remember that Romans is not a systematic theology that expresses all aspects of the writer's knowledge but a letter written to deal with understandings and misunderstandings in mid first-century Christianity.

Central to the letter and to Paul's ministry was the issue of how Jewish the church should be. On the one hand were those Jewish Christians who were apparently having a difficult time letting go of the ceremonial aspects of the Old Testament and were under the influence of those Jews who saw the law as a means to earn salvation. On the other hand were those who despised all things Jewish, including the law. Our discussion of the theological themes of Romans will take place within that tension-filled framework.

But before we look at the letter's various themes it is important to note that in the past 30 years E. P. Sanders and others have advocated that the Judaism of Paul's time was not legalistic and that the apostle was not arguing against those who sought to earn salvation by works of law. Sanders' thesis unleashed a major war among scholars. For critiques of the weaknesses of his position see the works of Stephen Westerholm and Peter Stuhlmacher under "List of Works Cited."

A reading of Paul's letter, it seems to me, clearly points to the correctness of the legalism understanding. That position best explains various passages on the topic, whereas the "new perspective" on Paul faces several serious difficulties.

Of course, it is true that the best representatives of Judaism in its ideal form undoubtedly held to a grace rather than a works-righteousness orientation. But too often many adherents of the faith failed to grasp the idea. Thus Paul had to deal with the impact of legalistic Jewish Christians in several of his letters—most notably in Galatians and Romans.

With those remarks in mind, we will turn to the major theological themes of the book of Romans.

1. *Unity in Christ and salvation for all.* John Brunt captured the essence of this theme when he wrote that "one of the most important theological terms in Romans is the simple term *all*" (Brunt, p. 23). Throughout the letter the apostle strives to bring into unity the members of the Roman church who had fractured on the racial line of Jew and Gentile.

Because *all* have sinned (Rom. 3:23) and *all* must stand before God's judgment seat (14:10), *all* have the same lostness and need of salvation.

Universal human need leads in Romans to God's provision for the salvation of all. Thus God extends salvation to *all* who have faith, both Jew and Gentile (1:16), and He will have mercy on *all* (11:32).

That unity of lostness and salvation lays the basis for much of Paul's practical counsel, such as not passing judgment on one another (14:13), loving each other (13:8-10), and living peaceably with *all* (12:18). Thus, as in so many cases in Paul's writings, we find theological conviction and day-to-day living united.

2. *Sin.* The fact of sin sets the stage for the entire letter. Romans 1:18-

32 lays out the guilt of the Gentiles while Romans 2 does the same for the Jews. Both groups are under the "power of sin" (3:9, RSV), because "all have sinned and fall short of the glory of God" (3:23, RSV). And since "the wages of sin is [eternal] death" (Rom. 6:23, RSV), the outlook for all humanity is hopeless.

People naturally, Paul argues, are not only sinners but they are slaves to sin (6:12-16). The only hope for them is to unite to Christ who can set them "free from the law of sin and death" (8:2, RSV) through His "grace" (6:14).

3. *Law.* The apostle's discussion of law in Romans is multifaceted. The major divide on the topic involves those statements that seem to be negative regarding the law and those that are positive.

Heading the negative category is the dictum that "no human being will be justified . . . by works of the law" (3:20, RSV). Closely related is Romans 7:4, in which the death of the sinful self releases believers from the condemnation and dominion of the law and frees them to join Christ. Thus they have "died to the law" as a way of redemption.

But believers are not free from the law. Rather, those of faith uphold the law (3:31), which is "holy and just and good" and "spiritual" (7:12, 16, 14, RSV). Thus the law has a place in the life of believers even though it is inadequate as a means of salvation.

A major function of the law is to point out human sin (3:20; 4:15; 7:7) and thus the need of God's justifying grace. Every human being has some form of law. Scripture reveals it for Jews (and Christians, 2:1-13), whereas those Gentiles who don't have the revealed law still have a law opened to some extent to their consciences (2:14, 15). In the end the law will form the standard of judgment (2:5, 6). Those who hear the law but do not obey it will be found wanting (2:13). Thus although the law is not the way to be saved (3:20), those who are saved and live the transformed life (12:2) will walk "with" Christ "in newness of life" as they obey the principles of God's law (6:1-8, RSV).

The basic principle of the law according to Romans is loving one's neighbor (13:8, 10), even if he or she is on the opposite side of the racial line dividing Jews and Gentiles. In a very helpful way Romans 13:8-10 shows how each of the commandments on the second table of the Decalogue flow out of Christ's second great love command (Matt. 22:36-

40). Paul could have done the same for the first table but his readers were having no problem in loving God.

His discussion of the law in Romans 13:8-10 demonstrates its spiritual and internal nature. That was important in a culture that focused on outward behavior rather than a person's inward spiritual status. Romans 7:7 also reflects on the spiritual nature of the law when Paul wrote that he really didn't understand sin until he grasped the meaning of "You shall not covet," the only commandment of the second table of the Decalogue that is an inward indicator of spiritual health rather than an outward action.

In summary, Romans presents the law as a guide for life, a convictor of sin, and a standard of God's judgment, but *not* a way to salvation.

4. *Grace.* Romans sets forth the path to salvation as one of grace (*charis*). Grace in Romans is God's free gift through Christ for human salvation (3:24). The apostle often contrasts grace with works as two alternative approaches to getting right with God (3:20-24; 6:14; 11:6). James Dunn is on target when he writes that "for Paul, behind the whole salvation process always lay the initiative of God. No other word expresses his theology so clearly on this point as grace (*charis*). . . . *Charis* joins *agap* ('love') at the very centre of Paul's gospel. . . . 'Grace' and 'love,' together sum up and most clearly characterise his whole theology" (Dunn, *Theology*, pp. 319, 320). Of the 155 uses of *charis* in the New Testament, 29 of them appear in the letter to the Romans.

5. *Justification by faith.* If grace is God's free gift for the salvation of sinners, Paul expresses that salvation in many metaphors. Romans 3:24, 25, for example, presents three of them, including "redemption" (signifying God's grace-filled purchase of those enslaved in sin that they might be set free), "propitiation" (a word having to do with the turning away of wrath, or God's judgment on sin), and "justification."

It is justification that forms the centerfold in Romans, providing the theme text for the letter in 1:16, 17 ("justification" and "righteousness" are two English translations of the same Greek word) and the primary substance of chapters 3, 4, and 5.

Paul coined the metaphor of justification to meet the problem of the legal curse of the law with its death penalty (3:23; 6:23). "Justification," Vincent Taylor claims, "is a question first and last of man's *standing* with God." Is a person righteous or guilty before the divine judge? (Taylor, *Forgiveness*, p. 68).

In Romans 3 justification does not mean "to make righteous," but rather "to declare righteous." "The root idea in justification," George Eldon Ladd writes, "is the declaration of God, the righteous judge, that the man who believes in Christ, sinful though he may be, . . . is viewed as being righteous, because in Christ he has come into a righteous relationship with God." Relationship, Ladd suggests, is the key to understanding justification. "The justified man has, in Christ, entered into a new relationship with God," who now regards such a person as righteous and treats that individual accordingly. *Justification is the opposite of condemnation.* "It is the decree of acquittal from all guilt and issues in freedom from all condemnation and punishment" (Ladd, pp. 437, 443, 445, 446).

And how, we might ask, do sinful humans receive such free gifts of grace? Paul is unequivocal on that question. All of God's salvific gifts of grace are always "received by faith" (Rom. 3:25, RSV; cf. 1:16, 17). Thus we have the phrases "justification by faith" and "righteousness by faith." At this point a word of caution is important. Faith is not some meritorious work that comes through human effort, but it is another free gift of God that makes it possible for people to accept His other gifts.

6. *Transformed living.* In Romans being justified, redeemed, and propitiated by grace is not the end of the salvation process. Rather, they stand near the beginning. Thus we find nothing of what Dietrich Bonhoffer called "cheap grace" (Bonhoeffer, p. 45). What we discover is transforming grace (12:2) that leads Christians to "walk in newness of life" (6:4, RSV) and to avoid a life of sin (6:1-14). At the heart of such sanctified or holy living in Romans is Christ's great law of love to neighbor (12:9-13) that flows out into a life in harmony with the Decalogue (13:8-10) and is not judgmental of other people (14:13).

Readers of Romans who see justification as the high point of Romans miss Paul's point. Justification never stands alone. To the contrary, it is inextricably linked with transformed or sanctified living. If you have the first you will have the last. And at the end of time people will be judged and eternally "justified" on the basis of how God's transforming grace impacted their daily lives (2:5, 6, 13). We should note that while Romans devotes three chapters (3-5) to justification, it provides six and one half chapters (6-8, 12-15a) to transformed or sanctified living. For Paul justification and sanctification form a unit. They are equally important, with the first leading to the second and the second being founded on the first. A Christian, according to Romans, is a person who is both justified *and* living the transformed life. Take away either part and we destroy the vision of salvation set forth in Romans.

7. *Hope and assurance.* "Hope" is another of the great words in Romans. Used 13 times, it appears in Romans more than any other New Testament book. Christians worship the God of hope (15:13), abound in hope (15:13), rejoice in hope (5:2; 12:12), and are saved by hope (8:24).

As a result, hope in Romans is not some wishful thinking about the future, but rather a certainty based upon what God has already done for believers in Christ. Thus hope provides the basis for confident daily Christian living and the knowledge that at the end of time God will make all things right (8:18-25).

Closely tied to hope is Romans' teaching on assurance. The Holy Spirit bears witness "with our spirit that we are children of God, and if children, then heirs, heirs of God" who will "be glorified" with Christ (8:16, 17, RSV). The letter's teaching on hope and assurance climaxes in Romans 8:31-39, in which Paul repeatedly promises Christians that nothing can separate them from the love of that God who is "for" them. With that thought in mind, perhaps we should see Romans' teaching on hope and assurance as the apex of the letter's discussion of salvation.

Structure and Outline of Romans

While some New Testament books, such as 1 John, are difficult to outline in a totally convincing manner, the structure of Romans (due to its tractate nature) is almost as clear-cut as the table of contents to a systematic theology. After an introduction (1:1-15) and a thematic statement (1:16, 17) the rest of the letter (1:18-15:13) flows logically from one major point to another until Paul binds it off with a postscript (15:14-33), greetings and commendations (16:1-23), and a doxology (16:25-27). The following outline reflects that structure:

I. Introductory matters (1:1-15)

    A. Greetings (1:1-7)

    B. Prayer and Paul's projected trip to Rome (1:8-15)

II. Theme statement: The gospel is the power of God for salvation to all who have faith (1:16, 17)

III. Universal sinfulness and the wrath of God (1:18-3:20)
   A. The guilt of the Gentile world (1:18-32)
   B. The principles of God's judgment, the sinfulness of the Jews, and the universality of sin (2:1-3:20)
      1. The principles of judgment (2:1-16)
      2. The Jews guilty before God (2:17-3:8)
      3. All people guilty before God (3:9-20)
IV. Justification by faith as God's solution to the problem of sin and guilt (3:21-5:21)
   A. God's better way of salvation: justification through faith in the sacrifice of Christ (3:21-31)
   B. Old Testament proof: Abraham was justified by faith (4:1-25)
   C. The benefits of justification by faith (5:1-11)
   D. The possibility of justification by faith for every person (5:12-21)
V. The believer's life in Christ (6:1-8:39)
   A. Born into a new way of life (6:1-11)
   B. Moving from being slaves of sin to slaves of righteousness (6:12-23)
   C. The Christian struggle with sin and law (7:1-25)
   D. The blessings of life in the Spirit (8:1-39)
      1. Liberation from the law of sin and death (8:1-17)
      2. The future hope and assurance of salvation (8:18-39)
VI. Salvation for everyone, both Jew and Gentile (9:1-11:36)
   A. Sorrow over Israel (9:1-5)
   B. Illustrations demonstrating that God's plan has not failed (9:6-33)
   C. Human responsibility in God's plan (10:1-21)
   D. The difference between the elect and the hardened (11:1-10)
   E. God will fulfill His promises (11:11-36)
VII. Living God's love (12:1-15:13)
   A. Ethical concerns (12:1-13:14)
      1. The transformed life (12:1, 2)
      2. Using God's gifts (12:3-8)
      3. Christian conduct in personal relations (12:9-21)
      4. Christian conduct in relation to the state (13:1-7)
      5. The law of love (13:8-10)

Romans' Relevance for the Twenty-first Century

While some people might question the relevance of such biblical books as Obadiah for living in today's world, no one doubts the importance of Romans for their life. All of us are daily confronted by the problems of sin and guilt. And every Christian rejoices in the amazing grace of God who welcomes us in spite of ourselves.

In addition, Romans presents guiding principles for many of the most important activities in life in terms of living the Christian life and relating to others of different beliefs and/or races, and it even provides guidance for the role of government in our individual and corporate existence. And then, of course, there is the issue of hope and assurance that buoy us up and give us confidence throughout the ups and downs of life. Hope as certainty in the covenant God fulfilling His promises is at the center of Romans. And a life without hope is by definition "hopeless." Thus it is not only true to say that Paul's letter to the Romans is relevant, but that its message is second to none in the Bible or elsewhere in importance for daily living in a complex and troubling world.

List of Works Cited

Achtemeier, Paul J. Romans. *Interpretation: A Bible Commentary for Teaching and Preaching.* Atlanta: John Knox, 1985.

Althaus, Paul. *The Theology of Martin Luther.* Philadelphia: Fortress, 1966.

Ante-Nicene Fathers, 10 vols. Ed. Alexander Roberts et al. Peabody, Mass.: Hendrickson, 1994.

Augustine. *The Confessions of St. Augustine.* Garden City, N. Y.: Image Books, 1960.

Badenas, R. *Christ the End of the Law: Romans 10:4 in Pauline Perspective.* Sheffield: JSOT Press, 1985.

Bainton, Roland H. *Here I Stand: A Life of Martin Luther.* New York: New American Library, 1950.

Balz, Horst, and Gerhard Schneider, eds. *Exegetical Dictionary of the New Testament,* 3 vols. Grand Rapids: Eerdmans, 1990-1993.

Barclay, William. *The Letter to the Romans.* 2nd ed., The Daily Study Bible. Edinburgh: Saint Andrew Press, 1957.

———. *The Letters to the Galatians and Ephesians.* 2nd ed. The Daily Study Bible. Edinburgh: Saint Andrew Press, 1958.

Barrett, C. K. *A Commentary on the Epistle to the Romans.* Harper's New Testament Commentaries. Peabody, Mass.: Hendrickson, 1957.

Barth, Karl. *The Epistle to the Romans,* 6th ed. London: Oxford University Press, 1968.

Barton, Bruce B. et al. *Romans. Life Application Bible Commentary.* Wheaton, Ill.: Tyndale House, 1992.

Bauer, Walter. *A Greek-English Lexicon of the New Testament and Other Early Christian Literature.* Rev. Frederick William Danker, 3rd. ed. Chicago: University of Chicago Press, 2000.

Beale, G. K., and D. A. Carson. *Commentary on the New Testament Use of the Old Testament.* Grand Rapids: Baker Academic, 2007.

Best, Ernest. *The Letter of Paul to the Romans.* Cambridge Bible Commentary. Cambridge, Eng.: Cambridge University Press, 1967.

Boice, James Montgomery. *Romans,* 4 vols. Grand Rapids: Baker, 1991-1995.

Bonhoeffer, Dietrich. *The Cost of Discipleship,* rev. ed. New York: Collier, 1963.

Braaten, Carl E. *Justification: The Article by Which the Church Stands or Falls.* Minneapolis: Fortress, 1990.

Bray, Gerald, ed. *Romans. Ancient Christian Commentary on Scripture.* Downers Grove, Ill.: InterVarsity, 1998.

Briscoe, D. Stuart. *Romans. The Communicator's Commentary.* Waco, Tex.: Wood Books, 1982.

Bromily, Geoffrey W., ed. *Theological Dictionary of the New Testament.* Abridged ed. Grand Rapids: Eerdmans, 1985.

Bruce, F. F. *The Letter of Paul to the Romans.* 2nd ed., Tyndale New Testament Commentaries. Grand Rapids: Eerdmans, 1985.

Brunner, Emil. *The Letter to the Romans.* Philadelphia: Westminster, 1959.

———. *The Mediator: A Study of the Central Doctrine of the Christian Faith.* New York: Macmillan, 1934.

Brunt, John C. *Romans: Mercy for All.* Bible Amplifier. Boise, Idaho: Pacific Press, 1996.

Calvin, John. *Commentaries on the Epistle of Paul the Apostle to the Romans.* Grand Rapids: Baker, n.d.

Carson, D. A., and John D. Woodbridge, eds. *Scripture and Truth.* Grand Rapids: Zondervan, 1983.

Carson, D. A., Peter T. O'Brien, and Mark A. Seifrid, eds. *Justification and Variegated Nomism,* 2 vols. Grand Rapids: Baker Academic, 2001, 2004.

Charlesworth, James H., ed. *The Old Testament Pseudepigrapha,* 2 vols. New York: Doubleday, 1983, 1985.

Cragg, Gerald R. "The Epistle to the Romans: Exposition." In *The Interpreter's Bible.* New York: Abingdon, 1954, vol. 9, pp. 379-668.

Cranfield, C. E. B. *The Epistle to the Romans,* 2 vols. The International Critical Commentary. Edinburgh: T & T Clark, 1975, 1979.

————. *Romans: A Shorter Commentary.* Grand Rapids: Eerdmans, 1985.

Denney, James. *The Christian Doctrine of Reconciliation.* London: James Clarke, 1959.

————. "St Paul's Epistle to the Romans." In *The Expositor's Greek Testament.* Grand Rapids: Eerdmans, n.d., vol. 2, pp. 555-725.

————. *Studies in Theology.* Grand Rapids: Baker, 1976.

Dodd, C. H. *The Epistle of Paul to the Romans.* London: Fontana Books, 1959.

Donfried, Karl P., ed. *The Romans Debate.* Minneapolis: Augsburg, 1977.

Douglass, Herbert E. *Why Jesus Waits,* rev. ed. Riverside, Calif.: Upward Way, 1987.

Dunn, James D. G. *Romans 1-8.* Word Biblical Commentary. Dallas: Word Books, 1988.

————. *Romans 9-16.* Word Biblical Commentary. Dallas: Word Books, 1988.

————. *The Theology of Paul the Apostle.* Grand Rapids: Eerdmans, 1998.

Durant, Will. *The Story of Philosophy.* New York: Simon and Schuster, 1961.

Earle, Ralph. *Word Meanings in the New Testament.* One vol. ed. Grand Rapids: Baker, n.d.

Edwards, James R. Romans. *New International Biblical Commentary.* Peabody, Mass.: Hendrickson, 1992.

Fitzmyer, Joseph A. Romans. *Anchor Bible.* New York: Doubleday, 1993.

Godet, F. *Commentary on the Epistle to the Romans.* Classic Commentary Library. Grand Rapids: Zondervan, 1956.

Greenman, Jeffrey P., and Timothy Larson, eds. *Reading Romans Through the Centuries: From the Early Church to Karl Barth.* Grand Rapids: Brazos, 2005.

Harrison, Everett F., and Donald A. Hagner. "Romans." In *The Expositor's Bible Commentary,* rev. ed. Grand Rapids, Zondervan, 2008, vol. 11, pp. 19-237.

Hauser, Marc D. "Is Morality Natural?" *Newsweek,* Sept. 22, 2008, p. 65.

Hawthorne, Gerald F., and Ralph P. Martin, eds. *Dictionary of Paul and His Letters.* Downers Grove, Ill.: InterVarsity, 1993.

Hodge, Charles. *Commentary on the Epistle to the Romans,* rev. ed. Grand Rapids: Eerdmans, 1950.

Huegli, Albert G., ed., *Church and State Under God.* Saint Louis: Concordia, 1964.

Hunter, A. M. *The Epistle to the Romans.* Torch Bible Commentaries. London: SCM Press, 1955.

Käsemann, Ernst. *Commentary on Romans.* Grand Rapids: Eerdmans, 1980.

Keck, Leander E. Romans. *Abingdon New Testament Commentaries.* Nashville: Abingdon, 2005.

Keener, Craig S. *The IVP Bible Background Commentary: New Testament.* Downers Grove, Ill.: InterVarsity, 1993.

Kittel, Gerhard, and Gerhard Friedrich, eds. *Theological Dictionary of the New Testament,* 10 vols. Grand Rapids: Eerdmans, 1964-1976.

Knox, John. "The Epistle to the Romans: Introduction and Exegesis." In *The Interpreter's Bible*. New York: Abingdon, 1954, vol. 9, pp. 353-668.

Ladd, George Eldon, *A Theology of the New Testament*. Grand Rapids: Eerdmans, 1974.

Leenhardt, Franz J. *The Epistle to the Romans*. London: Lutterworth, 1961.

Lewis, C. S. *Mere Christianity*. New York: Macmillan, 1960.

Lloyd-Jones, D. M. *Romans: An Exposition of Chapter 1: The Gospel of God*. Grand Rapids: Zondervan, 1985.

———. *Romans: An Exposition of Chapters 2:1-3:20: The Righteous Judgment of God*. Grand Rapids: Zondervan, 1989.

———. *Romans: An Exposition of Chapters 3:20-4:25: Atonement and Justification*. Grand Rapids: Zondervan, 1970.

———. *Romans: An Exposition of Chapter 6: The New Man*. Grand Rapids: Zondervan, 1972.

———. *Romans: An Exposition of Chapter 8:5-17: The Sons of God*. Grand Rapids: Zondervan, 1974.

———. *Romans: An Exposition of Chapter 8:17-39: The Final Perseverance of the Saints*. Grand Rapids: Zondervan, 1975.

Luther, Martin. *Commentary on Romans*. Grand Rapids: Kregel, 1976.

———. *A Commentary on St. Paul's Epistle to the Galatians*. London: James Clarke, 1953.

———. *Luther: Lectures on Romans*. Library of Christian Classics. Philadelphia: Westminster, 1961.

MacArthur, John, Jr. *Romans 1-8*. Chicago: Moody, 1991.

MacLaren, Alexander. *Romans. Expositions of Holy Scripture*. Grand Rapids: Eerdmans, 1938.

Macquarrie, John. *Principles of Christian Theology,* 2nd ed. New York: Charles Scribner's Sons, 1977.

McGrath, Alister E. *Justification by Faith*. Grand Rapids: Zondervan, 1990.

Mishnah. *Herbert Danby,* trans. London: Oxford, 1933.

Mishnah: *A New Translation*. Jacob Neusner, trans. New Haven, Conn.: Yale, 1988.

Moo, Douglas J. *The Epistle to the Romans*. New International Commentary on the New Testament. Grand Rapids: Eerdmans, 1996.

———. *Romans*. NIV Application Commentary. Grand Rapids: Zondervan, 2000.

———. "Romans." In *Zondervan Illustrated Bible Backgrounds Commentary*. Grand Rapids: Zondervan, 2002, vol. 3, pp. 2-99.

Mooneyham, Stan. *Dancing on the Strait and Narrow: A Gentle Call to a Radical Faith*. San Francisco: Harper & Row, 1989.

Morris, Leon. *The Atonement: Its Meaning and Significance*. Downers Grove, Ill.: InterVarsity, 1983.

———. *The Epistle to the Romans*. Pillar New Testament Commentary. Grand Rapids: Eerdmans, 1988.

Moule, Handley C. G. *The Epistle to the Romans*. New ed. London: Pickering & Inglis, n.d.

Mounce, Robert H. Romans. *The New American Commentary*. Nashville: Broadman and Holman, 1995.

Murray, John. *The Epistle to the Romans,* 2 vols. New International Commentary on the New

Testament. Grand Rapids: Eerdmans, 1959, 1965.

Newman, Barclay M., and Eugene A. Nida. *A Translator's Handbook on Paul's Letter to the Romans*. New York: United Bible Societies, 1973.

Nichol, Francis D., ed. "The Epistle of Paul the Apostle to the Romans." In *The Seventh-day Adventist Bible Commentary*. Washington, D. C.: Review and Herald, 1953-1957, vol. 6, pp. 465-652.

Niebuhr, Reinhold, *The Nature and Destiny of Man,* 2 vols., New York: Charles Scribner's Sons, 1964.

Nygren, Anders. *Commentary on Romans*. Philadelphia: Fortress, 1949.

Osborne, Grant R. *Romans*. The IVP New Testament Commentary Series. Downers Grove, Ill.: InterVarsity, 2004.

Packer, J. I. *Knowing God*. Downers Grove, Ill.: InterVarsity, 1973.

Pilgrim, Walter E. *Uneasy Neighbors: Church and State in the New Testament*. Minneapolis: Fortress, 1999.

Plumer, William S. *Commentary on Romans*. Grand Rapids: Kregel, 1993.

Richardson, Alan, ed. *A Theological Word Book of the Bible*. New York: Macmillan, 1950.

Rogers, Cleon L., Jr., and Cleon L. Rogers III. *The New Linguistic and Exegetical Key to the Greek New Testament*. Grand Rapids: Zondervan, 1998.

Sanday, William, and Arthur C. Headlam. *The Epistle to the Romans,* 5th ed. The International Critical Commentary. Edinburgh: T. & T. Clark, n.d.

Sanders, E. P. Paul and Palestinian Judaism: *A Comparison of Patterns of Religion*. Minneapolis: Fortress, 1977.

Sartre, Jean-Paul. *Existentialism and Human Emotions*. New York: Philosophical Library, 1957.

Schlatter, Adolf. *Romans: The Righteousness of God*. Peabody, Mass.: Hendrickson, 1995.

Schneemelcher, Wilhelm, ed. *New Testament Apocrypha,* 2 vols., rev. ed. Louisville: Westminster/John Knox, 1991, 1992.

Schreiner, Thomas R. *Romans*. Baker Exegetical Commentary on the New Testament. Grand Rapids: Baker Academic, 1998.

Steinbeck, John. *East of Eden*. New York: Bantam, 1955.

Stern, David H. *Jewish New Testament Commentary*. Clarksville, Md.: Jewish New Testament Publications, 1992.

Stewart, James S. *A Man in Christ: The Vital Elements of St. Paul's Religion*. New York: Harper & Row, n.d.

Stott, John. *Romans: God's Good News for the World*. Downers Grove, Ill.: InterVarsity, 1994.

Stuhlmacher, Peter. *Paul's Letter to the Romans*. Louisville: Westminster/John Knox, 1994.

———. *Revisiting Paul's Doctrine of Justification: A Challenge to the New Perspective*. Downers Grove, Ill.: InterVarsity, 2001.

Suetonius, vol. 2, Loeb Classical Library. Cambridge, Mass: Harvard University Press, 1914.

Taylor, Vincent. *The Epistle to the Romans*. Epworth Preacher's Commentaries. London: Epworth, 1955.

———. *Forgiveness and Reconciliation: A Study in New Testament Theology*. London: Macmillan, 1948.

Thayer, Joseph H. Thayer's *Greek-English Lexicon of the New Testament*. Peabody, Mass.: Hendrickson, n.d.

Thomas, W. H. Griffith. *Commentary on Romans*. Grand Rapids: Kregel, 1974.

Vanhoozer, Kevin J. ed. *Dictionary for Theological Interpretation of the Bible*. Grand Rapids: Baker Academic, 2005.

Walker, W. L. *The Gospel of Reconciliation: or At-one-ment*. Edinburgh: T. & T. Clark, 1909.

———. *What About the New Theology?* 2nd ed. Edinburgh. T&T Clark, 1907.

Wesley, John. *The Works of John Wesley*. 14 vols., 3rd ed. Peabody, Mass.: Hendrickson, 1984.

Westerholm, Stephen. "The 'New Perspective' at Twenty-Five." In D. A. Carson, Peter T. O'Brien, and Mark A. Seifrid, eds. *Justification and Variegated Nomism*. Grand Rapids: Baker Academic, vol. 2, pp. 1-38.

Whidden, Woodrow. *E. J. Waggoner: From the Physician of Good News to the Agent of Division*. Hagerstown, Md.: Review and Herald, 2008.

White, Ellen G. *Christ's Object Lessons*. Washington, D.C.: Review and Herald, 1941.

———. *The Desire of Ages*. Mountain View, Calif.: Pacific Press, 1940.

———. *Education*. Mountain View, Calif.: Pacific Press, 1952.

———. *Patriarchs and Prophets*. Mountain View, Calif.: Pacific Press, 1958.

———. *Thoughts From the Mount of Blessing*. Mountain View, Calif.: Pacific Press, 1956.

Wood, James E., Jr., E. Bruce Thompson, and Robert T. Miller. *Church and State in Scripture History, and Constitutional Law*. Waco, Tex.: Baylor, 1958.

Wright, N.T. "The Letter to the Romans." In *The New Interpreter's Bible*. Nashville: Abingdon, 2002, vol. 10, pp. 393-770.

Ziesler, John. *Paul's Letter to the Romans*. TPI New Testament Commentaries. London: SCM Press, 1989.

Part I

Meeting Paul

Romans 1:1-16

1. Greetings

Romans 1:1-7

> *¹Paul, a slave of Christ Jesus, called to be an apostle, having been set apart for the gospel of God, ²which He promised previously through His prophets in the holy Scriptures, ³concerning His Son, who descended from the seed of David according to the flesh, ⁴who was declared the Son of God in power according to the Spirit of holiness by His resurrection from the dead, Jesus Christ our Lord, ⁵through whom we have received grace and apostleship to bring about the obedience of faith among all the nations on behalf of His name, ⁶among whom you also are called ones of Jesus Christ; ⁷To all God's beloved in Rome, called as saints: Grace to you and peace from God our Father and the Lord Jesus Christ.*

What a way to begin a letter! Who in their right mind would lead off by claiming that they were a slave?

The apostle Paul for one. Never one to hide his allegiance, he indicates that the most important thing we can know about him is that he is a Christian—that everything that he is and has belongs to Jesus.

Many modern translators seek to soften the word "slave" by rendering it as "servant." But the Greek word *doulos* primarily means "slave." Paul tells us that he is not a hired man working with Christ for wages, but a slave who totally belongs to Him.

Concepts related to slavery stand at the heart of Paul's letter to the Romans. Thus when he talks in Romans 3:24 about God's redeeming sinners he uses the vocabulary of the marketplace. "Redemption" in his day meant to buy at the market, particularly to purchase a slave (see Bauer, p.

606). Central to Paul's life and message was the fact that he had been re-deemed by the blood of Jesus on Calvary's cross.

The idea of a Christian's slavery to God rises again in Romans 6, in which the apostle tells his readers that every human being is a slave to either Satan or Christ, that all belong to someone, that no person is a totally free agent, and that every individual becomes the slave of either "sin, which leads to death, or of obedience, which leads to righteousness" (see Rom. 6:16-23, RSV).

But slavery to Christ, Paul tells us, is not bondage. To the contrary, it is how a person gains freedom. It will climax in eternal life (verse 23). Thus even Paul's slavery is good news. In fact, it is one of the most important things about himself that he wants his readers to know.

But a second is close at hand. Paul describes himself as not only "a slave of Christ Jesus," but a person "called to be an apostle" (Rom. 1:1). Here we find a title connoting great authority. According to Acts 1:15-26, an apostle was one who had personally known the Lord and had been a "witness to his resurrection" (verse 22, RSV). In addition, an apostle was a disciple who had received a call "not from men nor through man, but through Jesus Christ and God the Father" (Gal. 1:1, RSV). Paul repeatedly asserts that God had called him to be an apostle (see, e.g., 1 Cor. 1:1; 2 Cor. 1:1).

Here we have an interesting juxtaposition, with Paul describing himself as a "slave" on one hand and an "apostle" on the other. The first is a term of great humility that expresses Paul's sense of personal insignificance. The second is a title of great authority—so much authority that he could claim equality with the disciples whom Jesus chose while on earth.

In actuality, Paul's claim to be an apostle lined up in one sense with his earlier one to be a slave of God, since the Old Testament also identified Joshua and other prophets as "slaves" of God (Joshua 24:29; Amos 3:7). Thus Paul in describing himself as both a slave and an apostle was placing himself in the succession of the prophets. As a result, he could assert that "the gospel which was preached by me is not man's gospel. For I did not receive it from man, nor was I taught it, but it came through revelation" (Gal. 1:11, 12, RSV). Thus in Roman's first verse Paul is alerting his read-ers that he has an authoritative word from God for them.

A third thing we discover about Paul in verse 1 is that he had "been set apart for the gospel of God." We find two significant ideas in that identi-fying factor. First, Paul was "set apart" for the gospel. That is an interesting phrase, since set apart has the same root meaning as Pharisee (one who is separated). With that in mind, Anders Nygren writes that "even before his becoming a Christian he had been 'set apart.' As a Pharisee he had set himself apart for the law. But now God had set him apart for something entirely different. . . . Paul, who had set himself apart for the law, is set apart by God for the gospel" (Nygren, pp. 45, 46). Thus the very first verse of the Epistle raises the tension between law and gospel as ways of approaching God, a tension that runs throughout the entire letter.

The second significant idea in Paul's third description of himself is "the gospel of God." In that phrase we not only meet the first usage of the word "gospel" in Romans but also the understanding that the gospel comes from God. "God" is the most important word in the letter. Not only did God call Paul, but He is the author of the gospel. Paul and the other apostles did not invent the good news. Rather, the God who called them and set them apart to preach it also revealed it to them.

The fact that God is the author of the gospel is the first point of a six-part analysis of it that Paul sets forth in Romans 1:1-6. The second is that the gospel had been "promised previously through [the] prophets" in the Hebrew scriptures (verse 22). The entire Old Testament points to the Christ and His work. The first allusion appears in Genesis 3:15, in which God declared that the seed of the woman would eventually defeat the devil. The last is in Malachi 4:5, which promises Elijah, the forerunner of the Messiah.

To put it bluntly, the gospel "promised previously through His prophets" is the key to understanding the entire Bible. The Old Testament points toward Christ, while the New expounds and expands upon the implication of God's good news in Jesus.

The fact that the Old Testament promised the gospel provides one of the major themes of the sermons in the New Testament (see, e.g., Acts 2; 13; 8:32, 33). Jesus Himself helped his followers recognize that the Old Testament pointed to His work. Describing Jesus' conversation with the two He met on the road to Emmaus, the Bible tells us that "beginning at Moses and all the prophets, he expounded unto them in all the scriptures the things concerning himself" (Luke 24:27, KJV).

The next point to note in Paul's six-point analysis of the gospel to which God had set him apart is that Jesus is its focal point. Jesus "descended from the seed of David according to the flesh" (Rom. 1:3). The words "according to

Six Important Facts About the Gospel

1. God is its author (Rom. 1:1).
2. It was prophesied in the Old Testament (verse 2).
3. It centers in Jesus, both the Son of David and the Son of God (verses 3, 4).
4. Jesus' resurrection demonstrated its power (verse 4).
5. It not only justifies but also leads to a faith-filled life of obedience (verse 5).
6. It is for "all the nations" rather than one specific nation (verse 5).

the flesh" remind us that He was not merely a human being. It is true that He was the Son of David, "according to the flesh," but He was also the unique Son of God. One of the great teachings of the Gospel of Matthew is that Jesus was Mary's son but not Joseph's—that is, He was the son of Mary and the Holy Spirit (Matt. 1:18). Thus Jesus was both human and divine—He was "God with us" (verse 23). As a result, the incarnate Jesus was in a position to "save his people from their sins" (verse 21).

Romans 1:4 makes it clear that the unique Jesus was God's Son. But the Son of David aspect of verse 3 is also crucial. "Son of David" was a universally recognized messianic title going back to 2 Samuel 7:12, 13, in which God promised to establish David's throne forever.

Jeremiah refers to that accepted understanding when he prophesies:

"'The days are coming,' declares the Lord,
'When I will raise up to David a righteous Branch.
A King who will reign wisely
and do what is just and right in the land. . .
This is the name by which he will be called:
The Lord Our Righteousness'" (Jer. 23:5, NIV).

Paul will build the book of Romans on the fact that Jesus is indeed "our righteousness," our hope, our Savior.

The apostle's fourth point is that Jesus "was declared the Son of God in power . . . by His resurrection from the dead" (Rom. 1:4). The good news centers not only on Jesus' incarnation but also on His resurrection.

Nothing is more useless than a dead Savior. If Jesus had come to earth and merely lived a good (even perfect) life and died a valiant death, He would have been just one more good and heroic person. But dead like the rest of them.

The good news, Paul reminds us, is about not merely another good man who came to an unjust end. To the contrary, His resurrection demonstrates Him to be the powerful Son of God. The good news is that Jesus lives on to continue His work for those who have accepted Him. His resurrection stands at the center of Paul's gospel message (1 Cor. 15:1-4, 14). That event is the hinge of history. "Before that" event, Nygren points out, Jesus "was the Son of God in weakness and lowliness. Through the resurrection He became the Son of God in power" (Nygren, p. 51).

The fifth point in Paul's initial analysis of the gospel is that its purpose is "the obedience of faith" (Rom. 1:5), a phrase also found in Romans 16:26, and one indicating that obedience based upon a saving relationship is a theme of Romans. Paul is quite clear on the importance of obedience in a Christian's life. While salvation does not come through obedience (3:20), obedience is a necessary fruit among those who have been justified by faith in Jesus. We will return to that topic since it is built into the very structure of the letter to the Romans.

Paul's sixth and final point in Romans 1:1-5 is that the gospel is not only for the Jews but for "all the nations" (verse 5).

The apostle closes his introductory remarks by noting that God took the initiative by calling each of his readers to the good news of salvation in Christ (verse 16) and that every Christian is a "saint"—is set apart to be holy (verse 7). Finally, he blesses each with grace and peace from the Father and the Son (verse 7).

2. Ministry at Its Best Is Two-edged

Romans 1:8-15

⁸First, I thank my God through Jesus Christ concerning all of you because your faith is being publicly reported in all the world. ⁹For God is my witness, whom I serve in my spirit in the gospel of His Son, how I constantly mention you, ¹⁰always in my prayers requesting that somehow I might now succeed by God's will in coming to you. ¹¹For I long to see you, in order that I might impart to you some spiritual gift so that you may be strengthened, ¹²that is, that we might be mutually encouraged through one another's faith, both yours and mine. ¹³Now I do not wish you to be unaware, brothers, that I often planned to come to you (but have

been hindered until now) so that I might also have some fruit among you,
even as among the rest of the Gentiles. [14]I am a debtor both to Greeks and
to non-Greeks, both to wise and to foolish. [15]So, for my part, I am eager
to proclaim the gospel to you also who are in Rome.

Thomas Schreiner is on target when he writes of Romans 1:1-7 that "this is easily the longest and most theologically complex of all the Pauline" introductions (Schreiner, p. 31). And for good reason. Paul directed all of his other letters at churches that he had been instrumental in establishing. But with the church in Rome he is dealing with a body of believers until now far outside of his sphere of influence. Thus his extensive greeting in which he not only set forth his credentials as a called of God apostle but also began to explore the texture of the gospel message that will dominate his letter.

By verse 8 Paul has finished with introductory generalities and is ready for the specifics of greeting the believers in Rome. He had made it abundantly clear in verses 5-7 that he was not only an apostle to the Gentiles or nations in general but that his ministry specifically included "all God's beloved in Rome." The apostle's thanksgiving and prayer in verses 8-15 are an expression of his commission with respect to the Roman Christians.

The word "first" in verse 8 is important even though Paul never gets to a second or third. Rather, his use of "first" is significant because "people reveal by their priorities what is genuinely important in their lives" (Mounce, p. 65). "First," Paul writes, "I thank my God." Thanksgiving and praise to God were central to his religious experience.

We should highlight several things in Paul's thanksgiving statement. One is that he addresses God as "my God," a reminder that religion at its best is a personal relationship. A second thing to note is that he offers his thanksgiving "through Jesus Christ," a phrase pointing to the mediatorial role that Christ performs for every believing Christian (see Rom. 8:34; 1 John 2:1). But above all Paul is thankful for the "faith" of the believers and that they have a good reputation. "Faith," of course, is a word that Paul will return to again and again in Romans.

His expression of thanksgiving has a lesson for each one of us. He started with the positive even though he probably could have found fault with something the Romans were doing or believing. All of us need to learn that lesson. I have known some church members who always have the negative at the tip of their tongue. In place of a good word, it is what is wrong with the world, the church, other people, or even me. Those things may be true, but the apostle understands the secret of successful communication. He began by noting the good in others. That element of appreciation helped him build a positive foundation with them that was of crucial importance since he would eventually have to deal with issues that were more disagreeable. We find that sequence in Romans and in most of Paul's other letters.

With verses 9 and 10 the apostle begins moving away from commendation to prayer for his readers. Paul believed in the power of intercessory prayer. He spent much time in prayer for other people because he knew that his ministry of prayer helped them.

But Paul not only prayed for the Roman believers, he also requested "that somehow I might now succeed by God's will in coming to you" (Rom. 1:10). Here we find an important indication for the apostle's purpose in writing his letter to the Romans. He had reached a critical juncture in his ministry. His evangelism thus far had covered the Roman provinces of Galatia, Asia, Macedonia, and Achaia (territories that cover roughly the modern nations of Turkey, Greece, and Macedonia), and he was preparing to shift the focus of his ministry to Spain (Rom. 15:24).

Before going to Spain, however, Paul needed to visit two other places. The first was Jerusalem, so that he could deliver the contribution for the poor among the Jewish Christians that he had collected from the Gentile churches. His second visit on the way to Spain would be Rome (15:23-28).

Those forthcoming journeys set the stage for Paul's letter to the Christians in Rome. Most specifically, he writes in Romans 15:24 that "I hope to visit you while passing through [on the way to Spain] and to have you assist me on my journey there, after I have enjoyed your company for a while" (NIV). In short, Paul was hoping that the Roman Christians would provide a base of support for his new ministry to the far west of the Mediterranean in the same way that Antioch had done during his early evangelization of the East.

Paul notes that he had often planned on visiting Rome but had been previously "hindered" for reasons that he does not state (Rom. 1:13). On the other hand, he is quite specific in what he hoped to achieve on such a visit. First, he wanted to impart to them "some spiritual gift" (verse 11). The term "spiritual gift" could imply a special charismatic gift, such as prophecy or the generosity that he later mentions in Romans 12:6-8, but the letter also uses the idea of spiritual gift in other ways. In Romans 5:15, for example, Paul speaks of justification by faith as a gift. It appears that he employs the phrase in Romans 1:11 in the sense of things that build up spiritual life.

Such a gift would strengthen them in their Christian walk (verse 11). Strengthening is an interesting concept since it indicates that "conversion is not an end" but "a beginning." As one author puts it, Paul's "epistles have been written because becoming a Christian is just a beginning." Young Christians need to be fed and trained and thus strengthened (Lloyd-Jones, *Chapter 1*, p. 182). We find an important lesson here. All too often we bring new converts into the church and then neglect them. But Paul has it right. Converted and baptized believers also need to be nurtured and strengthened, a task too often overlooked in most congregations.

Before moving away from the strengthening concept, we should observe that it has two edges, expressed by the words "that we might be mutually encouraged through one another's faith, both yours and mine" (verse 12). Here is a truly astounding idea. Most of us have no difficulty in understanding how the "great" apostle could help others. But Paul makes it plain that those who minister to others are also blessed by them. That is, we each bless each other as we share our faith and Christian experience and as we pray for one another. The good news is that the Pauls of the world not only give but also receive as they fellowship with the body of Christ, the church. We need to see the church not in terms of greater and lesser members but as a mutual-enhancement society in which every person is a servant and teacher to each of the others.

Another thing that Paul wanted to accomplish on his visit to the Roman Christians was to "have some fruit" among them, "even as among the rest of the Gentiles" (verse 13). It is in that context that he wrote that he was a "debtor both to Greeks and to non-Greeks, both to wise and to foolish" (verse 14) and that he was "eager to proclaim the gospel" to those in Rome (verse 15).

The surface meaning of verses 13-15 is clear enough. Paul wanted to evangelize both the Jewish and Gentile populations of Rome, as he had done in other great cities of the Roman world. But, we need to ask, what did Paul mean by saying that he was a "debtor" to them?

John Stott helps us answer that question when he writes that there are "two possible ways of getting into debt. The first is to borrow money *from* someone; the second is to be given money *for* someone by a third party." Thus if a friend handed me $10,000 to give to you, "I would be in your debt until I handed it over" (Stott, p. 59). It is in that sense that Paul was a debtor to all in Rome and all the world. God had entrusted him with the gospel message to give to everyone who would receive it. But debtorship didn't end with Paul. Every Christian is "a debtor both to Greeks and to non-Greeks, both to wise and to foolish" (i.e., everyone) in that we have an obligation to pass on the gospel of God in Christ Jesus.

In his next two verses Paul advances to the theme of the letter to the Romans as he defines more precisely the nature of God's good news.

3. The Gospel In a Nutshell

Romans 1:16, 17
> [16]*For I am not ashamed of the gospel, for it is the power of God unto salvation to everyone who believes, to the Jew first and also to the Greek.* [17]*For in it the righteousness of God is revealed from faith to faith; as it has been written, "Now the righteous man will live by faith."*

Why would anyone be ashamed of the gospel? Good question. Especially since Paul in other places asserted that he rejoiced in it (Rom. 5:2, 11).

Before examining the answer to our question we need to recognize that Paul's statement about not being ashamed is the third of three "I ams":

- *"I am* a debtor both to Greeks and to non-Greeks, both to wise and to foolish" (verse 14).
- *"I am* eager to proclaim the gospel to you also who are in Rome" (verse 15).
- *"I am* not ashamed of the gospel" (verse 16).

The results of the preaching of his gospel message in other places would certainly make a person with insufficient faith not only ashamed but also fearful. He had every reason to believe that many in Rome would despise the simplicity of his message. It certainly had been so in Corinth, where some saw the preaching of a crucified Savior to be "foolishness" (1 Cor.

1:18). In fact, he noted a few verses later, the preaching of "Christ crucified" was a "stumblingblock" to the Jews and "unto the Greeks foolishness" (verse 23, KJV). Again, in Athens "some mocked" "when they heard
of the resurrection of the dead" (Acts 17:32, KJV).

To preach a God who became a man through a virgin birth, died as a
criminal on a cross, rose bodily from the dead, went to live in heaven, and
would return to earth some day didn't exactly make sense to the sophisticates of that day. And the self-appointed sophisticates of any age can make
one feel a little squeamish with their "superior" attitudes and airs.

Another reason the people of Paul's time may have hesitated to preach
Christ was that in addition to verbal abuse, it often brought physical
persecution. William Barclay notes that "Paul had been imprisoned in
Philippi, chased out of Thessalonica, smuggled out of Beroea, laughed
at in Athens" (Barclay, *Romans*, p. 9).

Then again, the apostle may not have had an overly impressive physical
presence. Early tradition describes him as "a man of small stature, with a
bald head and crooked legs, . . . with eyebrows meeting and nose somewhat hooked" (Acts of Paul and Thecla, par. 2).

To put it bluntly, Paul probably had all the same problems as you and I
when it comes to testifying for our Lord. It has never been easy or pain-
less to witness. We always put ourselves in danger of ridicule and jest.

Yet Paul was "eager" to preach his message (Rom. 1:15). Beyond that, far
from being ashamed of the gospel, he was *proud* of it. Why? He answers that
question in verses 16, 17 as he talks about the power and salvation of God.

The first thing to note about the basis for Paul's confidence and boldness in
the face of opposition is that he defines the gospel as "the power of God unto
salvation" (verse 16). "Power," the operative word in that sentence, translates
the Greek *dunamis* from which we get the word "dynamite." I still remember my first experience with dynamite. Driving across the southern California
desert, the first thing I sensed was a blinding flash in the distance. Next I saw
a huge cloud of dirt and debris. At that point the sound waves shook my car,
and I realized that I had witnessed a mighty explosion.

Such is the *dunamis* of the gospel as it transforms the lives of men and
women by blowing away old ways and forming new. It was a power that
Paul knew from experience—his own on the road to Damascus and also in
the lives of countless others. To him the saving gospel of God "is demon-

strated, not by argument, but by what it does" (Denney, "Romans," p. 589).

One reason that Paul is not ashamed of the gospel is that it is backed by God's power. And one thing the apostle will make clear in the early chapters of Romans is that people are unable to save themselves from the ravages of sin. No matter how hard they try, they can't free themselves from the corruption of their very nature. That's where God's *dunamis* or power comes in. He can do what we can't do. And that is very good news—it is the gospel in a nutshell.

God's power, Paul claims, is aimed at salvation, a word meaning to "rescue," "preserve," "deliver," or "save." The basic idea is that the power of God in salvation rescues people from the penalties of sin.

"Salvation," the apostle said, is for "everyone who believes, to the Jew first and also to the Greek" (Rom. 1:16). In other words, it has universal scope. And that is important for the warring factions in his audience. As Leon Morris puts it, "the combination stands for the totality of mankind. The gospel is for all and knows no limitation by race" (Morris, *Romans*, p. 68). W. H. Griffith Thomas hit the nail on the head when he penned that "salvation is for everyone, from every sin, at every time, in every place, under every circumstance" (Thomas, p. 61). A worldwide need led God to make a worldwide provision. It is little wonder that Paul refers to his understanding of salvation as the gospel or good news. Nothing could be better.

> ### The Breadth of Salvation
>
> "Salvation is for everyone, from every sin, at every time, in every place, under every circumstance."
> —W. H. Griffith Thomas

Yet salvation has one condition: it is for "everyone who believes." God doesn't force it on anyone. People must accept it as they see their need in relation to the power of the gospel and its potential in their lives.

But all who accept God's salvation by faith are on one level—they become brothers and sisters in Christ. The Jews don't have one gospel and the Gentiles another. The community of Christ erases all racial, economic, and social barriers. As Paul wrote to the Galatians, "there is neither Jew nor Greek, there is neither slave nor free, there is neither male nor female; for you are all one in Christ Jesus" (Gal. 3:28, RSV).

The idea of salvation or mercy for all becomes a major theme throughout Romans. In fact, that very thought climaxes the letter's treatment of Jewish and Gentile inclusion in the gospel blessing that runs from Romans 9-11. Paul made it clear that God desires to have "mercy upon all" (Rom. 11:32, RSV).

On the other hand, the apostle is quite clear that in one sense Jews do have a priority. Jesus taught the same when He claimed that salvation came through Israel (John 4:22). After all, God not only used the Jewish nation to preserve the covenant in Old Testament times, but He also sent the Savior of the world through a Jewish mother.

The theme of the "firstness" of the Jewish nation runs throughout the New Testament. Thus in Acts 1:8 we read that after the disciples received the power of the Spirit they were to be God's witnesses beginning with the Jews and extending to the ends of the earth. Paul followed that command in his own ministry by always reaching out to the Jews first when he began work in a new community.

Pauline Faith

"For Paul faith is that attitude in which, acknowledging our complete insufficiency for any of the high ends of life, we rely utterly on the sufficiency of God. It is to cease from all assertion of the self, even by way of effort after righteousness, and to make room for the divine initiative" (C. H. Dodd, p. 43).

Romans 1:17 tells us that "in it [the gospel message] the righteousness of God is revealed from faith to faith." The phrase "the righteousness of God" has led to a great deal of discussion down through church history because one can interpret it as "the righteous standing which God gives," "the righteous character which God is," or "the righteous activity which comes from God" (Rogers, p. 316).

Both the immediate context and the argument in the first four chapters of Romans indicate that the proper interpretation in Romans 1:17 is the first. That is, the righteousness of God is something that God provides for His people when they accept it by faith. We will find the point easier to grasp when we realize that the Greek language uses the same word for both righteousness and justification. Thus righteousness by faith and justification by faith are exactly the same thing.

Another interesting aspect of verse 17 is the phrase "from faith to faith." It is another way of saying that salvation is a matter of faith from start to finish. Or, as Vincent Taylor points out, what Paul means is that "what God has done must be received by a faith which leads on to a larger and richer faith" (Taylor, *Romans*, p. 23). That is, a Christian life is dynamic faith on the march.

Part II

All Have Sinned

Romans 1:18-3:20

4. The Sin Problem and Human Responsibility

Romans 1:18-21a

> *¹⁸For God's wrath is revealed from heaven against all ungodliness and unrighteousness of men who suppress the truth in unrighteousness, ¹⁹because that which can be known about God is plain within them; for God made it plain to them. ²⁰For from the creation of the world His invisible attributes, both His eternal power and divine nature, have been clearly seen, being understood through the things that have been made. So they are without excuse. ²¹ᵃFor having known God, they did not honor Him as God or give thanks.*

Wow! What happened? In verses 16 and 17 we had been reading about grace, faith, and salvation. The highlight was mercy. But Romans 1:18 opens with the thunder of God's wrath.

The key to the transition is the word "for." "For" links the gospel presentation of Romans 1:16, 17 to the next couple chapters and their discussion of sin. The word "for" implies that we need the powerful gospel of salvation because of the depth of human sin.

Thus in Romans 1:18 we come to the first great transition in the book of Romans. We met Paul in verses 1-17, in which he introduced himself and his gospel and the purpose for writing his letter. With that foundation in place, the apostle is ready for the first segment of his formal argument.

It runs from Romans 1:18 through 3:20. In that extensive section Paul explores the depth and universality of the sin problem. He undertakes the task in three stages. First, Romans 1:18-32 demonstrates that "men in general" are sinners (Leenhardt, p. 59). While that is true, the main focal point of his treatment of sin in chapter 1 is the Gentiles, who do not have God's special revelation in the Scriptures as do the Jews. The second stage runs from Romans 2:1-29, which outlines the principles of judgment and the guilt of the Jews. The final stage appears found in Romans 3:9-20, in which the apostle demonstrates that all people (both Jews and Gentiles) are guilty before God. That conclusion he summarizes in Romans 3:23 with its proclamation that "all have sinned and fall short of the glory of God" (RSV). Paul utilizes that truth to indicate the universal human need for God's justification by grace through faith on the basis of Christ's death on the cross in Romans 3:21-26

A Four Step Argument

1. Gentiles are sinners (1:18-32).
2. The Jews have the same problem (2:1-29).
3. Thus all have sinned and fallen short (3:9-20, 23).
4. Therefore all people need justification (3:21-26).

While Romans 1:18-3:20 provides God's diagnosis of the sin problem, the rest of the letter deals with the cure. But before the cure people need to see the depth of the problem. Sin is serious. We can't just overlook it. It led to the death of Christ in the drama of God's solution for a lost world.

The first phrase that jumps off the page in Romans 1:18 is "God's wrath." Some people have a great deal of difficulty with that idea. They conjure up a furious God made in their own image, as one who in a fit of emotion lashes out in anger.

But that is not the biblical picture of divine wrath. A full reading of verse 18 helps us put the word in context: "For God's wrath is revealed from heaven against all ungodliness and unrighteousness of men who suppress the truth in unrighteousness." Sin and its results are the only things in the Bible that arouse God's wrath. His wrath is in part a holy reaction to the woe and misery resulting from rebellion against Himself and His principle. Thus God's "wrath only goes forth because God is Love, and because sin is that which injures His children and is opposed to the purpose of His love" (Walker, *What*, pp. 148, 149). From that perspective divine wrath is not in opposition to God's love but rather a natural fruit of it. In the long run, as the Bible pictures Him, God cannot and will not stand idly by while His creation suffers. His reaction is judgment of sin, and we should see such judgment as the real meaning of biblical wrath. God will someday put an end to the ongoing suffering that has resulted from sin. The good news of Romans is that Christ has born the penalty of God's judgment on sin for all who believe in Him (Rom. 3:21-26; John 3:36).

Having said those things about God's wrath in general, it is important to note that divine wrath in the Bible comes in two flavors. The one reflected in Romans 1 is that God lets judgment flow out of the natural consequences of wrong doing. That perspective appears in verses 24, 26, and 28, which indicate that "God gave them up to" sin and its results.

But the natural consequences aspect of wrath is not the full story. Some day God will put an end to the problem of sin and suffering. Like us, He is weary of dead babies, cancer, and blindness; rape, murder, and theft; holocausts, Rwandas, and Iraqs. The book of Revelation clearly reveals a second aspect of divine wrath, in which God will act to destroy sin and its results forever. It is in that context that John refers to "the wrath of the Lamb" (Rev. 6:16, RSV; cf. 19:1-21; 20:11-15; 21:1-5).

Romans 1:19-21 raises another issue vital to Paul's presentation. Put briefly, the apostle needs to make clear the basis of God's condemnation and judgment for those who do not know God's revealed will in Scripture. Said in another way, why should people be subject to God's wrath (verse 18) if they are ignorant of His ways?

Paul's answer is to the point. They are "without excuse" since "from the creation of the world" His "eternal power and divine nature" have been evident to all people (verse 20). That is, even people who don't have the Bible have some word from God, some knowledge of who He is and what He stands for. In the previous verse Paul noted that "what may be known about God is plain to them, because God has made it plain to them" (Rom. 1:19, NIV). Of course, not everything about God and morality can be deduced from nature. But the apostle is clear that people can at least understand that a powerful deity is behind the created world.

Here is an important point, since Paul in this section of Romans is demonstrating that Gentiles, in their relative ignorance, are still responsible for rebelling against what they know about God and goodness through what they see in nature and experience in their conscience.

God's revelation of Himself in nature is what theologians refer to as "general revelation." Such revelation, of course, is far from perfect. One author writes that "nature still speaks of her Creator. Yet these revelations are partial and imperfect. And in our fallen state, with weakened powers and restricted vision, we are incapable of interpreting aright. We need the fuller revelation of Himself that God has given in His written word" (White, *Education*, p. 17). Theologians describe God's fuller revelation of Himself in the Bible as "special revelation."

The Jews of Paul's day had both of God's books (general and special revelation), but the Gentiles had only the incomplete revelation through nature. Yet, Paul argues in Romans 1, even that partial revelation through nature and conscience left them accountable for their deeds.

Their real problem, he penned in verse 18, is that they preferred "ungodliness" and "unrighteousness" or "wickedness" to what they did know about God and goodness. As a result, they had elected to "suppress the truth in unrighteousness." Furthermore, even though they knew something about God, they chose not to "honor Him as God or give thanks" (verse 21). Rejecting God's general revelation, Paul makes clear in the last part of verse 20, leaves them "without excuse."

Paul has made his point clear. God has given every person some information about Himself and true goodness. Thus each of us, no matter how limited our knowledge, has a responsibility to live according to the understanding that God has provided.

5. Sin's Downward Path

Romans 1:21-32
>   [21]*For having known God, they did not honor Him as God or give thanks, but became futile in their thinking and their senseless heart [mind] was darkened.* [22]*Professing to be wise, they became foolish,* [23]*and exchanged the glory of the incorruptible God for an image of corruptible man and birds and four-footed animals and reptiles.*
>   [24]*Therefore God gave them over in the lusts of their hearts to impurity, to the dishonoring of their bodies among themselves,* [25]*who exchanged the truth of God for the lie and worshipped and served the creature instead of the Creator, who is blessed forever. Amen.*

26Because of this God gave them over to dishonorable passions; for even their women exchanged the natural function for that contrary to nature, 27and in the same way also the men gave up the natural function of the women and burned in their passionate desire toward one another, men with men performing the indecent act and receiving in their own persons the due penalty of their error.

28And since they did not see fit to acknowledge God, God gave them over to a degenerate mind, to do things that are not proper, 29being filled with all unrighteousness, wickedness, greediness, evil; full of envy, murder, strife, deceit, malice; they are gossips, 30slanderers, God haters, insolent, arrogant, boasters, inventors of evil, disobedient to parents, 31senseless, faithless, unloving, merciless; 32who knowing the just judgment of God, that those who practice such things are worthy of death, they not only do them but also heartily approve of those practicing them.

What are the fruits of people rebelling against what they know about God and neglecting praise of Him and thankfulness toward Him? (Rom. 1:18-21a). That is the topic of verses 21b through 32 as Paul presents the results of sin in a series of six downward consequences.

First, rejecting God darkens people's hearts and they become fools even as they proclaim their wisdom. Eugene Peterson translates verses 21 and 22 insightfully: "When they didn't treat him like God, refusing to worship him, they trivialized themselves into silliness and confusion so that there was neither sense nor direction left in their lives. They pretended to know it all, but were illiterate regarding life" (Message).

Paul was well aware of the philosophic contortions of the ancient world as it speculated on the meaning and purpose of life. And human philosophies haven't improved much in the 2,000 years since he wrote Romans. Take Friedrich Nietzche, for example. Sometime before his tragic suicide, he concluded that life had no meaning. For him the purpose of history was to develop the ruthless superman who did "right" by crushing those weaker than himself (see Durant, pp. 301-335). Adolf Hitler later used that philosophy to justify his actions. Then there was Jean-Paul Sartre who in mid-twentieth century decreed that "there is no human nature, since there is no God to conceive it. . . . Man is nothing else but what he makes of himself" (Sartre, p. 15).

Having given up a belief in the only true God, the world has endured a series of philosophic speculations that have led it into the nooks and crannies of darkness and futility.

A second result of rejecting God and a prominent example of the foolishness of verse 22 is idolatry, in which people exchange "the glory of the incorruptible God for an image" (verse 23). Isaiah captures the foolishness of idolatry when he speaks of kindling a fire with part of a tree and making a god to worship with the rest of it (Isa. 44:15-17).

The writer of the ancient book known as the Wisdom of Solomon takes the foolishness of idol worship a bit further when he speaks of creating a wooden idol, covering its defects with red paint, and making a shrine for it. He then "fixes it on the wall" with nails. However, the idol worshiper "has to take . . . precautions on its behalf to save it from falling. . . . *Yet he prays to it . . .* and feels no shame in addressing this inanimate object; *for health he appeals to a thing that is weak, for life he prays to a thing that is dead, for aid he asks help from something utterly incapable, for a prosperous journey from something that cannot put one foot before the other"* (Wis. of Sol. 13:15-18, REB, italics supplied). For Paul false worship was *"the lie"* (Rom. 1:25).

Now as twenty-first century people we see the foolishness of idolatry. Or have we? What do we put our trust in? Our things? Our beauty? Our wisdom? Those who continue to reject the true God, even though they may go to church each week, still find themselves locked up in the foolishness of idol worship.

A third consequence of rejecting God, Paul claims, is that God gives blatant sinners over to their "sinful desires," "shameful lusts," and "depraved mind" (Rom. 1:24, 26, 28, NIV). At first sight, it seems quite unlike God. Does God abandon people to evil?

The key to understanding the phrase "gave them over" seems to be in such words as "sinful desires." William Barclay points out that Paul is using a word that "makes men do nameless and shameless things. It is a kind of insanity which makes a man do things he would never have done if this desire had not taken away his sense of honor and prudence and decency" (Barclay, *Romans*, p. 21).

At the bottom of the issue is the fact that God allows us to make wrong choices and do hurtful things. But He doesn't rescue us from their harmful consequences. In fact, He "gave us over" to the frightful effects of sin. He lets us reap the results.

Why? Because he hates sinners? No, because He loves them and wants them to wake up to their need of His salvation.

Step four on the downward path of those who reject God is the massive list of perversions, dysfunctional attitudes, and behaviors in verses 26-31. Running all the way from unnatural sex (women with women and men with men [cf. Jude 7], which the apostle probably viewed in the light of the general revelation of verses 18-21 related to the obvious facts of human sexual anatomy) through the most comprehensive list of specified sins in the New Testament, Paul wants to show what happens to people when they leave God out of their lives. One of the grim facts of life is that sin gives birth to sin. Once a person or a society sets out on the path of sin it becomes easier and easier to practice evil. In fact, they soon come to view evil as normal.

Individuals begin sinning with what Barclay calls a kind of "shuddering awareness" of what they are doing, but as time passes they end up sinning "without a second thought" (Barclay, *Romans*, p. 22). Sinning becomes a way of life. The end result, as Paul points out later in Romans, is that a person under the rule of a depraved mind becomes a slave to sin (6:16). Thus we can use God's gift of free will in such a manner that in the end it obliterates our free will and we become slaves to sin.

> We can use God's gift of free will in such a manner that in the end it obliterates our free will and we become slaves to sin.

The fifth step on the plunging course of sin is that it leads to death. Sinners are not only justly worthy of death (verse 32), but Romans 6:23 is quite clear that their ultimate end will be eternal death. The good news regarding Romans 6:23 is that the verse doesn't end with a death sentence. It goes on to "the free gift of God" which "is eternal life in Christ Jesus our Lord" (RSV).

Paul's main agenda in Romans, however, is not the death that comes from sin but the life that results from a faith relationship to Jesus Christ (Rom. 3:24, 25). While it is true that the book of Romans cogently describes the sin that leads to death, it moves beyond that to the salvation which rescues men and women from both sin and its consequences.

The last downward step in the dreary journey running from verse 21 through verse 32 is the fact that some not only do evil things but "heartily approve" of such actions by others (verse 32b). The New English Bible captures the forcefulness of Paul's idea when it translates the phrase as "they actually *applaud* such practices." Here we find the lowest of the low points on the scale of sin.

Paul Achtemeier writes that "it may strike us as odd that Paul" in verse 32 "seems to think approving such acts is worse than doing them, but what he is pointing to is the fact that those who do things not only do them in their own lives but make them a matter of public encouragement for others to follow. Not content to let wrath take its course in their lives, such people, Paul says, seek to make the measure of their sinful conduct the norm for the conduct of others. It is the desire to make [their] private sin the measure of public conduct that Paul is condemning here" (Achtemeier, pp. 41, 42).

This is a serious issue. We live in a society that approves and applauds a great deal of evil. One only has to look at what the public generally calls "entertainment." If it isn't filled with action-packed sex and violence, it hardly rates in the popularity polls.

Modern society really hasn't moved beyond the ancient world in such matters. It is true, of course, that we no longer feed people to lions or let gladiators battle to the death. No, we are much more sophisticated in the sense that we do the same things in virtual reality through our media. But entertainment tells a great deal about a society. And it reveals much about Christian confusion on this topic.

The message of Romans 1:18-32 is that God finds sin to be sickening and death producing. He wants to help people move beyond approving evil. Not only does He long to save their souls but He wants to transform their minds and lives (Rom. 12:2). The Lord desires Christian influence to be on the side of approving and applauding that which is life-giving and upbuilding. As Christians, we have a part in shaping society through those things that we endorse.

6. Judgment for All

Romans 2:1-5

¹Therefore you are inexcusable, O man, everyone who judges, for in that which you judge another you condemn yourself; for you who judge are doing the same things. ²And we know that the judgment of God rightly falls upon those doing such things. ³But do you suppose, O man, that those who judge those doing such things yet are doing the same things will escape the judgment of God? ⁴Or do you scorn the riches of His kindness and forbearance and longsuffering, not realizing that the kindness of God leads you to repentance? ⁵But by the hardness of your unrepentant heart you are storing up wrath for yourself in the day of wrath and revelation of the righteous judgment of God.

It is easy to feel superior to others, especially for those living "good" lives. After all, we think, I don't do the kinds of sins Paul recorded in chapter 1.

That is just the attitude that he attacks in the first part of Romans 2. In the second half of chapter 1 he presented those who blatantly and obnoxiously sin. His depiction prompts those in the "front pew" to shout "amens" as loud as their judicious voices allow. But it is exactly that attitude of moral superiority that Paul now confronts in Romans 2:1-16.

The apostle is inexorably moving toward the conclusion that all have sinned (Rom. 3:23). He has dealt with what good church members and moralists see as the *real* sinners, an approach that won them over. They have sided with Paul. At the very point that he has them fully with him, however, he turns his guns on them.

They also, he points out, are sinners. Of course, they are nice church members. They don't let all their dirty laundry hang out. No, their sins are vegetarian sins. Compared with the really nasty people, they appear good in their own eyes.

But—and here is Paul's point in Romans 2:1—they don't look so good in God's sight. Their airs of moral superiority are also sin, even if it is invisible to them. Such people suffer from the *sin of goodness*, the most hopeless of all sins. One author correctly points out that "there is nothing so offensive to God or so dangerous to the human soul as pride and self-sufficiency. Of all sins it is the most hopeless, the most incurable" (White, *Christ's Object Lessons*, p, 154). Such goodness feels no need to repent or to seek God's grace.

Thus Romans 2 brings a major shift in Paul's argument. Finished with speaking to prostitutes, perverts, and thieves, he is now ready to speak to the morally superior, whether they be Jews, Gentiles, or just plain church members. It is time for those of us in the pews to wake up and to pay attention to what Paul is saying.

The message of Romans 2:1 is clear—that all humans are sinners. Here is the significance of Paul's statement that all are doing the same things. He doesn't necessarily mean the exact same deeds, but that all do sin. That brings us to verse 2 with its proclamation that "the judgment of God rightly falls upon those doing such things." Put another way, everyone comes under the same judgment, including both Jews and clean-living moralists.

That is the very concept many of his Jewish readers rejected, believing that since they were God's people they would not come under judgment in the same way as the Gentiles. Thus we read from the Wisdom of Solomon, "even if we sin, we are yours, since we acknowledge your power" (15:2, REB). Again, "so we are chastened by you, but you scourge our enemies ten thousand times more" (12:22, REB).

Those sentiments certainly lined up with Paul's own outlook before his conversion when in the context of his superior Hebrew, Pharisaic heritage he noted that he also had had "confidence in the flesh" (Phil. 3:4, 6, RSV). It is in that framework that we need to read Romans 2:3: "But do you suppose, O man, that those who judge those doing such things yet are doing the same things will escape the judgment of God?" James Dunn suggests that here "Paul the unconverted Pharisee," is "expressing attitudes Paul remembered so well as having been his own!" (Dunn, *Romans 1-8*, p. 91).

When it comes right down to it, one of the most effortless things in the world is to judge other people. In Romans 2:1-3 Paul exposes the rather twisted truth that it is easy to be critical of everybody except ourselves. For example, I can instantly work myself up into a state of moral indignation when my wife or children do some obnoxious thing (such as walking on a clean floor with muddy shoes) yet excuse myself. After all, I am in a hurry. John Stott points out that "we even gain a vicarious satisfaction from condemning in others the very faults we excuse in ourselves. . . . This device enables us simultaneously to retain our sins and our self-respect" (Stott, p. 82).

Well, you might be able to fool yourself, or even other people. But Paul tells us here that you can't mislead God, whose "judgment . . . is based on truth" (Rom. 2:2, NIV). The plain fact is, the apostle asserts, no one will escape God's judgment, no matter how often they go to church or how vegetarian their sins are. All of us are sinners, and all will stand before God's judgment seat. Each of us can choose to either present ourselves before Him in our own goodness or in Christ's righteousness. But we need to remember that even though our eyesight might be biased in our favor, God has 20/20 vision when it comes to reading not only our actions but the sentiments of our hearts and minds.

Romans 2:1-3 left Paul's highly moral readers with the thought that God's judgment is for everyone—Jew and Gentile, the nasty and the "righteous." In verse 4 he tells those with a Jewish heritage and other "good" people that they were in danger of despising God's "kindness," "forbearance," and "longsuffering." The apostle seeks to wake them up to their real needs. Just because God was gracious does not mean they had a right to keep on sinning. Just because He was forbearing with their perverse ways did not mean that they were safe from judgment. And just because God was longsuffering didn't mean that they were beyond punishment.

To the contrary, they needed to repent of their proud ways. They should not use God's kindness, forbearance, and longsuffering as an excuse to remain where they were spiritually, but should let God's graciousness inspire them to sincere repentance. As William Barclay puts it, "the mercy of God, the love of God, is not meant to make us feel that we can sin and get away with it; it is meant . . . to break our hearts in love" and lead us to repentance (Barclay, *Romans*, p. 37).

That thought brings us to Romans 2:5: "But by the hardness of your unrepentant heart you are storing up wrath for yourself in the day of wrath and revelation of the righteous judgment of God." The key word here is "but." It contrasts the passage with the counsel in verse 4. Thus instead of God's kindness and mercy leading to repentance, it had had the opposite effect—it had produced hardness or impenitence. The Greek word I translated as "hardness" is the same word from which we get the medical term "sclerosis." Thus arteriosclerosis refers to hardening of the arteries, a process also found in the spiritual realm. It represents the condition of those hearts that have become unresponsive and insensitive to God. But the spiritual condition has much more serious consequences than the physical. Physical arteriosclerosis may lead a person to the grave, but spiritual hardening may cause the loss of eternal life.

The Bible constantly warns about spiritual hardness. Thus when the self-righteous synagogue leaders waited to see if Jesus would heal on the Sabbath, He "looked round about on them with anger, being grieved for the hardness of their hearts" (Mark 3:5, KJV).

Paul put his comments about hard hearts in the context of the final judgment. Some Christians today seek to avoid any mention of the judgment. But the Bible writers had no such qualms. For Paul the final judgment was an absolute certainty that his readers needed to prepare for.

Each of them would be storing up one of two things: repentance or hardness. As with them, so with us. God's will is obvious. He wants us to let Him break up the fallow ground of our hearts—to have a new covenant experience of a softened and repentant heart. Through Ezekiel He promised: "A new heart I will give you, and a new spirit I will put within you; and I will take out of your flesh the heart of stone and give you a heart of flesh" (Eze. 36:26, RSV).

God is still making the offer of salvation, even to us "good" people as we read. But He forces no one. It is up to each of us either to harden our hearts by rejecting His offer or to respond with a yes to His gift of a new heart.

7. Judged by Works

Romans 2:6-11

⁶[On the day of judgment God] "will recompense each person according to his works": to ⁷those who by patience in good works seek for glory and honor and immortality, eternal life; ⁸but to those who are selfishly ambitious and who disobey the truth but obey iniquity, burning anger. ⁹There *will be tribulation and distress for every person who does evil, the Jew first and also the Greek, ¹⁰but glory and honor and peace to everyone doing good works, to the Jew first and also to the Greek. ¹¹For there is no partiality with God.*

Judgment is not a popular topic with many Christians. But God is of a different opinion. In Romans 2:1-16 we find what Anglican Bishop N. T. Wright identifies as "one of the fullest descriptions of the final judgment in all early Christian writing." He goes on to note that Paul treats the judgment in the light of the gospel, which "may come as a surprise to modern readers, for whom 'the gospel' has come to mean salvation from judgment." But for Paul, in line with the Old Testament, a part of the gospel is God putting things right at the end of time. Thus God's final judgment is an integral part of the good news (Wright, p. 438).

It is the basis of that judgment that Paul begins to set forth in Romans 2:6-11. But as we read that God "will recompense each person according to his works" (verse 6), we might be taken aback. Perhaps we may wonder if the apostle is a bit confused. After all, in the very next chapter he writes that "no human being will be justified in his sight by works of the law" (Rom. 3:20, RSV). And in Ephesians he points out that we are saved by grace through faith—"not because of works, lest any man should boast" (Eph. 2: 8, 9, RSV).

How can Paul then turn around and claim that people will be judged by what they have *done* or accomplished?

Before answering, we should note that his words come from Psalm 62:12, which reads: "You will reward each person according to what he has done" (NIV). Jesus picked up that idea when he noted that "the Son of Man is going to come in his Father's glory with his angels, and then he will reward each person according to what he has done" (Matt. 16:27, NIV).

Paul is not contradicting himself. It is true that in Romans 1:16 he claimed that salvation is by faith alone. But he is not now destroying his gospel by saying that salvation results from good works after all. To the contrary, he is affirming, as John Stott puts it, that "although justification is indeed by faith, judgment will be according to works." He goes on to argue that it is not difficult to discover the reason. The judgment is a public occasion, and its purpose is not so much to determine God's decision as to announce it and vindicate it.

"Such a public occasion," Stott writes, "on which a public verdict will be given and a public sentence passed, will require . . . verifiable evidence to support them. And the only public evidence available will be our works. . . . The presence or absence of saving faith in our hearts will be disclosed by the presence or absence of good works of love in our lives" (Stott, p. 84).

Thus Paul is teaching that good works are not the ground of our salvation but the fruit of a saving relationship with Jesus. The apostle called it the "obedience of faith" in Romans 1:5 and 16:26. A changed life results from giving one's heart to Jesus. Those who have died to sin will not continue to live in it. To the contrary, they will walk with Jesus "in newness of life" (Rom. 6:1-12, RSV).

Jesus himself sounded the same final judgment scene note when He said "not everyone who says to me, 'Lord, Lord,' shall enter the kingdom of heaven, but he who *does* the will of my Father" (Matt. 7:21-27, RSV).

Another thing we should note about Romans 2:6-11 is that no favored nation status exists in the final judgment. We see that indicated by the very flow of his argument itself, as outlined in the box below with the first and last points (a and a[1]) reflecting on the fact that all stand before God on the same basis and that God is impartial. But it is even more clearly pictured in verses 9 and 10, which focus on equality of distress and honor in relation to both Jews and Greeks.

That point must have raised eyebrows among some of Paul's Jewish readers. After all, hadn't God chosen Abraham, Isaac, and Jacob? Hadn't He selected Israel as His special covenant nation, His representative on earth?

He had, but that decision was not, so to speak, a blank check. To the contrary, God could bless Israel only if they followed His will. In Deuteronomy we read: "*If* you obey the voice of the Lord your God,

> ### Living Our Faith
>
> "We are not saved by good works, but when we commit our lives fully to God, we want to please him and do his will. As such, our good works are a grateful response to what God has done, not a prerequisite to earning his grace. . . . Think of what God has done for you. Then respond to God's loving acts by trusting and obeying him fully, living out your faith" (Barton, p. 47).

being careful to do all his commandments . . . , [then] the Lord your God will set you high above all the nations of the earth. And all these blessings shall come upon you. . . . But if you will not obey the voice of the Lord your God or be careful to do all his commandments and his statutes . . . , then all these curses shall come upon you" (Deut. 28:1-15, RSV).

Unfortunately, Israel never empha-sized the conditionality of God's blessings to them. Instead, they came to believe that they remained God's favored nation no matter how they lived. John the Baptist challenged that line of thought when he told the Jewish leaders that "God is able from these stones to raise up children to Abraham" (Matt. 3:9, RSV). And Jesus wept over the unresponsiveness of the Jewish leaders to His ministry (Matt. 23:37, 38). Then again, near the end of His ministry He told the parable of the wicked tenants with its frightful conclusion that "the king-dom of God will be taken away from you [Israel] and given to a nation pro-ducing the fruits of it" (Matt. 21:43, 45, RSV), but they never really believed Him. They still assumed that they had favored nation status.

> ## The Flow of Romans 2:6-11
>
> a God will recompense each according to their works (verse 6)
> > b Those who seek immortality will receive eternal life (verse 7)
> > > c Those who disobey the truth will
> > > c¹ get burning anger (verse 8)
> > b¹ There will be glory for everyone who does good (verse 10)
> a¹ There is no partiality with God (verse 11)

It is that very idea that Paul combats in Romans 2. The Lord always of-fers the kingdom to men and women on His conditions alone.

We miss a major point in Paul's presentation of the judgment if we view it only in terms of "tribulation and distress" and negativity (Rom. 2:9). Paul also emphasizes the positive—that there will be "glory and honor and peace to everyone doing good works" (verse 10).

All the way through the Bible judgment is two-edged, with condemna-tion going to those rebelling against God and unfathomable blessings and eternal life for those who love God with all their heart, mind, and soul. A merely negative view of judgment is a sign of a sort of "mental illness" that has afflicted some Christians down through the ages. But the big picture of Scripture features judgment as the greatest of all God's blessings to Christians. It is the occasion at which Jesus passes out eternal blessings. God's final judgment is the time of ultimate rejoicing (see, e.g., Dan. 7:22, 27; Rev. 6:10; 11:15-18; 14:6, 7; 18:20; 19:2).

Romans 2:10 portrays "glory and honor and peace" along with eternal life (verse 7) being bestowed upon God's faithful people in the final judgment. With that in mind, it is clear that God's judgment is not opposed to the gospel but *is* gospel.

Perhaps I should say a word about rewards before bringing this section to a close. Some Christians seem to consider it wrong to think, let alone to desire, rewards from God. But Paul doesn't have any problem with people having and seeking the goals of "glory and honor and immortality" in Romans 2:7. On the other hand, he would be the first to object to any idea that they can earn such rewards by their good conduct. Such things, he is clear, are God's gift (Rom. 6:23). Thus while it is impossible for humans to obtain such things by their own efforts at being good, the Bible is not against Christians contemplating such gifts during their daily struggles. God wants to give us all the encouragement that we need as we persevere in "the obedience of faith" (Rom. 1:5; 2:6, 7).

8. The Impartiality of Judgment

Romans 2:12-16

[12]For all who have sinned without the law will also perish without the law, and all who have sinned under the law will be judged by the law. [13]For it is not the hearers of the law who are righteous before God, but the doers of the law who will be justified. [14]For when Gentiles who do not have the law practice by nature the things of the law, these, not having the law, are a law unto themselves. [15]They demonstrate the requirements of the law written in their hearts, their conscience bearing witness and their thoughts sometimes accusing them and sometimes defending them [16]on the day when, according to my gospel, God judges the hidden things of men through Christ Jesus.

At first glance verse 12 may seem a bit confusing. Phillip's translation helps us see the meaning more clearly: "All who have sinned without knowledge of the Law will die without reference to the Law; and all who have sinned knowing the Law shall be judged according to the Law."

In order to understand Paul's meaning we need to remember the context. Romans 1:18-32 discussed the justifiable condemnation of the wicked Gentiles who sinned after rejecting their rather rudimentary knowledge of God (see especially verses 20-23). Then in the first half of chapter 2 Paul brought up the rather revolutionary idea that the Jews and other moralists (with the argument shifting more exclusively toward just the Jews in the first 11 verses) were equally guilty and equally subject to God's judgment.

That was a startling thought to the Jews. Could they be just as guilty as the uncouth Gentiles? Weren't they God's special people? Although Paul can agree on the point that they are a called-out people, at the same time he does not mean that they are exempt from sin or divine punishment. Here Jews and Gentiles stand on the same ground. Both are guilty. And all will be judged. After all, Paul concluded in Romans 2:11, "there is no partiality with God."

But that statement raised an objection in the Jewish mind. After all, they said to themselves, there exists a major difference between Jews and Gentiles. God has given the Jews His law. That proves that they are His favorites and in no way can He judge them in the same manner as the Gentiles.

Wrong! claims Paul in Romans 2:12. Although it is true that God cannot accuse the Gentiles of breaking a law that they never formally received, yet it is also true, as Paul argued in Romans 1:19, 20 and will do so more explicitly in Romans 2:15, that He has revealed to them a sense of right and wrong. That God-given sense will be the basis of their judgment. That is, He will demonstrate His impartiality in the judgment (2:11) by evaluating each group according to their response to the revelation that He has provided them—special revelation and the law for the Jews and general revelation (1:19, 20) and their conscience (2:15) for the Gentiles. Thus God is indeed impartial (2:11). He holds all individuals responsible for the light that He has provided them.

That conclusion brings us to Romans 2:13 and the claim that "it is not the hearers of the law who are righteous before God, but the doers of the law who will be justified." The word "hearers" is important here since it indicates that Paul is speaking about the Jews who heard God's law read week by week in the synagogue.

But—and here Paul makes the crucial point in his argument—"hearing" was not enough. Having the law is not sufficient. And neither is claiming Abraham as your father or Moses as your prophet.

Paul in these verses is making a concerted effort to break through Jewish exclusiveness, in which some apparently believed that the mere possession of the law meant eternal security.

But, the apostle lets them know, it is not those who hear or possess the law "who are righteous before God," but it is the "doers of the law who will be justified" (2:13). He had raised that point in verse 6 in which he wrote that God in the judgment "will recompense each person according to his works." Here, though, he specifically applies to the Jews responsibility to "do" or keep the law.

Taking Romans 2:13 out of context can be problematic since justification through law keeping obviously contradicts Romans 3:20, which teaches that "no human being will be justified in his sight by works of the law" (RSV). Of course, it is true that people could be justified or counted righteous by keeping the law if they obeyed it *perfectly*. But that is the very point that Paul is making. All are sinners because none keep it perfectly. One function of the law, he will argue in Romans 3:20-25, is to point out sin and lead people to justification through faith in Christ's sacrifice for them.

Well, then, if we are not justified by law keeping, what does Paul mean in Romans 2:13? We must always remember that the apostle is speaking in Romans 2:1-16 about God's final judgment. In that event God will look at "doing" and living the transformed life as an indicator that people have been walking with Jesus, that they have indeed been saved. Thus obedience to the law is important not as the way to get saved but as evidence of salvation. In that light the overall message of Romans is not "saved by grace and do as *you* please," but "saved by grace and do as *God* pleases."

That idea brings us to Romans 2:14, 15. Paul demonstrated in verse 13 that for the Jew the important issue was not having the law but rather keeping it. Yet that truth raises a question about the judgment of the Gentiles who will "perish without the Law" (verse 12). How will God, if He is truly impartial (verse 11), evaluate them? The short answer is that He will deal them according to what they know, just the same as the Jews.

The longer answer is that "the Gentile is not really outside the sphere of law, though he is of course outside the sphere of the law of Moses" (Barrett, p. 51). Paul's argument is that they "practice by nature the things of the law" (verse 14). He is not here making a universal claim, but stating that some Gentiles at times do some of what the law requires. Thus, for example, not all people are adulterers, thieves, or murderers. In fact, in a general sense people feel some need to honor their parents, acknowledge the sanctity of human life, and practice honesty, just as the last six of the commandments require. Thus even though Gentiles do not have the revealed law of Moses, their conduct often shows that they recognize right from wrong.

But on what basis do they have such knowledge? Through their conscience and the fact that God has written a sense of what the law requires in their hearts, Paul tells us in verse 15. Note that he is not claiming too much for human conscience. Rather, he is suggesting that conscience is informed to some extent by a divinely implanted (however minimal) sense of right and wrong. Along that line, Harvard's Marc Hauser reports that recent "studies suggest that nature handed us a moral grammar that fuels our intuitive judgments of right and wrong" and override a person's emotions, even though decisions are affected by emotions (Hauser, p. 65).

In Romans 2:12-15 Paul has demonstrated how God's judgments of both Jew and Gentile can be "impartial" even though one class has the revealed law while the other does not (verse 12). In one sense the situation will be the same for both groups since all will be judged on the basis of action or "doing" (see verses 13, 14, 6). But what informs the respective doing varies greatly between Jew and Gentile, with the former basing practice on the divinely given law and the latter on a divinely implanted sense of right and wrong that surfaces in people's consciences and which they find "sometimes accusing them and sometimes defending them" regarding their actions (verse 15).

Paul concludes his extensive treatment on the final judgment in verse 16: "We may be sure that all this will be taken into account in the day of true judgment, when God will judge men's secret lives by Christ Jesus" (Phillips).

And what does the apostle mean? In the context of Romans 2:11-15 he is indicating that God will judge all people impartially (verse 11) by basing His evaluation of them on their response to what they have known (verses 12-15).

But verse 16 raises two more aspects of God's judgment that need comment. The first is that judgment involves the "hidden things" of a person's life and not merely their outward actions. "On that day," Ernest Best writes, "the *secret* discussions of men's hearts and consciences will be brought to light and men's actions will be judged in relation to them" (Best, p. 29). That is, "God does not act upon superficialities, but upon the springs of character and action" (Ziesler, p. 89), a concept that harmonizes with Jesus' teaching on the spiritual nature of the law in the Sermon on the Mount and the heart as the motivational source for outward action in Matthew 15:18-20.

The final point to note in Romans 2:16 is that in Paul's mind judgment is not something opposed to his gospel but an integral part of it. Along that line, one aspect of the importance of judgment in the context of Romans 1-3 is Paul's argument that judgment shows up every person's (both Jew and Gentile) weakness and guilt. Thus he is in the process of developing the truth of universal condemnation so that all people will feel their deep need of the gospel message that he will begin presenting in Romans 3:21, immediately after bringing his argument that all people are sinners to a conclusion in verse 20.

The good news is that Paul's message always points beyond guilt and condemnation to salvation in Christ.

9. False Views of Assurance

Romans 2:17-29
> [17]*But if you are called a Jew and rely upon the law and boast in God* [18]*and know His will and approve what is excellent, being instructed from the law,* [19]*and have confidence in yourself to be a guide of the blind, a light to those in darkness,* [20]*an instructor of the foolish, a teacher of the immature, having in the law the embodiment of knowledge and of the truth—* [21]*you, therefore, who teach others, do you not need to teach yourself? You who preach against stealing, do you steal?* [22]*You who say do not commit adultery, do you commit adultery? You who abhor idols, do you rob temples?* [23]*You who boast in the law, through the transgression of the law do you dishonor God?* [24]*For, as it is written, "the name of God is blasphemed among the Gentiles because of you."*

> [25]*For indeed circumcision is of benefit if you practice the law. But if you are a transgressor of the law your circumcision has become uncircumcision. [26]If therefore the uncircumcised keeps the requirements of the law, will not his uncircumcision be regarded as circumcision? [27]And those who are physically uncircumcised yet keep the law will condemn those who are physically circumcised but transgress the law. [28]For he is not a Jew who is one outwardly, nor is circumcision something outward and physical. [29]But he is a Jew who is one inwardly, and true circumcision is of the heart and spirit and not literal. His praise is not from men but from God.*

Paul has finished with the topic of judgment, but not with pointing to the Jewish need for a greater righteousness than the heritage of their law. In fact, beginning with Romans 2:17 he actually increases the pressure on the Jews. He will do so in the rest of chapter 2 along two lines: First, the Jewish relationship to the law (verses 17-24), and second, the value of circumcision (verses 25-29).

He starts his first topic in verse 17 with the Jewish tendency to boast about their relationship to God and their reliance upon the law. Then he continues in verses 18-21 to chide them for their superior airs in things related to the law. If they are so full of wisdom and such great teachers of the world's lesser beings, he asks them, then why are they so ignorant? Or, to put it in his own words, "if you teach others, why don't you teach yourself?" (verse 21, NLT).

He picks up that line of thought in verses 21 through 23 in which he focuses on their hypocrisy in relation to the law. Their problem, Paul asserts, was not their message but that they didn't live up to it—that they said one thing but did another. Jesus pointed to the same trait when He noted that "they say, and do not do" (Matt. 23:3, NKJV).

The apostle highlights several examples of their problem. First, he asks: "You who preach against stealing, do you steal?" (verse 21). The implied answer is that they obviously do. Historically, the prophets had to face that problem in the Jewish nation. Ezekiel rebuked those who "have made profit" from their "neighbors by extortion" (Eze. 22:12. NKJV), Amos spoke of those who made their "bushel smaller and the shekel bigger" and "cheat with dishonest scales" (Amos 8:5, NASB), and Malachi accused his fellow Jews of robbing God through the withholding of tithes and offerings (Mal. 3:8, 9).

Things hadn't changed all that much by New Testament times. Jesus censured the Temple money changers and those who sold sacrifices in the Temple for making His Father's house into a robbers' den (Matt. 21:13). On another occasion He condemned the scribes and Pharisees (the self-appointed protectors of the law) for "shamelessly cheat[ing] widows out of their property, and then to cover up the kind of people they really are, they make long prayers in public" (Mark 12:40, NLT).

Paul's other examples were also pointed. He brought His series of questions to a conclusion by inferring that those who bragged about the law really didn't obey it (verse 23). Once again in the progressive argument of Romans 2, the Jews stood under the condemnation of God.

> ## Hypocrisy Is Not an Ancient "Sport"
>
> One of the easiest things in the world to become is a hypocrite. In fact, it seems natural to us humans, even to Christians. In line with the dictum in Romans 2:24 is the saying by the atheistic philosopher Friedrich Nietzsche that the best argument against Christianity is Christians. If Paul had to deal with some of today's church members he might say Amen! to that thought.

The apostle ends his section on Jewish hypocrisy with an Old Testament paraphrase based on such passages as Isaiah 52:5 and Ezekiel 36:22: "It is written, 'the name of God is blasphemed among the Gentiles because of you'" (Rom. 2:24). The ultimate difficulty with hypocrisy is that it reflects not only on the hypocrites themselves but also on the God they claim to be serving.

With Romans 2:25 the apostle has arrived at the next step in his extensive argument against Jewish exemption from God's judgment. If their possession of the law didn't protect them from divine judgment (verses 17-24), he goes on to argue in verses 25-29 that circumcision won't either.

The Jews put a great deal of stock in circumcision. The Jewish rite goes back to Abraham the father of the nation. When God established the covenant with Abraham that made his descendants the people of God's promises, He stipulated circumcision as the external sign of the covenant (Gen. 17:9-14).

As a result, the Jews regarded circumcision as having the utmost importance. Leon Morris points out that "it was unthinkable that a man, duly circumcised and admitted to the covenant, should fail of his salvation" (Morris, *Romans*, p. 139). We read in the Jewish *Mishnah* that "all Israelites have a share in the world to come" (M. Sanhedrin 10:1). And Rabbi Levi could state that "in the Hereafter Abraham will sit at the entrance to Gehenna [hell] and permit no circumcised Israelite to descend therein" (Gen. Rab. 48:8, in Morris, *Romans*, pp. 139, 140).

Beginning in Romans 2:25 Paul launches a concerted attack on such a belief. Attaching no saving value to the physical act of circumcision, he plainly states in Romans 2:25 and in Galatians 5:3 that circumcision had no significance unless a person obeys the "whole law" flawlessly.

His position directly challenged Jewish feelings of security, because he had just demonstrated in Romans 2:17-24 that the Jews were guilty before God because they were lawbreakers. Paul then came to the frightful conclusion in verse 25 that if they broke the law they had become as if they had not been circumcised.

That was serious. If they couldn't place their trust for salvation in either the law or in circumcision, what could they do? Paul knows the only answer to that question. But before he presents it he has to nail a few more points in place.

The apostle has not finished shaking up the Jewish mind. If in Romans 2:25 he argued that when they broke the law they had become as though they had never been circumcised, in verse 26 he looks at the other side of the coin, indicating that Gentiles would be regarded as though they were circumcised if they kept the law's requirements.

Paul is not arguing that the Gentiles could earn salvation by obeying the law, but rather that they stand on an equal footing with Jews when it comes to God's promises. The corollary to that position is that the Jews face God's judgment just as much as the Gentiles.

What Paul said would profoundly shock his Jewish readers. Traditionally they had pictured themselves as sitting in judgment on the uncircumcised pagans. But the roles could actually be reversed. What counts with God is not the external symbol of circumcision but an attitude of total surrender to doing His will.

This concept has a great deal of meaning for Christians in the twenty-first century. Many have thought of baptism or church membership in much the same way that the Jews did about circumcision, but such are merely outward signs of an inward dedication to God. Emil Brunner hits the point when he notes that "membership badges without loyalty and obedience are of no value. Attachment to the Church without discipleship is the husk without the kernel" (Brunner, *Romans*, p. 23).

Paul's depiction of the great reversal continues in Romans 2:27 and 28. In Romans 1 he made the Jews feel good by leading them to assume superiority over the wicked Gentiles. But throughout Romans 2 he has blasted away at Jewish self-confidence.

- First, he erased their confidence that they were beyond God's final judgment (verses 1-16).
- Second, he removed their confidence based upon their possession of the law (verses 17-24).
- Third, he undermined their confidence in the value of circumcision as guaranteeing entrance into God's kingdom (verses 25, 26).
- Then Paul had the audacity to say that Gentiles who obeyed the law would sit in judgment on the Jews (verse 27), completely reversing everything they had been taught about judgment.
- And now in verses 28 and 29 he redefines what it means to be a Jew.

His final nail in the coffin of Jewish confidence was that true circumcision is of the heart rather than of the body (verse 29). Talk of circumcised hearts was an Old Testament theme (see e.g., Deut. 30:6; 10:16; Lev. 26:41) as God had sought to teach the ancient Jews the spiritual nature of discipleship. But most of them hadn't caught that essential message, and, as a result, were still relying on externals.

But it is a message of utmost importance. It is the same one that Jesus sought to teach Nicodemus about being born from above of water and the spirit (John 3:3-7). And here we continue to face the same old problem. We still have too many "water" church members who have not met the "spirit." All such need to learn the lesson of the circumcised heart.

10. Objections to Paul's Teaching

Romans 3:1-8

¹Then what advantage has the Jew? Or what is the benefit of circumcision? ²Much in every way. In the first place, they were entrusted with the oracles of God. ³What then if some disbelieved? Surely their unbelief will not nullify the faithfulness of God? ⁴Certainly not! Rather, let God be true though every man be found a liar, as it is written,

"That You may be justified in Your words
and be victor when You are judged."

⁵But if our unrighteousness proves the righteousness of God, what shall we say? Is God unjust in inflicting wrath? (I am speaking in a human way.) ⁶Certainly not! Otherwise how will God judge the world? ⁷But if through my lie the truth of God abounds to His glory, why am I yet condemned as a sinner? ⁸And why not say (as we are slanderously charged and as some claim that we say) "Let us practice evil in order that good may come?" Their condemnation is just.

It is easy to agree with Frederick Godet that Romans 3:1-8 is "one of the most difficult" passages in the letter (Godet, p. 131). But if we follow the logic of what Paul was doing in Romans 1 and 2 it will help clarify what he is saying here. By the end of Romans 2 he had demonstrated that all people (both Gentiles and Jews) were sinners and thus needed Christ's righteousness.

At the beginning of chapter 3 we would expect him to summarize his conclusions. He will do that in verses 9-20, but first he takes us on an eight-verse digression. His plain speaking about the Jew has created some serious questions. The apostle places them in the mouth of a Jewish objector in verses 1-8, who raises four challenges to Paul's theology. Undoubtedly he had already met such objections in response to his preaching in various localities. In fact, Gerald Cragg suggests that "Paul knows the full force of his antagonist's questions because," given his pharisaic background, "he himself has often asked them" (Cragg, p. 421). In other words, here we have Paul the Pharisee debating Paul the Christian.

The debate itself in Romans 3:1-8 goes through four cycles, with four objections being presented, and Paul providing four answers in turn. The objections center on Jewish superiority in relation to God's faithfulness. The apostle

A Guide Through Romans 3:1-8

Objection number 1: Paul's teaching undermines God's covenant (verse 1).

Answer number 1: Not so! God continues to bless His people (verse 2).

Objection number 2: Paul's teaching leads to the conclusion that God is not faithful (verse 3).

Answer number 2: Not so! God is faithful and just even if all humans are messed up (verse 4).

Objection number 3: Paul's teaching undermines God's justice (verse 5).

Answer number 3: Not so! Both sides agree on God's justice and His right to judge. So there is no argument (verse 6).

Objection number 4: Paul's teaching leads to a cheap grace in which people ought to sin as much as possible so that the God of forgiveness can be glorified as much as possible (verses 7, 8).

Answer number 4: Not so! But people who spout such stupidity will get their just condemnation (verse 8).

touches briefly upon that topic in chapter 3, but he will treat it extensively in Romans 9-11. In chapter 3 he only has to deal with the issues to the extent that his opponents can't use them to set aside the powerful argument he made about Jewish sin and their liability to judgment in chapter 2.

The first argument arises in Romans 3:1, in which we find the objector asking in the light of chapter 2 what advantage being a Jew or being circumcised might possibly have. Paul will answer the first part of that question in Romans 3:2 and the second part in Romans 4, in which he deals with Abraham the father of the circumcised.

Here we find a question just as important for Christians as for Jews, except we might phrase it as "What advantage is there in being baptized or belonging to a church if those things don't save us?"

One might expect, given the argument in chapter 2 on the inadequacy of Jewish possession of the law and circumcision, a resounding no to the question on whether being a Jew had any advantage.

Instead we find a definite yes. A negative answer would have been problematic. After all, "if the Old Testament is to be believed God did choose the Jews out of all mankind and did bestow special privileges upon them. To reduce them therefore to the level of other nations is either to accuse the Old Testament of false-hood, or to accuse God of failing to carry out his plans. It is this theolog-ical objection to his thesis that Paul" must respond to (Barrett, p. 62).

His answer is forceful. Hadn't God entrusted them with His revelation (3:2)—a blessing that brings all others in its train? The primary advantage of being Jewish, Paul declares, is that God gave the Bible to the world through the Jewish nation. Through it they had received both the law and circumcision. But the Bible, Paul will point out from Romans 3:9 on-ward, contained much more—it also included God's teaching on the uni-versality of sin, the problems of outward religion, and the promises of the coming of Christ and the way of salvation.

Yes, the Jewish nation had received an inestimable blessing above other peoples (Rom. 3:2). Unfortunately, they had misused the blessing, as Paul pointed out in Romans 2. But that did not negate their privilege.

That very privilege leads to a second objection in the minds of Paul's op-ponents. What if some of the Jews lacked faith? Does that mean that God is free from His promises to the Jews?

Certainly not! Paul blasted out. Even if every person failed, God would re-main faithful (verse 4). To illustrate his point he cites Psalm 51:4 from the Greek translation of the Bible (the Septuagint) to indicate that "after being chastened for his sin [with Bathsheba] and refusal to confess it for a long pe-riod, David was ready to admit that God was in the right and he was in the wrong" (Harrison, p. 63). Thus God vindicated His covenant faithfulness. He had been true to His promises in spite of David's faithlessness.

That conclusion sets the stage for objection number three in Romans 3:5, which in its essence suggests that Paul's teaching frustrates divine jus-tice. The force of the objection is that if human wickedness brings God's justice or righteousness into focus and magnifies His glory, then it couldn't possibly be right for God to punish sinners. After all, the objection implies, if we didn't sin, God couldn't be shown to be just. And if we have thereby done God such a good favor by sinning, how can He turn around and punish us for helping Him?

The apostle appears to be embarrassed for even raising such a ridiculous ob-jection. Thus he adds the words, "I am speaking in a human way" (verse 5).

While Paul may have been uncomfortable about the way he had to state such a foolish objection, he was more than bold in answering it. "Certainly not!" he thunders in response to such foolishness (verse 6). He then adds that "if God is not just, how is he qualified to judge the world?" (NLT). That affirmation put an end to the objection since all Jews were convinced of God's justice and His final judgment of the world, even if they restricted the negative aspects of that judgment to the Gentiles. But the point has been made and the objection neutralized. "The basic message is the same as in 2:1-3:4: when God judges his people, he is faithful to his covenant promises because evil works demand judgment" (Osborne, p. 83).

Romans 3:7, 8 brings us to the final objection, one related to the issues of verse 4, but now Paul more clearly states the human side of it. The basic idea is that if human sin leads to God's glory as He saves by grace, what right does God have to condemn sinners? (verse 7). Or as the apostle puts it even more sharply in verse 8, "Let us practice evil in order that good may come." For the present the apostle refuses to even consider such a ridiculous proposition. He merely says that such is what some people are saying about him. And all such will get their just condemnation for their slander (verse 8).

But Paul eventually will take up the issue of increasing sin so that grace might abound in Romans 6, in which he will deal with it thoroughly, since the accusation of cheap grace is one that many raise when they discover that salvation is a gift.

But, first, however, he has to get to the gift itself in Romans 3:21-5:21. And before he does that he has to put the finishing touches on his treatment of the universality of sin (3:9-19) and the helplessness of humans to do anything about it (verse 20).

Meanwhile, some extremely positive conclusions flow out of Romans 3:1-8.

1. It is indeed a blessing to be a part of the people of God, since God has given us His Word as a guide to life (Rom. 3:1, 2).
2. God is always faithful to His covenant promises, even when we sin. He can be trusted even when we prove untrustworthy and let Him down (verses 3, 4). The Lord is not only merciful but He is just and He will judge the world in righteousness (verses 5, 6).
3. God does not suffer fools, but His arms are wide open to His repentant children (verses 7, 8).

11. "Sinner" Means Everybody

Romans 3:9-19
⁹What then? Are we [Jews] better than others? Not at all; for we have already incriminated both Jews and Greeks. All are under sin. ¹⁰As it is written,
"None is righteous, not one;
¹¹No one understands,
No one seeks God.
¹²All have turned away, together they became worthless;
No one does good,
Not so much as one."
¹³"Their throat is an open grave,
With their tongues they work deceit."
"The poison of asps is under their lips."
¹⁴"Whose mouth is full of cursing and bitterness."
¹⁵"Their feet are swift to shed blood,
¹⁶In their paths are ruin and misery,
¹⁷And they have not known the way of peace."
¹⁸"There is no fear of God before their eyes."
¹⁹Now we know that whatever the law says, it speaks to those under the law, so that every mouth may be stopped and all the world may come under judgment by God.

What shall we conclude then?" is the New International Version's interpretative rendering of the first part of Romans 3:9. And most readers by this time are ready for some concluding remarks about human sinfulness. It has seemed as if Paul would never get finished with the topic. But He had his reasons for his extensive treatment. Leon Morris indicates it when he claims that "unless there is something to be saved from, there is no point in preaching salvation," or embracing it for that matter (Morris, *Romans*, p. 163).

The apostle's extensive treatment of universal sin and condemnation has paved the way for him to discuss God's great plan of salvation. And just as he has repeatedly stressed the fact that both Jew and Gentile are sinners, so he will repeatedly emphasize that salvation is for everyone. God's great salvation has no racial, ethnic, or other barriers. His grace is free to all.

That thought brings us back to Paul's concluding remarks in Romans 3:9. At first glance, the apostle might sound as if he is contradicting himself when he says that the Jews are no better off than other people when he has already said in verse 1 that they had greater advantages. But in verse 1 he was referring to privileges and responsibilities, not favoritism, since even God's people are not exempt from judgment.

Romans 3:9 is actually a continuation of the line of argument left off in Romans 2:29, since 3:1-8 was a digression that dealt with a series of objections to Paul's teaching. But with verse 9 Paul is back on track, and his conclusions are not only forceful but devastating to Jewish thoughts of favored nation status. The truth, he says, is that the Jews are no better than others. He notes that he has already demonstrated that "*all* are under sin" in chapters 1 and 2, with "all" including the Jews.

Just to make certain that no one has any misunderstandings on the point, Paul presents a barrage of quotations from the Jewish Scripture. Each of the six quotations drives home the point that the Jews aren't quite as good as they think they are.

The first quotation, a paraphrase of Psalm 14:1-3, lists six indictments.

1. First, "there is no one righteous, not even one" (Rom. 3:10, NIV). "Righteousness" is a key word in Romans. In its essence it means being right before God. None fit that category.

2. "No one understands" (verse 11). Thus as humans we are not only morally evil, we are also spiritually ignorant.

3. "No one seeks God" (verse 11). In addition to being universally evil and spiritually ignorant, Paul now claims that people are rebellious. They avoid God. Of course, they don't shirk the duties of religion. People like pageantry and they enjoy doing things that make them feel religious. But seeking God with all one's heart is a bit more threatening than our human solutions.

4. People not only fail to seek God, but they deliberately turn away from Him (verse 12), like a soldier running the wrong way in the midst of battle.

5. Paul charges that the natural person is "worthless" (verse 12), a word used of milk when it sours (Dunn, *Romans 1-8*, p. 150). Human nature without God, he is saying, is sour and useless.

6. "No one does good, not so much as one" (verse 12). That condemnation is both a repetition of the first one and a summary of the previous five.

Given the power and breadth of that first quotation, it seems that Paul doesn't need to cite any more. But in order to leave absolutely no doubt as to human sinfulness he produces a list of five more, utilizing a Jewish method that they referred to as "stringing pearls."

An examination of the next five "pearls" finds the apostle systematically listing the various parts of the human body. Thus sinners' *throats* are as open graves, their *tongues* practice deceit, their *lips* spread snakelike poison, their *mouths* utter bitter curses, and their *feet* don't merely pursue violence, but are swift to do so (verses 13-16). Verse 18 deals with the shortcoming of their *eyes*.

Paul is teaching his readers that sin affects every part of humanity. He is presenting what theologians label as "total depravity." Total depravity does not mean that people are as wicked as they could be, but rather that sin has affected their entire being. Thus they use bodily organs that God gave them to bless other humans to harm them and rebel against God.

Romans 3:19 is the conclusion of Paul's understanding of sin. Here he needs to plug one last possible Jewish loophole. Sixteenth-century Reformer John Calvin highlights the issue when he points out that "whatever was said in the law unfavourably of mankind, [the Jews] usually applied to the Gentiles, as though they were exempt from the common condition of men" (Calvin, p. 129).

With that evasive logic in mind, Paul writes that "we know that whatever the law says, it speaks to those under the law" (verse 19). "Those under the law" is Paul's way of referring to the Jews. Thus Paul's string of pearls is for them also and not merely for the Gentiles. That, he asserts, ought to "stop" their mouths on the topic and help them to face up to the ultimate facts of life. "The reference to the stopped mouth," C.E.B. Cranfield notes, "evokes the image of the

> **Total Depravity and Total Redemption**
>
> Just as sin affects every part of human life including body, heart, and mind, so God aims His redemptive activity at the total person. He isn't merely interested in saving our souls, but also in renewing our minds, transforming our attitudes, and eventually resurrecting our bodies. Just as sin affects us totally, so does salvation.

defendant in court, who, when given the opportunity to speak in his own defence, remains silent, overwhelmed by the weight of the evidence against him" (Cranfield, *Shorter Commentary*, p. 67).

And what is the ultimate fact of life that Paul has been moving toward ever since Romans 1:18? That "all the world," including both Jews and Gentiles, is "under judgment by God" (3:19). None can rest on their spiritual pedigrees.

Of course, we can be thankful that the final words of verse 19 are not the only "ultimate fact" of the book of Romans. Paul has rigorously laid the foundation of humanity's great need. Now he will present God's provision for it in the rest of the letter to the Romans. But before getting to the real solution in Romans 3:21, the apostle needs to seal off one final attractive false path in verse 20.

12. What the Law Can't Do

Romans 3:20

20because by works of the law no flesh will be justified before Him. For through the law comes the knowledge of sin.

The careful reader has probably noticed that I did not begin the first word in verse 20 with a capital letter. My reason is that in actuality verses 19 and 20 are one long Greek sentence with verse 19 pointing out that no one really has anything that they can say in their defense because they are under God's judgment on sin and thus guilty before Him.

The "because" of verse 20 is the glue that holds it to verse 19. That is, all are guilty "because by works of the law no flesh will be justified before Him."

The first thing we must recognize about verse 20 is that it is dealing with a legal situation found in the context of words familiar to a court of law. Judgment, guilt, and silent witnesses are central to verse 19 in which Paul sums up the argument he began in Romans 1:18—that all humanity is under "the wrath of God" because of its sin. It is the *guilt* of the "whole world" that Paul has established in the extensive passage running from Romans 1:18–3:18.

D. Martyn Lloyd-Jones argues perceptively that universal human guilt is what Paul has demonstrated rather than that "we are in a rotten state inside ourselves and that we are polluted as the result of sin." While those things are true, the apostle's main point is that humans "are answerable" to God and stand "under the condemnation . . . of God" (Lloyd-Jones, *Chapters 2:1-3:20*, p. 225).

Thus the problem Paul deals with here is guilt rather than pollution. Although he will extensively treat the pollution of sin later in the book, that is not his topic in the legal context of Romans 3:19, 20.

It is because of the all-important topic of human guilt that the apostle uses the word "justification" in verse 20. Justification is a legal term that meshes perfectly with the law-court related ideas of judgment, law, and guilt. Paul utilized the metaphor of justification to meet the problem of the legal curse of the law with its death penalty (Rom. 3:23; 6:23). "Justification," Vincent Taylor asserts, "is a question first and last of man's *standing* with God." Is a person righteous or guilty before the divine judge? (Taylor, *Forgiveness*, p. 68).

The problem that Paul confronts in Romans 3:20 is not guilt or condemnation. He has already demonstrated that all are guilty and stand condemned before God. What he now needs to address is how a person can be justified before God. And here we must be careful and very specific. The first and most important human requirement is not help in becoming better people or a Christ that can enable them to be conquerors in life's battles. To follow such priorities is to totally miss the meaning of Paul's gospel. Those "improvement" and aid for a better life types of issues have their place, but they are not primary. "The first trouble with man," Lloyd-Jones writes, "is that he is guilty. He does need to be better. He does need help. He does need to get rid of self. I know he does, but before any one of those things, he needs to be put right with God" (Lloyd-Jones, *Chapters 2:1-3:20*, p. 226).

But *how* does a person become right with God? That issue will consume the apostle Paul from Romans 3:20 through 5:21. His first approach to the topic is to tell his readers how *not* to do it. "By works of the law," he writes in Romans 3:20, "no flesh will be justified before Him."

His statement has caused a great deal of discussion. What is it that Paul is saying? Some have pointed out that Judaism at its best did not hold to salvation by works of law. While that is true, the New Testament makes a great deal of what we might call "a popular pervision [of Judaism] which *did* think of earning God's favour" (Ziesler, p. 105). That attitude shows up in the question of the rich young ruler who asked Jesus what he needed to do in order to be saved (Matt. 19:16-22) and in the superior airs of the Pharisees who had achieved so much more than the publican who frankly admitted to God that he was a sinner (Luke 18:9-14). In fact, works of righteousness appears as a subtheme to the class of Pharisees that Jesus dealt with in the gospels.

From the immediate context of Romans 3:20 it appears that Paul is at the very least telling the Jews that they cannot earn God's favor by works of the law. But the larger context of Romans 1:18-3:20 of necessity broadens out the implications to include both Jews and Gentiles since the force of his argument has been to demonstrate the guilt of both groups. Thus the significance of his "all the world" in Romans 3:19 and "no flesh" in verse 20. Paul is making a statement that refers to all sinners at all times. In no case can works of law free anyone from the problem of guilt. But we should add that Paul specifically "uses the phrase 'works of the law' instead of the simple 'works' because he is particularly concerned" in the context of Romans 2:1-3:18 "to deny to Jews an escape from the general sentence" of guilt promised in verse 19 (Moo, *Epistle*, p. 209).

On the other hand, "since 'works of the law' are simply what we might call 'good works' defined in Jewish terms, the principle enunciated here has universal application; nothing a person does, whatever the object of obedience or motivation of that obedience, can bring him or her into favor with God. It is just at this point that the significance of the meaning" of "'works of the law' emerges so clearly. Any restricted definition of 'works of the law' *can* have the effect of opening the door to the possibility of justification by works—'good' deeds that are done in the right spirit, with God's enabling grace, or something of the sort. This, we are convinced, would be to misunderstand Paul at a vital point. The heart of his contention in this section of Romans is that *no one* is capable of doing *anything* to gain acceptance with God" (*ibid.*).

That conclusion brings us to Paul's remark on the law in Romans 3:20. In the first half of the verse he tells what the law cannot do—keeping it cannot make sinful humans right with God, no matter how sincere they are or how well one obeys it or how much energy and time a person spends in the endeavor. Now Paul is ready to treat what the law can do: "For through the law comes the knowledge of sin" (Rom. 3:20). That is a sentiment he will return to again in Romans 4:15 and 7:7. Here we find what we might call the diagnostic function of the law. The law provides the divine standard against which people measure themselves and come to conclusions regarding their guilt. Phillips' rendering of Romans 3:20 is helpful here: "Indeed it is the straight-edge of the Law that shows us how crooked we are." The New Living Translation is also insightful: "For no one can ever be made right in God's sight by doing what his law commands. For the more we know God's law, the clearer it becomes that we aren't obeying it."

> ### Martin Luther on the Function of the Law
>
> "The principle point . . . of the law . . . is to make men not better but worse; that is to say, it sheweth unto them their sin, that by the knowledge thereof they may be humbled, terrified, bruised and broken, and by this means may be driven to seek grace, and so come to that blessed Seed [i.e. Christ]"—Luther, *Galatians*, p. 316.

James 1:23-25 captures Paul's idea of both the strengths and weaknesses of the law when it compares the law to a mirror. Before I leave for work in the morning I go to the mirror to discover what is right and wrong with my face and hair. The mirror tells me that not all is quite ready for public exposure, that I have egg on my face or that my hair is only half combed.

Now, the function of the mirror is to point out things that need improvement. With that knowledge I can go to the soap, washcloth, and comb. But it won't do to rub the mirror on my face to get the egg off or to run the mirror through my hair to comb it. The purpose of the mirror is to remind me of shortfalls and needed improvements.

So it is with the law. When I compare myself with God's law I find that I have problems in my life. But the law cannot correct them. It has another function: to tell me that I am a sinner.

Thus the law is not a ladder to heaven. But in the theology of Romans it makes me aware of such a ladder. In the end the law points beyond itself to Jesus and the real solution to sin, guilt, and condemnation. It is to that topic that Paul now turns as he moves beyond his extensive analysis of the sin problem to the good news of justification.

Part III

The Good News of Justification

Romans 3:21-5:21

13. Righteousness by Faith

Romans 3:21, 22a

²¹But now apart from the law the righteousness of God has been man-ifested, although the law and the prophets bear witness to it, ²²ᵃ righteous-ness of God through faith in Christ Jesus for all those who believe.

"But now." With those two words we have arrived at a major turning point in the book of Romans. During the first step (1:1-17) we met Paul and his gospel. At the second step (1:18-3:20) he demonstrated, at times in excruciating detail, that every person is a sinner headed for judgment, the wrath of God, and eventual death.

Not a very bright future. That's where Paul's "but now" comes in. D. Martyn Lloyd-Jones claims that "there are no more wonderful words in the whole of the Scripture than just these two words 'But now'" (Lloyd-Jones, *Chapters 3:20-4:25*, p. 25).

Why make such an emphatic statement? The answer lies in the context. Paul has left his readers in a state of hopelessness and helplessness. In Romans 3:19 he noted that every person stands under God's just condemnation. Then in verse 20 he emphatically stated that people couldn't get right with God even if they wanted to be good and zealously kept the law. At that very point Paul drops in his "but now."

"But now," he writes, "apart from the law the righteousness of God has been manifested." With those words Paul introduces his gospel and sets the agenda for step three in his presentation in Romans. This stage picks up the righteousness by faith theme of Romans 1:16 and 17 and fills out its meaning in a mighty passage that runs from Romans 3:21 through 5:21.

His initial treatment of the topic extends from Romans 3:21 through 3:31 in what Leon Morris claims might be "the most important single paragraph ever written" (Morris, *Romans*, p. 173).

The good news is that God has intervened in human affairs. He has done for us what we could not do through the law. "But now" reflects the fact that God's saving work through Christ has transformed the human predicament.

The plan of salvation through Christ that we discover in Romans 3:21 was not an afterthought. To the contrary, "the law and the prophets [i.e. the Hebrew Scriptures] bear witness to it." The first glimmer of the Old Testament witness to righteousness apart from the law comes in Genesis 3:15, in which God tells us that the Seed (i.e. Christ—Gal. 3:16) would bruise the head of the serpent (cf. Rev. 12:7-11). That glimmer becomes brighter in the experience of Abraham, whom God counted righteous because he believed Him (Gen. 15:6), a topic that Paul treats extensively in Romans 4. But perhaps the most explicit showcase of the plan of salvation in the books of Moses is the sacrificial system. Along that line, it is of interest that John the Baptist refers to Jesus as the "Lamb of God, who takes away the sin of the world" (John 1:29, RSV) and Paul describes Christ as "our paschal lamb" who "has been sacrificed" for us (1 Cor. 5:7, RSV).

And David speaks of the "righteousness from God, apart from law" (Rom. 3:21, NIV) when he relies on God's mercy to "blot out" his "transgressions" and to wash him from his iniquity (Ps. 51:1, 2, KJV). Isaiah 53 foretells the One who will justify individuals by bearing their "iniquities" (Isa. 53:11). Again, the same chapter notes that "he was wounded for our transgressions, he was bruised for our iniquities: the chastisement of our peace was upon him; and with his stripes we are healed" (verse 5, KJV).

Jeremiah also treated the topic, referring to the coming Branch of David who would be called "THE LORD OUR RIGHTEOUSNESS" (Jer. 23:5, 6, KJV). And the great prophetic chapter of Daniel 9 notes: "Seventy weeks of years are decreed concerning your people and your holy city, to finish the transgression, to put an end to sin, and to atone for iniquity, to bring in everlasting righteousness" (Dan. 9:24, RSV).

Paul knew what he was talking about. God's plan for saving people by means other than obedience to the law is a theme that runs throughout the Old Testament.

With Romans 3:22 and its statement that "this righteousness from God comes through faith in Jesus Christ" (NIV) we have come to the beginning of an absolutely central part of Paul's argument in Romans. Verse 21 noted that God had a righteousness "apart from the law." That is the negative side—what righteousness is not. But with verse 22 we come to the positive explanation that Paul has been wanting to get to ever since Romans 1:16, 17.

In that passage the apostle said that he was "not ashamed of the gospel, for it is the power of God unto salvation to everyone who believes, to the Jew first and also to the Greek. For in it the righteousness of God is revealed from faith to faith."

Paul did not stop to explain what he meant because he had a task that he had to accomplish first. He wanted to make clear that *everybody* needed God's righteousness, and that we could not obtain it by any human condition or achievement—not by birth into the covenant people or by having or keeping the law.

Since the law's function was to point out sin (Rom. 3:20), it had no power to save, but could only condemn. Everybody—even the good synagogue attending Jews—was under condemnation, with no way out.

Now that Paul has made those points he can pick up on his statement about the gospel or righteousness by faith that he had set forth in Romans 1:16, 17. He is now ready to explain what he meant by the phrase. And by now everybody should be ready to listen since they now know that they have no hope outside of God's gracious offer.

> "Righteousness" is an important word in Romans, appearing 37 times. The next-highest usages are seven times in 2 Corinthians and six in Hebrews. The phrase "a righteousness of God," as found in Romans 3:22, shows up eight times in Romans, but only twice in all the rest of Paul's letters combined.

Now we should point out that "God's righteousness" or "righteousness of God" can refer to either God's character or His gift. In the context of Romans 3:21, 22 it primarily means that righteousness which God provided and offered to sinful humans. To Paul such righteousness is humanity's greatest need. Thus it stands at the very center of his presentation of the gospel message.

But receiving that righteousness is not automatic. It must be accepted. It has a condition, and that stipulation according to Romans 3:22 is "faith in Christ Jesus" described as "all those who believe."

But what is faith? C. K. Barrett helps us to understand its meaning in the context of Romans when he writes that faith "can hardly be better defined than as the opposite of man's self-confident or self-despairing attempt to establish a proper relationship between himself and God by legal (that is, by moral or religious) means. Instead of concentrating his hope upon himself he directs it towards God." Particularly toward His saving act of grace through Jesus Christ (Barrett, p. 74).

Faith, Frederick Godet suggests, "is nothing else than the simple acceptance" of God's salvation. In another connection he describes it as "the hand of the heart" (Godet, p. 92). Thus it is believing faith that appropriates God's free gift. Here we must beware of understanding faith as some kind of human work. People are not saved *on account of* their faith but rather *through* their faith as it takes hold of God's gift in Christ. Thus "faith receives what God bestows but adds nothing to the gift" (Harrison, p. 70). Paul even describes faith itself as a gift from God (Rom. 12:3). The only function of the individual is to decide how to use the gift.

Biblical faith includes both believing and trusting. In fact, we might think of it as trust based on belief. Just as the first step in sin involved distrust in God (Gen. 3:1-6), so the first step toward Him is trusting faith. Faith is coming to grips with the fact that we must trust God because He has our best interests at heart, and because there exists nothing else completely trustworthy. Thus "God's righteousness" or "righteousness of God" in its secondary sense also helps us understand Romans 3:22. That is, God is a fit object of faith because He is trustworthy in His relationships to humanity. As a result, accepting righteousness through faith is not faith in an abstraction but trusting faith in a person. In that sense, "because Jesus is the personal manifestation of God's righteousness, righteousness must be received through a relationship of faith in God's Son" (Edwards, p. 99).

Finally, we should note that saving faith is single minded in its fixation on Christ as one's only hope. James Denney can therefore write that "faith is not the acceptance of a legal arrangement; it is the abandonment of the soul, which has no hope but in the Saviour, to the Saviour. . . . It includes the absolute renunciation of everything else, to lay hold on Christ"

(Denney, *Studies*, p. 155). Again, faith is a "passion in which the whole being of man is caught up and abandoned unconditionally to the love revealed in the Saviour" (Denney, *Reconciliation*, p. 303).

Such was the faith of that Paul whose life was "captured" and transformed on the road to Damascus. So it will be in the experience of each of those who truly accept Christ as their only hope.

14. The Place of Grace

Romans 3:22b-24a
 [22]For there is no distinction;[23]since all have sinned and continue to fall short of the glory of God, [24]they are justified freely by His grace.

"There is no distinction."

No distinction in what? That every human being who has ever lived (except Jesus) has been a sinner and fallen short of what he or she should be.

But, you may be thinking, *I am better than some people.* Are you? Read Paul in his context. Oh, it's true that your sins aren't as open and visible as those of the most disgraceful and notorious lawbreakers, but you are just as hopelessly different from "the glory of God" as they are.

As Handley Moule notes, God's "moral 'glory,' the inexorable perfectness of His Character, with its inherent demand that you must perfectly correspond to Him in order so to be at peace with Him—you are indeed *'short of'* this. The harlot, the liar, the murderer, are short of it; but so are you. Perhaps they [from our faulty perspective] stand at the bottom of a mine, and you on the crest of an Alp; but you are as little able to touch the stars as they" (Moule, p. 97).

Thus "no distinction" refers to every human being that has ever lived, including, in the flow of Paul's presentation in Romans, both Jew and Gentile. "All have sinned and continue to fall short of the glory of God" (Rom. 3:23).

The verb tenses in that verse hold a lesson for us. All "have sinned" is a Greek aorist that pictures sinning as being in humanity's past. But that doesn't mean that sin is merely universal in the past. Unlike most translations, I have rendered "fall short" in such a way as to bring out the full force of the verb's present tense to indicate that the falling is continuous and ongoing. Paul is not only saying that all "have fallen" in the past but that they also "continue to fall short" in the present. The sin problem, therefore, is truly universal in time as well as comprehensive in the sense that it includes all people.

A first reading of Romans 3:23 might make us think that the verse is out of place, an intrusion in the flow of the text, since Romans 3:21-31 is not talking about sin but about the way of salvation. It seems that verse 23 should have been a part of Paul's concluding statement on the sin problem that ran from Romans 1:18 through 3:20.

But a look at Romans 3:23 in its immediate context makes the verse even more forceful than it would have been earlier. After all, Paul has embedded it right in the middle of his treatment of righteousness by grace through faith. It is that context that highlights the full meaning of "no distinction." Just as we are all sinners, even so (both Jew and Greek) need God's grace. And only when we realize that in God's sight there is no distinction between us "good" church members and the wildest profligate can we be saved.

Thus it is that "all" without distinction "are justified freely by His grace" (Rom. 3:24). Justification, a legal term, is the opposite of condemnation. Both are pronouncements by a judge. Justification in Paul's general usage does not mean "to make righteous," but rather "to declare righteous." "It is the decree of acquittal from all guilt and issues in freedom from all condemnation and punishment." But it is more than a mere pardon, which is the remission of a penalty or debt. To the contrary, justification includes a positive pronouncement of righteous status on the repentant sinner (Ladd, pp. 437, 446, 443). We see that point illustrated in the parable of the prodigal son, in which the father not only forgives his son but welcomes him fully back into the family at the very instant of confession. "Quick!" exclaimed the father, "bring the best robe" (Luke 15:22, NIV).

Martin Luther viewed justification as the central scriptural doctrine. It is, he claimed, "the master and ruler, lord, governor and judge over all other doctrines" (in McGrath, p. 147). And it is the unique Christian doctrine that "distinguishes [the Christian] religion from all others" (in Althaus, p.

224). Paul also put justification by faith at the core of his gospel (see, e.g., Rom. 1:16, 17; 3:24-26; Gal. 2:16-21).

Part of the reason that he and Luther saw justification as central to the plan of salvation was undoubtedly the judgment theme that runs throughout the Bible (e.g., Eccl. 12:14; Dan. 7:10, 22, 26; Matt. 25:31-46; Rom. 2:5; Rev. 14:7). But beyond the judgment imagery were the two men's own personal experiences. Early in their lives both were Pharisees at heart. Both had hoped to win God's favor through amassing merits on the balance scale of judgment. But that attempt, as both learned, was an impossible task.

Paul and Luther in their Pharisaic days were not altogether wrong. After all, righteousness does demand perfect lawkeeping. And the automatic penalty for failure is condemnation and death (see Rom. 6:23; 4:15). They were also correct about their shortcomings in obeying the law as God demanded. The great breakthrough for both of them came when they understood justification as God's free gift.

That realization brings us to how God justifies, which Romans 3:24 describes as "freely by His grace." The two key words in that phrase are "freely" and "grace." The word I have translated as "freely" means "as a gift without payment, gratis, for nothing" (Rogers, p. 322). The wonder of wonders is that the greatest gift in the universe is absolutely free.

"Grace" is another word central to both Romans 3:21-25 and to the plan of salvation as Paul describes it. Of the 156 uses of *charis* in the New Testament, 30 occur in Romans. The formal definition of *charis* is "a beneficent disposition toward someone, *favor, . . . care/help, goodwill*" and "the action of one who volunteers to do something" for another "not otherwise obligatory" (Bauer, p. 1079). And what does God freely do for sinners that makes grace central to the gospel? According to Paul, He gives people justification and forgiveness rather than condemnation. Now if

> **Thoughts on Grace**
>
> "The free gift of God is a 'spontaneous' and 'unmotivated' love. God loves human beings because of his own inclination to do so. There are no love-worthy qualities within us that drive God to love us. God loves the unlovable. God even loves the ungodly, the enemies of religion and morality, the publicans and sinners of every age" (Braaten, p. 88).

people deserve a severe punishment and they receive a beautiful, priceless gift, they are *getting something they do not deserve*. And that is the everyday meaning of what Paul calls "grace" in Romans 3:24.

It is difficult to overestimate the importance of Romans 3:21-24 to the Christian understanding of God's salvation. He does indeed have a way of saving all people "apart from the law." It is His righteous gift freely offered to both Jews and Gentiles (all humanity). When they accept it by faith they are justified or accounted righteous. The apostle said it differently in Ephesians 2:8, 9 but the meaning is the same: "For by grace you have been saved through faith; and this is not your own doing, it is the gift of God—not because of works, lest any man should boast" (RSV).

What a salvation! What a God!

But Paul isn't finished yet. In the rest of Romans 3:24 and on through verse 26 he will continue to set forth his understanding of God's salvation in Christ.

15. The Vindication of God

Romans 3:24-26
> [24]*They are justified freely by His grace through the redemption which is in Christ Jesus;* [25]*whom God publicly set forth as a propitiation [atoning sacrifice] through faith in His blood. This was a demonstration of His righteousness, because in God's forbearance He had passed over the sins previously committed.* [26]*It is a demonstration of His righteousness at the present time so that He might be just in justifying the one who has faith in Jesus.*

The first part of Romans 3:24 (discussed in section 14 above) set forth the mode of justification with the words "freely by His grace." "Through the redemption which is in Christ Jesus" illuminates the means by which God made His acquitting verdict possible.

With the word "redemption" we have come to a metaphor of the marketplace. Its most basic meaning is "to redeem one by paying the price, . . . to let one go free on receiving the price" or "*a releasing effected by payment of ransom;*" or "*liberation procured by the payment of a ransom*" (Thayer,

p. 65). The ancient world used it in connection with the freeing of military captives or slaves. When the ransom or redemption price was paid, they were free (see Lev. 25:47-49).

The New Testament applies the redemption concept to Christ. Romans 6:16 speaks of sinners as being slaves of sin. But unlike the Old Testament Jew who might become rich and thus redeem himself (Lev. 25:49), Satan's captives struggle in vain against the bondage of sin.

It is in that context that Paul tells us that Christ became our redemption (Rom. 3:24). As Jesus told His disciples, "the Son of man" came "to give his life as a ransom for many" (Mark 10:45, RSV), so also Paul notes that "Christ redeemed us from the curse of the law, having become a curse for us" on Calvary's "tree" (Gal. 3:13, RSV). And Peter reminds us that we were not ransomed with silver or gold, "but with the precious blood of Christ, like that of a lamb without blemish or spot" (1 Peter 1:18, 19, RSV).

The first words of Romans 3:25 shifts the focus from the redemptive price that made justification a possibility ("through the redemption which is in Christ Jesus") to God's initiative in providing the means of redemption. Thus we read that "God publicly set forth" Christ as "a propitiation" (verse 25).

With "propitiation" we encounter a challenging word of the first order. The basic meaning of propitiation is "turning away wrath" (Richardson, p. 25; Kittel, vol. 3, pp. 310, 311). In the Greek world in which the New Testament arose, propitiation had the flavor of bribing the gods, demons, or the dead in an attempt to win their favor. Since the gods were mad they needed to be appeased (see 2 Kings 3:26, 27 for a biblical example).

But we must not confuse Paul's use of the word with that of the pagans. Rather than Christ shedding His blood to appease the Father's wrath, Romans 3:25 claims that it was God Himself who "set forth" the propitiatory sacrifice. That point is in agreement with John, who writes: "Herein is love, not that we loved God, but that he loved us, and sent his Son to be the propitiation for our sins" (1 John 4:10, KJV). That passage agrees with John 3:16, which asserts that God sent Christ because He so loved the world.

Since "propitiation" has misleading overtones, the New International Version's rendering of the Greek word as "atoning sacrifice" is both insightful and a definition that captures the essence of the biblical understanding of propitiation (see Moo, *Romans*, pp. 128, 129, for a helpful discussion).

The "atoning sacrifice" rendering is illuminating in two ways. First, it indicates that God takes sin and His condemnation of sinners seriously; that God just didn't say "so what" and ignore His own proclamations and sense of justice, but that He sent Christ as the Lamb of God who died to take away the penalty of sin (John 1:29) and the curse of the broken law (Gal. 3:10-13); and that He sent Christ who died in our place and absorbed the death sentence (Rom. 6:23) of God's just condemnation for those who through faith accept His sacrifice. Thus it is significant that Romans 3:25 ties "propitiation" to "faith in His beloved."

And the explicit mention of Christ's "blood" in verse 25 is the second way that the "atoning sacrifice" translation is helpful. It explicitly centers God's redeeming act through Christ on the cross as the focal point of the "demonstration of His righteousness" that becomes the topic for the last part of Romans 3:25 and all of verse 26.

According to the text, God's sending Christ to be the propitiation or atoning sacrifice exhibited His righteousness at two levels. First, God needed to demonstrate His justice for the past because he did not immediately visit His wrath on sinners in the Old Testament period (Rom. 3:25) even though He had told Adam and Eve that the very day that they ate the forbidden fruit they would die (Gen. 2:17).

But they obviously didn't perish as soon as expected. Rather God in His "forbearance" (patience) granted them full lives in which to discover His grace. In a similar manner, He put up with the Israelites of Moses' time, even giving them the sacrificial system as an illustration of grace, showing that help was on its way in the form of the real Lamb who would die once for all. God didn't act against sin right away because He knew that He would send Christ, whose "atoning sacrifice" would absorb the penalty for sin (Rom. 3:25a). His death would be not only for those born after the cross, but for the whole human race from the beginning of earthly time. Thus the eventual sending of Christ demonstrates that in spite of appearances God was acting justly in past history.

There was, however, a more serious problem in Paul's day that dealt with "present time" realities and the future. He raises that issue and the second aspect of God's demonstration in Romans 3:26. Underlying that verse is the question of how God can be just and yet treat people as if they had never sinned (i.e., justify sinners).

The natural thing to say "would be, 'God is just, and, therefore, condemns the sinner as a criminal'" (Barclay, *Romans*, p. 56). Such reasoning is fully in harmony with the instructions that He gave to human judges, who were to "justify the righteous, and condemn the wicked" (Deut. 25:1, KJV). Anyone who justifies the wicked, we read in Proverbs, and "condemns the righteous" is "an abomination to the Lord" (Prov. 17:15, RSV).

How can God break the rules He set up for human judges and still be just? How can He justify sinners by grace, which by definition means giving them what they don't deserve, and still be righteous? That is one of the questions that Paul felt that he must deal with in his outlining of God's provision for the salvation of sinners in Romans 3:21-26.

God's unmerited forgiveness through grace demonstrates that God is merciful and compassionate. But, Leon Morris suggests, some would be tempted to doubt His justice. "Not any more," Paul is saying in Romans 3:24-26. "The cross demonstrates the

The Significance of the Cross for God

D. Martyn Lloyd-Jones sets forth the importance of Romans 3:26 when he points out that verses 25 and 26 highlight something "infinitely more important" than the justification of human beings. "The Cross is the vindication of the character of God. The Cross not only shows the love of God more gloriously than anything else, it shows His righteousness, His justice, His holiness.... On Calvary God was making a way of salvation so that you and I might be forgiven. But He had to do so in a way that will leave His character inviolate.... God was declaring publicly once and for ever His eternal justice and His eternal love. Never separate them, for they belong together"—Lloyd-Jones, *Chapters 3:20-4:25*, pp. 106-108.

... justice of God. ... It is not the fact that God forgives that shows him to be righteous, but the fact that he forgives in a certain way, the way of the cross. ... God does not set aside the moral law when he forgives" (Morris, *Atonement*, p. 195). Neither does He abolish the penalty (see Rom. 6:23) of the broken law. To the contrary, Christ not only kept God's law, but He became "sin for us" (KJV) and died the death that was ours that we might have His righteousness (see 2 Cor. 5:21).

It was in the brutal fact of the cross that God demonstrated that He was both just and loving and that we could trust His way since He was willing to sacrifice of Himself for the good of the universe. There at the cross the Godhead laid the foundation for forgiveness and justification. Because of the cross God can justify sinners yet still be just Himself (Rom. 3:26b).

16. The Consequences of God's Plan

Roxmans 3:27-31

[27]*Where then is boasting? It has been excluded. By a law of works? No, but by a law of faith.* [28]*For we consider a man to be justified by faith apart from works of law.* [29]*Or is He the God of Jews only? And not of Gentiles? Yes also to Gentiles,* [30]*since there is one God who will justify the circumcised by faith and the uncircumcised through faith.* [31]*Do we therefore nullify the law through faith? Certainly not! On the contrary, we establish the law.*

Romans 3:21-26 presented Paul's most profound discussion of the plan of salvation. He left no doubt in the minds of his readers that justification is by grace accepted through faith based upon Christ's atoning sacrifice on the cross.

Verses 27-31 take up three implications of that explanation. The first issue is that justification by faith sounds the death knoll to a certain type of boasting. I say a certain type because Christians should always boast of their gracious God who has provided for them in every way, both temporally and eternally. And the Jews of course had a legitimate pride that they had a special relationship to God in the sense that He had elected their nation in ancient times as His people to whom He had revealed His law. Such were occasions for legitimate pride because no other people had been granted such great gifts. But from such a position "it was an easy step, and a very natural one, to pride in the extent to which one kept the law" (Morris, *Romans*, p. 185). That was the kind of pride Paul is driving at in Romans 3:27, in which he states that all reason for pride has been excluded. It is the context that highlights the apostle's remark on boasting.

He has just finished explaining in verses 21-26 that none have been justified because of their own goodness. To the contrary, Paul's gospel teaches that it is their acceptance of the goodness of Christ that opens the door of salvation to them. But, it isn't only accepting His goodness—it is accepting His death in our place. As we saw in our discussion of verses 24 and 25, that death provided the grounds for God to freely give each of those who by faith receive from Jesus what they don't deserve—grace, life, forgiveness, justification. We aren't entitled to any of them. Yet God provides them to us as a gift. Thus the principle of faith, Paul declares, precludes Christians from boasting regarding their salvation (verse 27). All we sinful humans can do is come to God thanking Him for His mercy on us. As a result, the saints in heaven will have boundless praise for God and the "Lamb that was slain" (Rev. 5:12, KJV), but none for themselves.

And that in itself is good news. After all, one of the most disgusting things that I can think of is having to listen for about 10,000 heavenly years to Aunt Mary or Uncle Charlie brag about how good they were. Such a rendition is repulsive for even 10 minutes. Having to hear such endless self-praise would be closer to hell than to heaven, and it would certainly remind us of some of the things we had to endure on earth.

We despise nothing in others as much as boasting. Yet here is a paradox, since we find our own quite pleasant. In a sinful world boasting is quite natural. It is that very tendency that prompts Paul to proclaim that all boasting related to salvation is totally excluded (Rom. 3:27). Why? Because a person is justified by faith *alone* apart from any works of law (verse 28).

Dwight L. Moody was fond of noting that if anybody ever got to heaven by what they had done, we would never hear the end of it.

The second implication that Paul addresses in Romans 3:27-31 related to his explanation of God's work in justification is that salvation is for everyone (verses 29, 30). He raises the topic by asking whether God is the diety of the Jews only, or whether the Gentiles were also included. Here he brings Jewish covenant consciousness into focus.

One of the great texts of Judaism was Deuteronomy 6:4: "The Lord our God is one Lord" (RSV). Every day every male Jew recited that passage as part of the Shema. They had no doubt in their minds on the topic of monotheism. Not only were they convinced that there was only one God, but that that one God had only one people—Israel. The Canaanites had their gods, and the Egyptians theirs, but Israel belonged to the only true God—Yahweh, who had created heaven and earth and everything in them.

It is at that very point that Paul challenges them to think in Romans 3:29. After all, if only one true God exists, and if that Being created everything, isn't He also God of the Gentiles?

Most Jews hadn't thought of it that way. But Paul's logic has a crushing forcefulness. What they had forgotten was that their special privilege as God's chosen ones did not exclude Gentiles, but was meant for their inclusion, since all the peoples of the earth were to be blessed through Abraham (see Gen. 12:3).

Having made his crucial point, the apostle goes on to note in Romans 3:30 that not only is the Lord the God of the entire world, but that the plan of salvation is also for the entire world—both Jew and Gentile. Not only is the plan of salvation for all humanity, but, Paul concludes, it saves both Jew and Gentile in the same way. All are saved through faith in God's gift—the exact same type of faith—without exception. That was an important point for Paul to make, given the divisions that had grown up in the Roman Christian community over racial issues.

The third implication that Paul addresses in Romans 3:27-31 in relation to his explanation of justification by grace through faith in verses 21-26 is the place of the law in Christianity. "Do we therefore nullify the law through faith?" "Certainly not!" he exclaims. Rather "we establish the law" (verse 30).

Here we have an issue that troubles people to the present day, since some of his readers perceive him as placing "law" and "faith" in opposition to each other. Some even fear that his emphasis on faith actually does away with the law. Anticipating that response to his theology, the apostle quickly and firmly asserts that salvation by grace through faith actually establishes the law.

But what does he mean? The answer depends on how he uses the term "law" in verse 30. We can think of three possible interpretations. First, if he is referring to the Old Testament in general (which the Jews often thought of as the Law and the Prophets) then his gospel of justification by faith would be seen as upholding the law in the sense that the Old Testament itself taught the truth of justifying faith. He has already set forth that interpretation in Romans 3:21. If it is correct, it sets the stage for Romans 4, which asserts that both Abraham and David were justified by faith.

Second, if law refers to its more restricted meaning as being the law of Moses, then Paul is saying that faith upholds the law by assigning to it its proper place in the plan of salvation. As he saw it, the law's role was to expose and condemn sin (Rom. 3:20) and to direct sinners to that salvation "apart from the law" (verse 21). In that way the gospel and the law are united in the sense that the gospel justifies those whom the law condemns.

A third possibility is to view the law of verse 31 as being God's moral requirements, such as the Ten Commandments. This interpretation gains strength from the fact that some of his readers might fear that Paul's teachings lead to antinomianism, that is, that Christians don't need any law, that they are free to live in sin since they are saved by grace. Such a charge, one which Paul has already alluded to in Romans 3:8 and will deal with extensively in chapters 6-8, is the most likely problem under-girding his statement in verse 31. In this sense the saved-by-grace Christian will fulfill the "just requirement of the law" in their lives through the power of the Holy Spirit.

Stating that the third interpretation is the most likely meaning of Paul's statement about establishing the law should not lead us to neglect the other two possible interpretations. After all, all three have contextual support and all are true. Perhaps the apostle's ambiguity on the exact meaning of law in verse 31 was by design so that we might explore all of his possible meanings. Before moving to Romans 4 we should note an insight made by Douglas Moo. He finds that the topics treated in Romans 3:27-31 mirror those to be taken up in chapter 4:

Romans 3:27-34

1. Boasting is excluded (verse 27).

2. Individuals are justified by faith, not works of law (verse 28).

3. The circumcised and uncircumcised are united under one God through faith (verses 29, 30).

Romans 4

Abraham had no right to boast (verses 1, 2).

Abraham was justified by faith not works (verses 3-8).

The circumcised and uncircumcised are united as children of Abraham through faith (verses 9-17).

"What Paul does in 3:27-31," Moo concludes, is to "touch on the basic points he wants to make about faith before developing them at greater length with respect to Abraham" (Moo, *Romans*, p. 137).

17. Old Testament Proof of Justification by Faith

Romans 4:1-8

¹What then shall we say that Abraham, our forefather according to the flesh, has discovered? ²For if Abraham was justified by works, he has reason to boast, but not before God. ³For what does the scripture say? "And Abraham believed God, and it was credited to him for righteousness." ⁴Now to the one who works, the reward is not credited as a gift but as what he is owed. ⁵But to the one not working, but believes in Him who justifies the ungodly, his faith is credited as righteousness, ⁶just as David also speaks of the blessing of the man to whom God credits righteousness apart from works:

⁷"Blessed are those whose lawless deeds have been forgiven,
and whose sins have been covered;
⁸blessed is the man whose sin the Lord does not credit to him."

Paul has set forth his basic understanding of how people are saved (Rom. 3:21-26) and defended it against certain criticisms (verses 27-31). In making his presentation he had been quite emphatic that justification by faith had been an Old Testament understanding (3:21; 1:2). But he had not yet supplied the evidence. And that was an important task because he knew some Jews doubted it.

Thus he anticipates their objection by asking a question about what Abraham "discovered" on the topic (Rom. 4:1). Selecting Abraham as his first witness was an absolutely essential decision on Paul's part because Abraham as the acknowledged father of the Jewish people was the most important figure in the Old Testament.

Here is a test case for Paul's doctrine of salvation. If he can demonstrate that Abraham is in harmony with justification by faith, he wins his case.

The apostle begins his treatment of Abraham by alluding to the Jewish belief that the great patriarch's works had justified him (verse 2). Basing their thoughts on Genesis 26:5 (that God blessed Abraham because "Abraham obeyed my voice and kept my charge, my commandments, my statutes, and my laws" [RSV]) the Jews reasoned that the patriarch "had performed the whole Law before it was given" (M. Kiddushin 4:14). Again in the Jewish book of Jubilees we read that "Abraham was perfect in all of his actions with the Lord and was pleasing through righteousness all the days of his life" (Jubilees 23:10). Another Jewish book, the Prayer of Manasseh, mentions that Abraham, Isaac, and Jacob didn't have to repent to God because they were righteous and "did not sin against you" (Prayer of Manasseh 8, REB). Lastly, the Wisdom of Sirach states that "Abraham was the great father of a multitude of nations, and no one has been found equal to him in glory. He observed the Law of the Most High, and entered into an agreement with him. He certified the agreement in his flesh, and, when he was tested, he proved faithful" (Wisdom of Sirach 44:19, 20, Goodspeed).

If all that is true, then Abraham certainly did have something to boast about! But Paul dismisses the possibility as soon as he raises it. "It is unthinkable that anyone, even Abraham, could have matter for boasting in God's presence" (Morris, *Romans*, p. 195). Thus Paul's exclamation "but not before God" (4:2).

The apostle then turns to the Bible to prove his point: "And Abraham believed God, and it was credited to him for righteousness" (verse 3). His text is Genesis 15:6, in which Abraham believed God's promise that the aged and barren Sarah would have a son, and that his offspring would be as numerous as the stars of heaven. Abraham believed God's promise, Scripture tells us, "and it was credited to him as righteousness" (NIV).

Clearly Paul is using Genesis 15:6 to prove that Abraham was justified by faith rather than works. But that interpretation, the apostle knew, was not the one held by the Jews of his day. In 1 Maccabees 2:52, for example, we find the following question: "Did not Abraham prove faithful under trial, and so win credit as a righteous man?" (REB). That passage changes the idea of faith into faithfulness and thus a meritoriousness that deserved a re-ward. Again Rabbi Shemaiah, who lived about 50 B.C., represents God as saying: "The faith with which their father Abraham believed in Me . . . merits that I should divide the [Red] sea for them, as it is written: 'And he believed in the LORD, and he counted it to him for righteousness'" (in Cranfield, *Romans*, vol. 1, p. 229).

Thus the Jews by the time of Christ had begun to consistently interpret Abraham's faith as a type of merit-earning faithfulness.

Paul knew that. Yet he deliberately chose Genesis 15:6 to prove just the opposite. That is not surprising since "it was clearly essential to the credibility of his argument that he should not by-pass a text which would seem to many of his fellow Jews the conclusive disproof of the point he was trying to establish" (*Ibid.*, pp. 229, 230).

Rather than avoid the disputed passage, Paul needed to demonstrate that rightly interpreted it confirmed his contention that Abraham had nothing to boast about because he had been justified by dependent faith apart from good works. The apostle undertakes his demonstration in Romans 4:4-8.

Verses 4 and 5 provide the first step in his argument: "Now to the one who works, the reward is not credited as a gift but as what he is owed. But to the one not working, but believes Him who justifies the ungodly, his faith is credited as righteousness."

The idea underlying that rather complex explanation of Genesis 15:6 is that the Old Testament text makes no mention of any work by Abraham, but only his faith. Had good works been mentioned, then they could have been credited to Abraham for righteousness as something justly "owed" to him. But that is Paul's point. There were no works. Thus God owed him nothing. To the contrary, in the context of Genesis 15:6, Abraham's astounding faith that an old barren woman would not only conceive (a human impossibility) but make Abraham the father of many nations could only be due to the gift or grace of God. That faith in God's gift of grace was then, Genesis 15:6 tells us, credited to the patriarch as righteousness. Thus he was justified by faith in God's gracious gift rather than works.

By the end of verse 5 the apostle has made his point. But he is not going to let his case rest there, lest some of his detractors not see the point. He will bring David on board to clinch his case.

But before we go to David we need to examine the concept of "credited" ("reckoned" [RSV], "accounted" [Phillips], "counted" or "imputed" [KJV]). Paul uses the word 10 times in chapter 4, with five of them in verses 3-8. When employed in a financial context, it signifies to put something to somebody's account. And Paul employs the word that way when he writes to Philemon about Onesimus: "If he has wronged you at all, or owes you anything, charge that to my account" (Philemon 18, RSV).

The apostle's use of credited is clear: God justifies the wicked not by what they have done, but through their faith and trust in Him. Their faith is thus counted or imputed as righteousness. It is that usage in light of the King James Version that gave birth to the phrase "imputed righteousness." Romans 4:1-8 is one of Paul's clearest presentations on how Christ's righteousness is transferred to a sinner who comes to Jesus. It happens not by works of any type, but by faith in Jesus. At the very moment that a person accepts Jesus by faith, God accounts him or her as righteous.

That thought brings us back to David. To say the least, Paul is mustering his big guns as he aims at his fellow Jew's objections to justification by faith. If Abraham was the most important person in Jewish history, David wasn't far behind. Next to Abraham and Moses he was probably the most revered. The first verse of the New Testament highlights that fact: "The book of the genealogy of Jesus Christ, the son of David, the son of Abraham" (Matt. 1:1, RSV). David, like Abraham, was a central figure in Israel's covenant history.

Thus Romans 4 calls on the two most important witnesses available to prove its point that righteousness is by faith without works. And in the Jewish mind it was important to have two witnesses, since Deuteronomy 19:15 explicitly states that "a matter must be established by the testimony of two or three witnesses" (NIV).

So in Romans 4:6-8 Paul calls upon David to validate the point he made from Abraham's witness in verses 1-5. And what a witness he is. While Abraham, though he had his faults, might possibly be thought of as one who had enough goodness to merit salvation, no one had the same suspicions about David. All knew, including David himself (see Ps. 51), that the only way he could be saved was by God's grace. Thus he presents an excellent case in Paul's argument.

Quoting in Romans 4:7, 8 from Psalm 32:1, 2 with its usage of "credited" or "imputed," the apostle nails down his case. Yet that all-important word is employed in a different sense with the forgiven David than it was for Abraham. For the latter, Paul tells us that God credited his faith as righteousness. But for David we find that God *did not* credit his sin to his account. Thus the apostle in a few short verses explains justification as having two aspects—a positive and a negative. First God counts our faith as righteousness. Second, He does not count our sins against us. As a result, those who come to God through faith in Christ are truly "clean." So it was with David. Paul in Romans 4:6-8 equates his experience with righteousness and justification. And the good news, of course, is that God's grace is still available in our day as we appropriate it to our lives by faith.

18. Abraham's Multicultural Family

Romans 4:9-15
> ⁹*Is this blessing then upon the circumcised or also upon the uncircumcised? For we say, "His faith was credited to Abraham for righteousness." ¹⁰How then was it credited? While he was circumcised or uncircumcised? Not while circumcised, but while uncircumcised. ¹¹And he received the sign of circumcision, a seal of the righteousness of his faith while uncircumcised, so that he might be the father of all who believe without being circumcised. For righteousness is also credited to them. ¹²He is also father to those circumcised who are not merely circumcised but who also follow the steps of the faith of our father Abraham which he had before being circumcised.*
>
> ¹³*For the promise to Abraham or to his seed that he should be heir of the world did not come through the law but through the righteousness of faith. ¹⁴For if those of the law are heirs, faith has been made empty and the promise has been nullified, ¹⁵for the law works wrath, but where there is no law there is no transgression.*

Romans 4:9-12 continues Paul's treatment of Abraham. But whereas verses 1-8 argued that he was justified by faith rather than works, verses 9-12 shift the focus to the topic of the identity of the children of

Abraham. We always need to remember that the apostle is dealing with a warring church in Rome divided along the fault line of Jew and Gentile. Thus in the process of healing it is crucial for Paul to demonstrate that not only are both groups justified before God in exactly the same way (by faith) but that both have Abraham for their father.

The apostle picks up the word "blessing" in verse 9 from the previous two verses, in which he quoted David as saying "blessed are those whose lawless deeds have been forgiven."

That may be true, but who may receive the blessing? Jews only or also Gentiles (verse 9)? Paul was undoubtedly aware of the fact that some Jewish leaders considered blessedness to be only for the circumcised Jew. It is difficult for most of us to comprehend the importance that the ancient Jew placed on circumcision. It was so vital in their understanding that it divided the world into two segments—Jews and everybody else.

As the Jew saw it, circumcision had a direct relationship to salvation. Thus we read in the apocryphal book of Jubilees that "anyone who is born whose own flesh is not circumcised on the eighth day is not from the sons of the covenant which the LORD made for Abraham since (he is) from the children of destruction. And there is therefore no sign upon him so that he might belong to the LORD because (he is destined) to be destroyed and annihilated from the earth" (Jubilees 15:25). On the other hand, the Jews held that "no Israelite man who is circumcised will go down to Gehinnom [hell]" (Ex. R. 19:4 in Morris, *Romans*, p. 201).

Such beliefs were so strong in Judaism that many Jewish converts carried them over into Christianity. That whole set of beliefs raised two questions that Paul will have to answer in Romans 4:9-12:

1. What about Abraham? Wasn't he blessed because of his circumcision?
2. What about the Gentiles? Are they even candidates for God's blessing if they don't become Jews through circumcision?

The apostle answers the first of those questions in verses 9-11. His point of departure is to reiterate that Abraham's faith was credited to him for righteousness (verse 9). That may be true, Paul's Jewish audience reasoned, but God accepted his faith only because he had been circumcised. Not so, Paul asserts. He received the blessing *before* he was circumcised. That is not difficult to prove since Genesis 15:6 declared the patriarch to be justified by faith even though the circumcision command did not come until Genesis 17, 14 years later.

Thus God blessed Abraham prior to his circumcision. The Lord later gave him the rite of circumcision as a "sign" that he had indeed been blessed of God and as a "seal" that his experience was genuine (Rom. 4:11). It is therefore clear from history, Paul argues, that Abraham was not blessed because of his circumcision.

That conclusion allows the apostle to address the question about the Gentiles. The fact that Abraham was blessed before he was circumcised makes him the "father of all who believe without being circumcised. For righteousness is also credited to them" (verse 11). In short, Gentiles don't need to be circumcised to be accepted by God or to become full members of the church.

> While "the Jews looked upon Abraham as the great dividing point in the history of mankind," to Paul "Abraham through his faith became the great rallying [uniting] point for all who believe," whether Jew or Gentile, circumcised or uncircumcised. (Nygren, p. 175).

But what about those already circumcised? What is their status? Paul addresses that question in verse 12. His answer is that mere outward circumcision avails nothing. Rather, they must have the same faith as the uncircumcised patriarch when he received God's blessing. But if they have that faith then Abraham is their father also (cf. Gal. 3:28, 29). The upshot of Paul's argument is that Abraham is the father of both believing Jews and believing Gentiles, that in Christ both groups are one.

Romans 4:13-15 provides the foundation on which Abraham is father to both Jews and Gentiles. The picture is clear to Paul. The promise to both the patriarch and his descendants came through faith not law (verse 13). According to the apostle's logic, that promise can do what the law cannot, since a promise implies grace. The promises to Abraham were based not on the fact that he was a perfect man, but upon the reality that he was a needy sinner who had faith. That faith runs all the way through his life. Thus when he took Isaac to the land of Moriah for a sacrifice, Abraham had faith that God would provide a lamb for a burnt offering (Gen. 22:8). The book of Hebrews notes that "by faith Abraham, when he was tested, offered up Isaac, and he who had received the promises was ready to offer up his only son, of whom it was said, 'Through Isaac shall your descendants be named.' He considered that God was able to raise men even from the dead" (Heb. 11:17-19, RSV). Abraham didn't know how God would fulfill His promises, but he believed that the Lord could and would. His faith transcended his sight. It is that dynamic faith expressed throughout his life that made Abraham the recipient of God's promise and that made him the father of those who live by faith.

The promise was not something he had earned. No, it was God's gift to him. Abraham received it not through law but by God's grace.

Having made it plain in Romans 4:13 that the blessing to Abraham came through faith rather than the law, Paul next demonstrated in verses 14 and 15 why it could never be the product of law. Verse 14 begins the presentation with the affirmation that if the blessing comes through the law the promise has reached a dead end, it is "nullified" and faith is made of none effect. Why? Because "the law works wrath" (verse 15).

In order to grasp Paul's argument we need to remember that he is addressing legalistic Jews who believed they could obtain God's promise through law-keeping. He is telling them that such a path offers no hope. Why? Watch his logic:

1. It is true that they have God's law.
2. But it is also true that they have all transgressed its requirements (see Romans 2:1-29; 3:1-20, 23).
3. Consequently, they face the penalty for transgression.
4. Therefore, if they don't get help through accepting God's grace by their faith, they are certainly without hope.

Faith, Paul has argued, is the only way to hope since the function of the law is to point out one's sin (Rom. 3:20), and the reward of sin is wrath (4:15). At that point in his presentation he reverts to the function of the law as a detector of sin: "where there is no law there is no transgression." The apostle is not saying that places exist without any law or that people cannot sin without revealed law. He covered those issues in Romans 1 and 2. Nor is he suggesting that there is anything wrong with lawkeeping in its proper context, a topic he will take up in chapters 6 and 7.

What he does mean is that there can be no transgression without law. That brings us to the distinction between sin and transgression. Sin (*hamartia*) includes all actions that miss the mark of God's ideal. But transgression (*parabasis*) is a special type of sin. The Greek word itself means to step over a boundary (see Bauer, p. 758). If people are to step over a boundary, they need to know where the boundary marker is. That's where the law comes in. The Ten Commandment law, for example, tells people not to steal. When they know that law yet steal anyway they have crossed the boundary and become transgressors and thereby deserve "wrath" or punishment. That is why the law can't lead to the blessing of the promise. It's very purpose is to point out sin (Rom. 3:20) and transgression (4:15) and lead needy people to faith in Christ as their only hope.

Along with Paul, we can thank God for the hope of the gospel and that it unites all people since all are saved in exactly the same way—by grace through faith in God's gift made possible on Calvary. The truth of Romans 4:9-15 is that we are all on flat land before the cross. All who have faith are God's children no matter what their pedigree or their past life. The formula for acceptance into God's family is not faith + circumcision or faith + baptism or faith + any other activity, but faith alone. That faith God "credits" to the believer's account. Such is the radical good news of justification by faith according to the apostle Paul.

19. The Faith of Abraham

Romans 4:16-25

[16]*That is why it depends on faith in order that it may be in accordance with grace so that the promise will be guaranteed to all the descendants, not only to those of the law, but also to the descendants of the faith of Abraham, who is father of us all,* [17]*as it is written: "A father of many nations I have appointed you"—in the presence of God whom he believed, the one who gives life to the dead and calls into existence that which does not exist.* [18]*In hope he believed against hope that he would become a father of many nations according to that which had been spoken:*

"So will your descendants be." [19]*Yet he did not weaken in faith when he considered his own body, it being as good as dead since he was about 100 years old, and the deadness of Sarah's womb.* [20]*Yet he did not waver in unbelief at the promise of God, but was strengthened by faith, giving glory to God,* [21]*fully convinced that God was also able to do what He had promised.* [22]*Therefore it was also "credited to him for righteousness."* [23]*Now not only for him was it written that it was credited to him,* [24]*but also for us, to whom it shall be credited; that is, those believing in Him*

who raised Jesus our Lord from the dead, 25who was delivered over [to death] because of our transgressions and was raised for our justification.

This complex paragraph breaks down into three sections as Paul completes his extended treatment of Abraham. Verse 16 deals with the way of faith as the guarantee of God's promise, verses 17-22 explore the nature of Abraham's faith, and verses 23-25 apply the lessons of that faith to Paul's readers.

In Romans 4:13-15 the apostle demonstrated why the "righteousness of faith" is the only way to receive the promise of God. Verse 16 takes that point further with its claim that the way of faith in God's grace "guarantees" or "makes certain" the promise to all of Abraham's descendants, both Jewish and Gentile. The way of faith is a guarantee because it is something that we can trust. Human performance and human promises are far from secure. But the fact that it is God's grace that makes His salvation available to those who have faith puts the gift beyond the realm of human untrustworthiness.

However, it is important to know what kind of faith Abraham had if it was to be meaningful to Paul's readers. He takes up that important topic beginning in verse 17, stating that Abraham believed in a God who gives life to the dead and "calls into existence that which does not exist."

Possibilities for interpreting those ideas are many, but the one that best fits the context reflects verse 19, in which we read that Abraham's body and Sarah's womb were "as good as dead." In order to receive the promise Abraham had to believe in a God who could take their "dead" organs and bring life out of a situation in which there was no life. That interpretation also fits the fact that God "calls into existence that which does not exist" (verse 26), which would include not only the son of promise but the fatherhood of many nations.

Verse 17, Leander Keck points out, "is the closest the New Testament comes to stating the doctrine of *creatio ex nihilo.*" And it is significant that Paul "connects creation [verse 17], resurrection [verse 25], and Sarah's conceiving Isaac [verse 19]," all topics related to the absolute power of God to guarantee the promise (Keck, p. 128).

Abraham's faith was in a Being who could truly do the impossible. But that didn't necessarily mean that faith came easy to the patriarch. Romans 4:18 tells us that "he believed against hope." There is always a tension in faith, because faith must always transcend sight and even common sense in many cases.

And that was certainly true in Abraham's situation. Verse 19 tells us that there was deadness everywhere (cf. Heb. 11:11, 12). Yet Paul asserts that the patriarch's faith did not weaken even though the promise of an heir looked impossible from a purely human perspective.

Here is a lesson for each of us on the nature of faith: While it never closes its eyes to life's realties, it at the same time refuses to be limited by human estimates of what is possible. As Leon Morris points out, "in view of all this deadness it was not possible for the couple to have a child in the normal human fashion, and to believe God's promise under those circumstances was more than a passive acquiescence in a conventional religious posture; it was the active exercise of a profound faith" (Morris, *Romans*, p. 212).

In verse 20 Paul writes that Abraham "did not waver in unbelief at the promise of God, but was strengthened by faith, giving glory to God." The next verse goes on to add that the reason that his faith never faltered was because he "was fully convinced that God was also able to do what He had promised." Both verses highlight something very important about faith as lived out in daily life.

Even though Paul claims that Abraham's faith never wavered, that is not the picture presented by Genesis. There we read that after God's promise of a son "Abraham fell on his face and laughed, and said to himself, 'Shall a child be born to a man who is a hundred years old? Shall Sarah, who is ninety years old, bear a child?'" Then the good patriarch offered to help God out of the scrape by substituting Ishmael (his son through Hagar) as the promised son (Gen. 17:17, 18, RSV).

At that point God jumped back into the picture and said: "Sarah your wife shall bear you a son, and you shall call his name Isaac. I will establish my covenant with him as an everlasting covenant for his descendents after him" (verse 19, RSV).

The actual history of that experience tells us a great deal about the quality of Abraham's faith in the real world of everyday life. Faith for him apparently didn't come any easier than it does for the rest of humanity. It was not automatic for him. He knew the problems and realities that all of us face. "Yet he did not waver" (Rom. 4:20). Taken in the light of the whole biblical picture of Abraham, not wavering apparently means that despite the ups and downs of daily life, he kept his faith on track. It wasn't a perfect faith, but it was steady and upward as he moved along life's path. Paul captures that upward drift in Romans 4:20 with the idea that Abraham was "strengthened by faith." The *New American Standard Bible's* translation is helpful here when it notes that he "grew strong in faith."

True faith is dynamic rather than static. Through the years it develops and deepens as people walk with God. Maturing Christians ought day by day to be growing in faith as they come closer to God and experience His watch care over time. That appears to have been Abraham's experience in the book of Genesis. Scripture pictures him as a man of many faults, but one who let God strengthen him over time. Years passed between God's giving of the promise in Genesis 15:5 and its fulfillment in Genesis 21:2. During those long years the patriarch had his moments of doubt. But his faith grew, and God was able to strengthen him (Rom. 4:20, 21). And when Paul tells us that Abraham was "fully convinced that God was also able to do what He had promised" (verse 21), he was talking about his mature faith, not his immediate reaction at the time he first heard it. Abraham had genuine faith in God's promises within the context of the real world. And it was "credited to him for righteousness" (Rom. 4:22).

What Kind of Faith Did Abraham Really Have?

It was far from being perfect or flawless faith as he faced genuine problems in the "real world," but it was steady and upward as he progressed along life's path. It was a faith that faltering humans can identify with.

That conclusion brings us to the application section. Paul is very clear that God's commendation of Abraham was not only for his benefit (verse 23), but also for his first readers and the rest of us (verse 24) who face the challenge of how to relate to God's promise.

The apostle closes chapter 4 with a gospel statement certifying that Christ was "delivered over [to death] because of our transgressions and was raised for our justification" (Rom. 4:25). The function of that statement in its context is to certify that the promises made to Abraham have been realized through the death and resurrection of Christ.

Verse 25 presents several points as we think about God's great salvific promise through Christ. First, the apostle tells us that Jesus was "delivered over," or as Romans 8:32 puts it, God "did not spare His own Son, but delivered Him over for us all" (NASB). The implication of God's delivering of Christ is that God Himself is the active agent in human salvation. The cross wasn't an accident or merely the doing of evil people, but a part of God's plan to accomplish our salvation through the death of Christ. That is why Revelation 13:8 refers to Jesus as "the Lamb that was slain from the creation of the world" (NIV). The second thing to note about Romans 4:25 is that Jesus died in our place on the cross, and the third is that He was "raised for our justification." That is an interesting reality, since it wasn't merely Christ's death but also His resurrection that rounds out God's promise (cf. 1 Cor. 15:1-4). Reformer John Calvin makes an interesting suggestion regarding Christ's resurrection for our justification when he notes that it was not enough that Christ died. He also needed to be "received into celestial glory," so that by His "intercession" He might as a "conqueror" apply the fruits of His sacrifice on our behalf (Calvin, p. 185). Paul presents a similar thought in Romans 8:34 as he pictures the risen Christ at the right hand of God in His heavenly ministry of intercession. Part of the good news to both Abraham and ourselves is that God is always on the side of His children as He reaches out to make the promise effective in their lives.

20. The Fruit of Justification

Romans 5:1-5

¹Therefore, having been justified by faith we have peace with God through our Lord Jesus Christ, ²through whom also we have access by faith into this grace in which we stand; and we rejoice in hope of the glory of God. ³And not only that, but we rejoice also in hardships, knowing that hardship produces patient endurance; ⁴and patient endurance [produces] proven character; and proven character produces hope; ⁵and hope does not disappoint, because the love of God has been poured out in our hearts through the Holy Spirit which has been given to us.

Romans 3:21-4:25 set forth the blessing of justification by faith for both Jews and Gentiles. Romans 5:1-5 begins to treat the fruits of justification for believers in the sense that all the "blessings, which belonged to Israel as God's people, are now the portion of those who are in Christ" (Schreiner, p. 250).

The first of those blessings is "peace," a concept that comes from the Hebrew *shalom*, a term meaning complete well-being. Obtaining peace of heart and mind is a universal desire. It is the goal of all religions as people seek relief from the sense of guilt and alienation from God that comes from having a less than flawless life. Secular people sense the same gut level anxieties about life and search for security and peace in wealth, prestige, human relationships, and a lot of other things. But nothing really satisfies. Things pass away as does beauty and life itself. Even the ongoing quest to satisfy the "gods" merely leads to the need for more satisfaction in a sinful world. Peace is at best elusive.

But there is an answer, Paul claims. A Christian has genuine, lasting "peace with God through our Lord Jesus Christ" (Rom. 5:1), who died for our "transgressions and was raised for our justification" (4:25). Accepting God's gift of justification through faith, the apostle points out, is the secret of genuine and lasting peace with both God and our inner turmoil. Thus Christian peace rests on objective fact rather than subjective feelings. Christ's death and resurrection put it on firm ground.

A second fruit of justification is "access" to God "by faith into this grace in which we stand" (5:2). Here is an important truth that we too often fail to recognize. A sense of alienation from God plagues the human heart, but believers in Christ have direct access to the Father through the Son. It was not so in the Old Testament services connected to the Temple. Only the priest could enter the Temple proper. And only the high priest once a year had access to God's throne room—the holy of holies. But through Jesus we can approach God any time we desire it.

The death and resurrection of Christ that resulted in the justification that Paul reflected upon in Romans 4:24, 25 opened the way for His followers into the very throne room of God. As the book of Hebrews puts it, as Christ's followers we can "come boldly unto the throne of grace, that we may obtain mercy, and find grace to help in time of need" (Heb. 4:16, KJV). Paul presents the same thought in Ephesians when he writes that in Christ "and through faith in him we may approach God with freedom and confidence" (Eph. 3:12, NIV; cf. 2:18, 19).

A third major fruit of justification by faith is that Christians have joy: "We rejoice in hope of the glory of God" (Rom. 5:2). Note the pronoun "we."

This is not a universal joy, but only for those who "by faith" enter "into this grace in which we stand." The interesting thing about the word I have translated as "rejoice" is that it is the same word rendered "boast" in Romans 2:17 and 4:2. William Plumer is quite correct that the word "is used in both a good and bad sense, the context determines which" (Plumer, p. 196). The passages about boasting in chapters 2 and 4 tell us that no one has room for boasting in relation to their accomplishments in lawkeeping, and that even Abraham couldn't boast about his works. The fact that righteousness comes through God's gift rather than human accomplishment leaves people no room to brag about their spiritual condition.

But there is a difference in Romans 5. Verse 2 urges us to boast. Why the change? Because Christians are not exalting their own accomplishments but rather what the Lord already has done for them and will do for them in Christ in the future. Christians boast in the goodness and graciousness of their Lord, who has given them peace with God and continual access to Him. That is something to proclaim with the greatest possible enthusiasm. It is that sense of the word that has led Bible translators to seek to express the meaning implied in the word usually rendered boasting as being an attitude of rejoicing. Thus C. K. Barrett suggests that in its Romans 5:2 context "it means a triumphant, rejoicing confidence . . . in God" (Barrett, p. 103).

The fourth fruit of justification by faith is hope, a gift that comes to all who are right with God. Paul takes up the topic of hope in the last part of Romans 5:2 and extends his initial treatment of it through verse 5.

Before we examine those verses it is important to look at the meaning of hope for Paul. For many of us hope is something we wish for or think might happen. But that is not the way Paul employs the word. For him hope is certitude. Hope implies not the slightest doubt. Thus when he speaks of the "blessed hope" of the Second Advent (Titus 2:13), he is not suggesting that such an event is merely wishful thinking that might or might not take place. No! The Advent was a certainty. The question was not if it would take place, but when. The apostle uses hope the same way in Romans 5:5, in which he states that "hope does not disappoint." Of course, Christian hope is not just hope in general but rather it is rooted in "the glory of God" (verse 2).

Hope in the ultimate outcome of life's journey is central to Paul's thought, but he doesn't neglect those struggles in day-to-day living that can crowd out hope and destroy faith if people do not have a Christian understanding of the developmental aspect of Christian existence. Thus the apostle raises the issue of suffering in verse 3, in which he suggests that Christians should "rejoice also in hardships." *Wait a minute,* you may be thinking, *if believers have peace with God, access to Him, and joy, then how come they have troubles and sufferings like other people?* That was an important topic for his readers, since being a Christian in the Roman Empire wasn't always easy. And then there was the Jewish understanding that suffering and disease resulted from sin. Even worse, sufferings and hardships probably cause some Christians to doubt the reality of their so-called blessings.

Paul in his usual manner took a positive approach to the topic by claiming that Christians should rejoice in their hardships. Now the word translated as "hardships" is a forceful one. It does not refer to minor inconveniences, but to real suffering. The Greek original is *thlipsis,* which literally means "pressure." It was the word used for crushing olives in a press or for squeezing grapes to extract the juice. Other meanings of the word include "trouble that inflicts distress, *oppression, affliction, tribulation*" (Bauer, p. 457).

In a similar manner, life's troubles pressure and squeeze Christians. The Bible is clear that people of faith are not immune from suffering and tragedy. For example, John the Baptist's head ended up on a platter, the apostle John purportedly was dipped in boiling oil, Paul was repeatedly beaten, and Jesus had His cross.

Suffering, of course, can do one of two things to people. It can crush them as the olive in the press. Or they can view hardships as instruments to open up new opportunities for growth and development.

Paul focuses on the second option, writing that Christians can rejoice in hardship because it produces "patient endurance," which in time creates "character," which ultimately generates "hope." The first link in that chain is "patient endurance," translating two Greek words that literally mean "to abide" or "stay under." The idea is that a person not only learns to abide in Christ when all is well, but also in troublesome times. It is all too easy to quit when life becomes difficult. But Christians discover through hardship that instead of sufferings being causes of quitting, they can be the means of utilizing their faith to enter a deeper relationship with Jesus. A Christian in a Communist country, pressured to give up his faith and conform, declared, "We are like nails: the harder you hit us the deeper you drive us." That is perseverance, that is "staying under" the rule of Christ.

But perseverance, Paul tells us, is not an end in itself. Rather, it develops character (Rom. 5:4). Character was the word used of testing precious metals to purify them and to demonstrate their purity. Just as the metal smith uses intense heat to melt silver and gold in order to remove physical impurities, so God uses hardships and suffering to rid His children of spiritual impurities or to develop their characters. Strength of character does not come through avoidance or whining, but through meeting problems head-on in a faith relationship to God through Jesus.

That thought brings the apostle to the final link in his chain: "proven" or tested "character produces hope" (verse 4). Thus the Christian can "rejoice in hope" (verse 2) because "hope does not disappoint" (verse 5). Why? Here we come to the last fruit of justification in Romans 5:1-5. "Hope does not disappoint, *because* the love of God has been poured out in our hearts through the Holy Spirit." The ultimate hope of Christians is grounded on God's abundant love for them. His love will never give them up. *Amen!*

21. Reason to Rejoice

Romans 5:6-11

> [6]*For when we were still helpless, at the right time, Christ died for the ungodly. [7]For one will scarcely die for a righteous person; though perhaps for the good person one might even dare to die. [8]But God demonstrates His own love for us in that Christ died for us while we were still sinners. [9]Much more then, having now been justified by His blood, we will be saved from wrath through Him. [10]For if while we were enemies we were reconciled to God through the death of His Son, much more, having been reconciled, we shall be saved by His life. [11]And not only so, but we also rejoice in God through our Lord Jesus Christ through whom we have now received the reconciliation.*

The word "for" is important in verse 6. It refers us back to verse 5, which spoke of the revelation of God's love flooded into the believer's heart by the Holy Spirit. Romans 5:6-8 explores the objective basis for that subjective experience as God's love is expressed by the cross of Christ.

Douglas Moo summarizes the apostle's argument as follows:

"a. Human love, at its best, will motivate a person to give his or her life for a truly 'good' person (v. 7);

"b. Christ, sent by God, died, not for 'righteous' people, or even for 'good' people, but for rebellious and undeserving people (v. 6);

"c. Therefore: God's love is far greater in its magnitude and dependability than even the greatest human love (v. 8)" (Moo, *Epistle*, p. 306).

Thus Paul provides further evidence that the Christian's hope cannot fail. A God who loved people enough to die for them while they were at war with Him will never let them go.

Romans 5:6 tells us that Christ died for the helpless and the ungodly. In chapters 1-4 he has already demonstrated how helpless human beings are to earn or achieve their own salvation. The King James Version of Acts 4:9 translates the Greek word for "helpless" as "impotent." And one commentator notes that impotent is not an "unsuitable description of the condition of a sinner before his acceptance of the saving grace and power of God. Paul's reference to the impotence or helplessness of the unregenerate sinner stands in contrast to his picture of the justified believer, now rejoicing [Rom. 5:1-5] as he grows stronger in hope, in endurance, in character, and in the assurance of God's love" (Nichol, vol. 6, p. 526).

Christ, we read in Romans 5:6, died not only for the helpless, but for the "ungodly." By ungodly he does not mean that Christ died for some people who were worse than others. To the contrary, all were ungodly and needed His grace. Nor does ungodly mean powerless or helpless. People may be powerless to earn salvation, but as both the Bible and the daily news demonstrate, they have plenty of energy to rebel against God. It is one of the wonders of the universe that God died for the ungodly—those who did not deserve it.

That thought brings Paul to Romans 5:7 and the human approach to giving our life for someone or even helping them. Our first question when asked to help someone even at the financial level is "Are they worthy? Do they deserve help? Will they appreciate it or merely squander the fruit of my gift?" It is only in the light of our human attitudes that the absolute radicalness of God's love shines forth. Romans 5 tells us that Jesus did not die for the worthy but for those out of harmony with Him and the Father. It is that kind of love that undergirds the Christian hope.

Verse 8 continues Paul's thought by telling us that "Christ died for us while we were still sinners." Now, a sinner is not merely out of harmony with God's will, but in active rebellion against God. The Bible describes sin as being against God personally. "The mind that is set on the flesh" (unconverted human nature), Paul writes, "is *hostile* to God" (Rom. 8:7, RSV; Ps. 51:4).

Beyond being personal, sin is moral. It is a deliberate act of the will to rebel against God. Sin is a choice, a conscious rejection of God. Thus Herbert Douglass can correctly say that "sin is a created being's clenched fist in the face of his Creator; sin is the creature distrusting God, deposing Him as the Lord of his life" (Douglass, p. 53). Emil Brunner puts it succinctly when he claims that sin "is like the son who strikes his father's face in anger, . . . it is the bold self-assertion of the son's will above that of the father" (Brunner, *Meditator*, p. 462). It is with those thoughts in mind that we can begin to see the height and depth and breadth of God's love.

> ## The Great Exchange
>
> "Christ was treated as we deserve, that we might be treated as He deserves. He was condemned for our sins, in which He had no share, that we might be justified by His righteousness, in which we had no share. He suffered the death which was ours, that we might receive the life which was His" (White, *The Desire of Ages*, p. 25).

Romans 5:9-11 fleshes out the conclusions that can be drawn from the revelation of the love of God at the cross. Verses 9 and 10 each focus on a "much more" than statement that parallel each other. "Much more than," we read in verse 9, "having now been justified by His blood, we will be saved from wrath through Him." The focal point in the first half of the verse is justification "by His blood," a reference to Christ's substitutionary sacrifice that laid the foundation for God's justification of sinners (previously presented in Rom. 3:24, 25). Paul never tires of reflecting on "the Lamb of God, who takes away the sin of the world" (John 1:29, RSV). "For our sakes," he wrote to the Corinthians, "he made him to be sin who knew no sin, so that in him we might become the righteousness of God" (2 Cor. 5:21, RSV). And, he pointed out in Galatians, "Christ redeemed us from the curse of the [broken] law, having become a curse for us—for it is written, 'Cursed be every one who hangs on a tree'" (Gal. 3:13, RSV).

That dying for human sin is at the very center of Paul's gospel (1 Cor. 15:1-3). What we find in Romans 5:9 is an extension of Paul's thinking on the topic signaled by the words "much more then." C.E.B. Cranfield helps us understand the apostle's thinking when he writes that "since God has already done the really difficult thing, that is, justified impious sinners, we may be absolutely confident that He will do what is by comparison very easy, namely, save from His wrath at the last those who are already righteous in His sight" (Cranfield, *Romans*, vol. 1, p. 266).

That brings us to the second "much more" in Romans 5:10: "For if while we were enemies we were reconciled to God through the death of His Son, much more, having been reconciled, we shall be saved by His life." The first word we should highlight in that verse is "enemies." We have seen in Romans 5:6-10 a progression of Paul's categorization of the lost from "helpless" (verse 6a) to "ungodly" (verse 6b) to "sinners" (verse 8) to "enemies" (verse 10). Each term in that sequence is more serious and more explicitly descriptive than those before. With "enemies" Paul has come to the apex of his description of the lost. "Enemy" is a strong word. "An enemy," Leon Morris points out, "is not simply someone who falls a little short of being a good and faithful friend. He belongs in the opposite camp. He is opposed to what one is doing. Sinners are putting their efforts into the opposite direction to that of God" (Morris, *Atonement*, pp. 136, 137). Thus an enemy is, as in the case of war, out to destroy the other.

Now it is clear all through the Bible that sinners are God's enemies, that they oppose the principles of His kingdom. But, we need to ask, does the phrase "God's enemies" say anything about His attitude toward sinners? The contrasts in Romans 5:9, 10 provide a definite yes to our question. The fact that those who cling to their rebellion will eventually experience God's wrath (verse 9) indicates His hatred of the sin that destroys people's lives.

On the other hand, we must beware of a fine line here. God hates sin but He loves sinners, so much so that He sent Jesus to heal the broken relationship and thus to reconcile them to Himself. To reconcile means to bring together two estranged parties. But like justification, reconciliation is a two-sided affair. Paul makes it clear that God (in this case the wronged party) has taken all the necessary steps to heal the conflict between Himself and those at war with Him. But the other side or aspect is for them to accept His offer through Christ of both peace and salvation. When His "enemies" refuse the offer they come under His legitimate wrath (Rom. 5:9; cf. John 3:36; Rev. 6:16). Since He will not force compliance, He can do nothing to help those who continue to "spit in His face" and live by destructive principles.

But those who accept God's reconciliation made possible "through the death of His Son" (Rom. 5:10) will discover the second "much more." If the first had to do with being "saved from wrath through Him" (verse 9), the second is that those reconciled "shall be saved by His life" (verse 10).

Here we find a statement akin to that of Romans 4:25, which states that Christ was "raised for our justification." The resurrection is an essential part of Paul's gospel (1 Cor. 15:3, 4) because Christ's salvific work was not completed at the cross. Subsequent to His death there is not only His high priestly ministry for His children in the heavenly sanctuary (Rom. 8:34; Heb. 7:25; 1 John 2:1, 2) but His Second Advent at which time He will save His people from the presence of sin eternally. Thus there exists a future aspect to salvation when the reconciled ones "shall be saved by His life." Reflecting on that passage, Charles Hodge writes that "if while we were enemies, we were restored to the favour of God by the death of his Son, the fact that he lives will certainly secure our final salvation" at the end of time (Hodge, p. 140).

With that thought Paul returns to the imperative to rejoice in God's salvation which he had raised in verse 2. There is no doubt about it in his mind that Christians ought to be the happiest people on earth. Pickle-faced church members need to catch the point and join the host of those who have been reconciled to God and can't hold back the joy in their hearts.

22. The Adam Way or the Christ Way? (part 1)

Romans 5:12-14
> [12]*Therefore as sin entered into the world through one man and death through sin, so also death came to all men because all sinned—*[13]*for sin was in the world before the law, but sin is not credited when there is no law.* [14]*But death reigned from Adam until Moses, even over those who had not sinned in the likeness of the transgression of Adam, who is a type of the One who was to come.*

The Adam Way or the Christ Way? (part 1)

One thing you never have to teach your children is how to sin! It seems to come naturally. Everyone does it. Thus Paul's earlier conclusion in Romans 3:23 that all have sinned and fallen short of God's ideal.

Sin and its effects are universal. One commentary to its power and prevalence is that every state must have its army, police, judges, courts, and penal system. Theologian John MacQuarrie highlights the problem when he writes that when we "look at actual human existing, we perceive a massive disorder in existence, a pathology that seems to extend all through existence, whether we consider the community or the individual" (MacQuarrie, p. 69). Reinhold Niebuhr was just as succinct when he wrote that "where there is history . . . there is sin" (Niebuhr, vol. 2, p. 80).

But you don't have to be a theologian to reach that conclusion. Even if the Bible did not exist, we would still have a doctrine of sin. Written on the fabric of existence, we find its universality attested to by the pagan writers of antiquity as well as by the philosophical, literary, sociological, psychological, political, and other theorists of the present day.

Secular novelist John Steinbeck put it accurately when he penned: "I believe that there is one story in the world, and only one. . . . Humans are caught—in their lives, in their thoughts, in their hungers and ambitions, in their avarice and cruelty, and in their kindness and generosity too—in a net of good and evil. . . . There is no other story" (Steinbeck, p. 366).

In Romans 5:12 Paul explains the obvious universality of sin by the simple phrase that "sin entered into the world through one man"—Adam. He goes on to add that sin resulted in death, and that "death came to [or 'spread to,' RSV] all men because all sinned." The implication is clear that all people are sinners through some connection to Adam.

But please note that Paul, although he deals with the universality of sin and death and the fact that Adam was the fountainhead of the problem, does not in any way seek to explain how sin and death spread to everyone. He just treats it as a fact.

Romans 5:12-21, rather than trying to explore how sin and death took over humanity, focuses on Adam and Christ as models of two types of life. John Brunt is quite correct when he writes that "what Paul is most interested in showing us . . . is that no matter how big a mess Adam got us into, Christ's solution not only cleaned up the mess but went far beyond. Yes, Adam got everyone into a mess. . . . But now Christ brings a solution for everyone as well. . . . Adam brings the problem, but Christ brings an even bigger solution, for grace is greater than sin" (Brunt, p. 122).

One of the most obvious things about Romans 5:12 is that it doesn't have a proper ending. I have represented that fact by a dash at the end of the verse. What appears to be happening is that as Paul is laying out the sentence he begins to think of objections that some might have to the idea that all people have sinned. After all, not everyone had the law of Moses. And hadn't the apostle just mentioned in Romans 4:15 that "where there is no law there is no transgression" (RSV)?

Paul, as usual in the face of such objections, responds aggressively in verse 13: Of course sin was in the world before the coming of the law. He could have pulled up some illustrations since sin and its results are major themes of the Bible throughout the patriarchal period. But the existence of sin before the giving of the law on Sinai is a fact that none of Paul's readers would have doubted.

> "Christ is much more powerful to save, than Adam was to destroy" (Calvin, p. 206).

At that point the apostle notes that "sin is not credited when there is no law" (verse 13). What does Paul mean? He can't be suggesting that people were not held responsible. After all, they *did* die ("death reigned from Adam until Moses," verse 14). And, beyond that, as he noted in Romans 1 and 2, everybody through nature and conscience has a knowledge of right and wrong. C.E.B. Cranfield's translation helps us to see Paul's point better: "in the absence of the law, sin is not registered *with full clarity*." He added the italicized words to indicate that Paul is saying that "in the absence of the law sin is not the clearly defined thing, starkly shown up in its true character, that it becomes when the law is present" (Cranfield, *Shorter Commentary*, p. 116). That interpretation builds upon Paul's previous comment in Romans 3:20 that it is through the law that we know sin. Thus the command "thou shalt not kill" is much clearer than merely having an uneasy conscience about such actions. The law given on Sinai makes God's will quite explicit. In that sense the apostle can say in Romans 5:20 that "the law came in to increase the trespass" (ESV) or "God's law was given so that all people could see how sinful they were" (NLT).

The "but" at the beginning of Romans 5:14 indicates that there was a sense in which sin was "credited" (verse 13) in spite of the fact that God had not yet given the law to Moses. Thus Paul reemphasizes the fact that death still reigned during the interim between Adam and Moses, even though people living at that time didn't have a definite commandment in the same sense that Adam did in Genesis 2:17 (not to eat of the tree) or that Israel had after Moses received the Ten Commandments. Thus "though sins were not 'charged up separately' as in the case of Adam and Israel—both [having been] confronted with direct 'law'—still, 'death reigned from Adam until Moses'" (Moo, *Epistle*, p. 333).

Once again Paul has driven home the purpose of the law. Clarifying God's will, it holds people accountable. And breaking it means not only temporal death but eternal death (see Rom. 6:23). The apostle never ceases to point out that it is from that dreary ending that Christ wants to save us. All have sinned, and all need Christ's atonement.

Paul's mention of not sinning in the likeness of Adam (Rom. 5:14) raises an interesting idea in his mind that leads him into the provocative concept that Adam "is a type ['pattern,' NIV] of the One who was to come," or Christ.

"How is it," we are forced to ask, "that Adam the sinner is a pattern of Christ the sinless? What is Paul talking about?"

One way to get at the question is to ask ourselves what is the most important event in human history. Would it be the invention of the wheel? the discovery of fire? the introduction of printing? the development of the computer? the testing of atomic power?

Those are all important, but from Paul's point of view they pale into insignificance in the light of the two events he cites in Romans 5:12–19 the fall of the race through Adam and its redemption through Christ. The significance of what Christ and Adam did touches every human being who has ever lived. Thus Adam is a type or pattern of Christ in the sense that both affected the entire race. They came to represent two ways of facing life. Brunt (pp. 120, 121) has outlined the results of our relationship to Adam and to Christ in the following way:

Adam	**Christ**
Sin entered through him (verse 12)	Through Him God's grace overflows (verse 15)
By his trespass the many died (verse 15)	He brings justification (verse 16)

He brings condemnation (verse 16)	He brings life to all (verse 18)
Through him death reigned (verse 17)	Through His obedience the many will be made righteous (verse 19)
He brings condemnation to all (verse 18)	Through Him, we reign in life (verse 17)
Through his disobedience the many were made sinners (verse 19)	

Paul in Romans 5:12-21 is really writing about two ways of life—the Adam way and the Christ way. Beyond that, in the entire context of Romans with its emphasis on faith, he implies that all people choose whether they will align with Adam or Christ. In the end every person will either remain in Adam and the sin life with its inglorious ending, or will unite by faith to Christ and receive both justification and life everlasting.

23. The Adam Way or the Christ Way? (part 2)

Romans 5:15-21

[15]But the grace gift is not like the transgression. For if by the transgression of the one the many died, much more did the grace of God and the gift in grace of the one Man, Jesus Christ, abound to the many. [16]And the gift is not like the effect of the one who sinned. For on the one hand judgment from one transgression resulted in condemnation, on the other hand the grace gift following many transgressions resulted in justification. [17]For if by the transgression of the one, death reigned; much more will those who accept the abundance of grace and of the gift of righteousness reign in life through the One, Jesus Christ.

[18]So then as one's transgression resulted in condemnation for all men, so also One's righteous act resulted in justification and life for all men. [19]For as by the disobedience of the one man the many were made sinners, so also by the obedience of the One the many will be made righteous. [20]Law came in to increase the transgression, but where sin increased grace abounded even

more, ^{21}so that just as sin reigned in death, so also grace might reign through righteousness to eternal life through Jesus Christ our Lord.

One of the keys to understanding Romans 5:15 and 16 is "not like." In verse 15 Paul asserts that "the grace gift is not like the transgression." In what way are they unlike? The apostle's vigorous reply is that the gift of grace is greater than all the effects of sin. As *The Revised English Bible* puts it: "God's act of grace is out of all proportion to Adam's wrongdoing. For if the wrongdoing of that one man brought death upon so many, its effect is vastly exceeded by the grace of God and the gift that came to so many by the grace of the one man, Jesus Christ."

The apostle continues to exhibit grace's unlikeness to sin and its superiority in verse 16. "Again, the gift of God is not to be compared [not like] in its effect with that one man's sin; for the judicial action, following on the one offence, resulted in a verdict of condemnation, but the act of grace, following on so many misdeeds, resulted in a verdict of acquittal" (REB).

What Paul is claiming is that if the effects of sin were powerful, the effects of God's gift are even more powerful. Thus the gift more than conquers the sin problem.

Sin is not the last word, Paul points out in verses 15 and 16, because the grace gift changes the sinner's entire situation. The gift provides a way of escape. It opens up an avenue that releases sinners from the penalty of judgment and provides for their justification full and free.

The word "gift" is significant in Romans 5. It appears 5 times in verses 15-17 and Paul picks it up again in Romans 6:23, in which he tells us that eternal life is the gift of God.

"Gift" not only points to the freeness of salvation, but also to the fact that those who accept the gift do not have to strain heroically against Adam's legacy of sin as the price of acceptance. Acceptance does not come through struggle. Rather we receive it as a gift from God through Christ, who paid the redemption price (see Rom. 3:23-25).

The message of Romans 5:15 and 16 is that greater by far than sin and all its results is God's gift to those willing to accept it. The good news is that the gift is "not like" the curse—it is supremely greater.

That conclusion we find reinforced by the "much more" of verse 17 (see also verse 15), which once again contrasts the superior achievements of

Christ to the penalty of death as the heritage of Adam (verses 12-14). In his repeated use of "much more" in Romans (5:10, 15, 17) the apostle is seeking to express the Father's extreme love and generosity for His children. Paul is telling us that God wants to do more for us than we can even imagine. He not only intends to save us from the penalty of sin, but longs to give and give and give more and more to those who accept His gift through faith in Christ.

That overflowing generosity concept is especially evident in the "much more" of verse 17, in which Paul ties it to "the abundance of grace" or "God's abundant provision of grace" (NIV). Translations have struggled with that phrase. Goodspeed renders it "God's overflowing mercy," Moffat as "the overflowing grace and free gift of righteousness," and *The Message* as "this wildly extravagant life-gift."

But no matter how we translate the Greek, Paul's idea is clear. Not only does grace defeat sin, but we have a "much more" kind of God who wants to fill His children's every need. Today we can be thankful for the "much more" of the Diety we serve.

With Romans 5:18 and 19 Paul is ready to conclude the argument that he began in Romans 5:12, in which he pointed out that death came to all because of the infection of sin that tainted all human beings. The words "so then" signal that he is about to sharpen the point of what has gone before. He has not the slightest doubt in verse 18 that just as condemnation came upon all humanity because of Adam, so justification can reach all through Christ.

But, we need to ask, what does he mean in each case by "all men"? There is not the slightest uncertainty that the judgment of condemnation has come upon every individual because all have sinned. That has been Paul's theme since Romans 1:18, and he explicitly states it in Romans 3:23.

But that is not the only theme in the first five chapters of Romans. A second one follows from the conclusion that all have sinned (Rom. 3:23) and stand condemned (6:23). Immediately following in Romans 3:24 and 25 and on into chapters 4 and 5 the apostle begins to emphasize justification by faith as a solution to universal sinfulness and condemnation. Paul couldn't be plainer that it is those who have faith who are justified. He sets forth faith as the condition of their justification. Without it they are not justified, but still remain under condemnation. Paul doesn't suddenly change that model in Romans 5:18. While Christ died to provide justification for all people, they still need to accept it before it is theirs.

Some are not happy with that explanation. They point out that it says that Christ's righteous act resulted in justification and for "all." But an interpretation that implies that Christ justifies all people irrespective of faith not only removes verse 18 from its context in Romans 3 through 5, which sets forth faith as God's way of justifying people, but it also faces the challenge of the parallel passage in 1 Corinthians 15:22.

The latter text claims, in the context of the resurrection of the righteous, that "as in Adam *all* die, so in Christ shall *all* be made alive" (RSV). Thus to claim that the "alls" of Romans 5:18 and 1 Corinthians 15:22, 23 mean everybody would result in universalism (the theory that everyone will be saved)—a teaching that flatly contradicts the Bible, which tells us that some individuals will reap eternal destruction.

Paul's point in his use of "all" in verse 18, Douglas Moo notes, "is not so much that the groups affected by Christ and Adam, respectively, are co-extensive, but that Christ affects those who are his just as certainly as Adam does those who are his. When we ask who belongs to, or is 'in,' Adam and Christ, respectively, Paul makes his answer clear: every person, without exception, is 'in Adam' (cf. vv. 12d-14); but only those who 'receive the gift' (v. 17; 'those who believe,' according to Rom. 1:16-5:11) are 'in Christ'" (Moo, *Epistle*, p. 343). Moo's explanation of "all" in Romans 5:18 as not meaning "every single human being" is in harmony with other passages in Romans where Paul uses *pas* (all) in the same limited way (see, e.g. Rom. 8:32b; 12:17, 18; 14:2; 16:19).

A similar situation to the "all" of verse 18 is the "many" of verse 19. We can have no doubt in the context of Romans that the "many" who "were made sinners" through the fall of Adam means every person (see Rom. 3:23). But it is also true to the overall flow of Romans that the "many" who "will be made righteous" are those who accept Christ by faith (see Rom. 1:16, 17; 3:24, 25; 4:1-25; 5:1). Verse 19's immediate context, in which verse 17 plainly states that it is only those who "*accept*" the gift who are blessed in Christ, supports such an interpretation. While many translations render *lamban* as "receive," that receiving is the same as accepting. Thus Walter Bauer sets forth to "receive, accept," "take hold of," and "grasp" as possible meanings (Bauer, pp. 584, 583), while the *Theological Dictionary of the New Testament* suggests such renderings as "to grasp," "to seize," and "to take," as well as "to receive" (Kittel, vol. 4, p. 5).

The good news is that Christ died for every human being who has ever lived. The bad news is that not all receive or accept God's gracious gift. His sacrifice made provision for the justification of the entire human race. But some choose to follow the Adam way rather than the Christ way.

Ellen White, speaking in a slightly different context, makes essentially the same point: "The *provisions* of redemption are free to all; the *results* of redemption will be enjoyed by those who have complied with the conditions" (White, *Patriarchs and Prophets*, p. 208). The condition of justification in Romans 3-5, of course, is acceptance by faith. Thus "many" is not "all" in its fullest sense when it comes to justification and salvation. It is our privilege right now to accept through the gift of God's Spirit His abounding grace (Rom. 5:20) and the way of Christ as we at the same time turn our backs on the reign of death connected to the Adam way (verse 21). Thank God for the choice.

Part IV

The Way of Godliness

Romans 6:1-8:39

24. Dead to Sin and Alive to God

Romans 6:1-11

¹What then shall we say? Should we continue in sin that grace may increase? ²May it never be! How can we who died to sin still live in it? ³Or do you not know that as many as were baptized into Christ Jesus were baptized into His death? ⁴Therefore we were buried with Him through baptism into death, so that just as Christ was raised from the dead through the glory of the Father, so also we may walk in newness of life. ⁵For if we have been united with Him in the likeness of His death, we shall also be united with Him in the likeness of His resurrection. ⁶We know that our old self was crucified with Him so that our sinful body might be made inactive, and that we should no longer be slaves to sin, ⁷for he who has died has been freed from sin. ⁸Now if we have died with Christ, we believe that we shall also live with Him, ⁹knowing that Christ, having been raised from the dead, will never die again. Death no longer rules over Him. ¹⁰For in dying He died to sin once for all, but the life that He lives He lives to God. ¹¹So you also must consider yourselves to be dead to sin but alive to God in Christ Jesus.

The first five chapters of Romans present a powerful argument. Paul first dealt with the all-pervasive problem of sin among both Jews and Gentiles, who thereby stood condemned and subject to death (Rom. 1:18-3:20). Then the apostle vigorously set forth God's solution to the sin problem—justification by grace through faith. He left no stones unturned in demonstrating that salvation is a free gift from God (Rom. 3:21-5:21).

His teaching was clear and helpful, but it raised questions in the minds of some. One quite natural response was this: "If everything depends upon what God has done, if our achievements don't bring about our justification or even aid God in granting it, then what does it matter how we live?" That question is inevitable once a person realizes that God has made full provision for our justification.

Of course, it can be asked for different reasons. Sometimes the question comes from genuine believers who honestly want to know how they should live if they have been saved by grace. At other times those who are confused about what it means to be saved by grace utilize it as a justification to continue a sinful life. And others who oppose the idea of justification as a free gift raise it to demonstrate the irresponsibility of Paul's theology. From their perspective "cheap grace" leads to antinomianism or lawlessness.

It is the latter two groups that Paul probably has in mind in Romans 6:1, although he most certainly also wants to instruct those who desire to know how justified Christians should persue their lives.

The logic of those who are against Paul's teaching on grace or are confused on the topic runs something like this:

1. Paul claimed in Romans 5:20 that the law identifies sin and thereby increases it;
2. more sin means more grace;
3. therefore, let's go on sinning so that grace may increase and God will be glorified all the more because of His ever more extensive graciousness (Rom. 6:1; 3:8).

Such reasoning, of course, would invalidate Paul's theology among serious thinkers and provide a basis for profligate living among the irresponsible and insincere.

To both head off his detractors and to instruct true believers Paul raises the question himself in Romans 6:1: "Should we continue in sin that grace may increase?"

His reaction to it borders on violence: "By no means!" (RSV). "May it never be!" (NASB). "God forbid" (KJV). "What a terrible thought!" (Phillips). "Never!" (Moffat).

No matter how we translate the Greek words, they depict the fact that Paul stands totally aghast at the idea that a Christian should go on living in a state of sin. They represent the strongest idiom of repudiation in the Greek New Testament. The phrase projects a sense of *outrage* that anyone could ever consider such a foolish idea as being true.

The very thought that sin could in any conceivable way be pleasing to God or be to His honor absolutely appalled the apostle. He doesn't even stop to reason with such stupidity. Rather than providing an argument against it, he asks a rhetorical question: "How can we who died to sin still live in it?" (Rom. 6:2).

The answer was obvious. It was impossible for one who has died to sin to continue to live in sin as a way of life. "Previously," Leon Morris points out, "they had been dead *in* sin (Eph. 2:1); now they were dead *to* sin" (Morris, *Romans*, p. 245). Only the most perverted logic would conclude that a life of sin was the way for Christians to exist.

Paul illustrates his meaning in Romans 6:3 through the baptism experience, since it provides the perfect image for what he wants to illustrate. "Baptize" is not a warm fuzzy word in history. It means "to dip in or under," "to immerse," "to sink," "to drown" (Bromiley, p. 92). Writers in the ancient world used it to describe sinking ships or drowning people. Jesus picked up on that rather violent aspect of the word when He referred to His death as a baptism (Mark 10:38; Luke 12:50).

Paul follows that lead in Romans 6, in which he employs the term to signify death to a way of life (verse 4). Thus becoming a Christian is a violent sort of thing. We enter it through baptism, a symbol of death to the old ways. Now Paul tells us in Romans 6:2, 3 that if a person has died to the old ways, it is ridiculous to claim that he or she would still want to live in them. No genuine Christian would desire to continue a life of sin.

Yet, we know that death was not the end for Christ. Resurrection followed it. Continuing to use the baptism metaphor in verse 4, Paul goes on to say that "just as Christ was raised from the dead through the glory of the Father, so also we may walk in newness of life." Thus "as Christ was raised from among the dead by a majestic exercise of Divine power, so we also must from henceforth conduct ourselves as men in whom has been implanted a new principle of life. For it is not to be supposed that we can join with Christ in one thing [death] and not join with Him in another [a new life]" (Sanday, p. 154).

Baptism is the perfect symbol of death to the old way and resurrection to a new way of life. After all, as C. H. Dodd aptly notes, baptism by "immersion is a sort of burial; emergence from the water is a sort of resurrection" (Dodd, p. 107).

Before leaving Romans 6:4, we need to examine the idea of walking in newness of life. The word "walk" is important here, because it not only expresses a process of ongoing fellowship with God, but signifies directionality, since every walker has a goal. The book of 1 John highlights the implications of the verb when it notes that "if we say we have fellowship with him while we *walk* in darkness, we lie and do not live according to the truth; but if we *walk* in the light, as he is in the light, we have fellowship with one another, and the blood of Jesus his Son cleanses us from all sin" (1 John 1:6, 7, RSV).

Thus it is that Paul describes the beginning of the Christian life as the start of the new journey in which it is impossible to tread the path of sin as a way of life.

A reader of Romans 6:1-11 will notice that Paul repeats himself several times on the themes of death to the old ways and life to the new. And with good reason. "As a good teacher he knew that truth once stated is not necessarily absorbed" (Mounce, p. 151). And it was of the utmost importance in the apostle's mind that this particular lesson be not only learned but put into practice.

A Look at the Nature of Baptism

Romans 6:3, 4 is one of the clearest passages in the New Testament on the meaning of baptism. Not only are those being baptized "buried with Him" in the watery grave, but they are "raised" out of the watery grave just as God raised Christ from the dead. Any other form of baptism would completely miss the meaning of Paul's symbols. In fact, if baptism in Paul's day were of any other form than immersion (such as sprinkling or dipping), Paul would never have used the illustration. He couldn't have employed it, since it would have made no sense. But immersion perfectly illustrates the death, burial, and resurrection process as reenacted by all new Christians when they become a part of the body of Christ.

Before moving to verses 12-14 we should note that some people become confused with the thoughts in verses 7 and 10 which, respectively, teach that Christians are "freed from sin" and dead to sin. Some have interpreted these concepts to mean that a true Christian will be totally insensitive to sin and its attractions, somewhat like a dead dog lying in the road, which is completely unresponsive to a kick in its ribs. Thus for them sin should hold no attraction and is no real temptation.

Such an understanding overlooks the fact that it wasn't so in the life of Jesus. In His life on earth He was genuinely tempted in that He felt Himself drawn toward some aspects of the wilderness temptation and His mind and body found going to the cross repulsive. And universal human experience identifies with Christ's reaction. To put it bluntly, born-again Christians still feel such things as the pull of appetite and unlawful sexual attraction.

Paul's point, if we look at the context of Romans 6:7, 10, is not that Christians are dead to and free from sinful impulses, but that they will not be walking in the way of sin. The apostle highlights his major point in Romans 6:12, in which he noted that Christians do not let sin "reign" in their lives. It is one thing to be tempted or even to commit an act of sin and repent of it (see 1 John 1:9) and quite another to be a slave of sin (Rom. 6:17).

We will return to that topic in our next chapter. But first we should note that John Wesley caught Paul's idea when he wrote that sin "*remains, though it does not *reign*" (Wesley, vol. 5, p. 151). Thus Christians no longer live lives characterized by sin, but when they do sin John tells us that "we have an advocate with the Father, Jesus Christ the Righteous" (1 John 2:1, KJV).

25. And Who Is the Ruler of My Life?

Romans 6:12-14
[12]Therefore let not sin reign in your mortal body so that you obey its lusts. [13]Neither go on offering your bodily parts to sin as weapons of unrighteousness, but offer yourselves to God as those brought from death to life, and your bodily parts as weapons of righteousness to God. [14]For sin will not lord it over you, for you are not under law but under grace.

Romans 6:12 is very realistic in the sense that on one hand it holds in tension the fact that Christians do not need to allow sin to reign or control their lives because of Christ's victory, while on the other hand it raises the issue that even born-again Christians still find themselves tempted by the lusts of the flesh.

Paul exhorts his readers not to let sin rule. That very exhortation assumes that sin is still there, that believers do not have a serene existence that excludes the possibility of sin. Even though they are "in Christ" they still remain "in the flesh." They still feel its "twitches."

Paul personifies sin in Romans 5:21 and chapter 6 as a dethroned but still powerful monarch determined to reign in Christians' lives just as he did before their conversion. Thus the apostle urges believers not to let sin have its old place of superiority, because it no longer has a right to rule. In fact, sin has no power to control a believer unless that person chooses to "obey its lusts" (Rom. 6:12). Peter makes a similar appeal: "You are a chosen people, a royal priesthood, a holy nation, a people belonging to God. . . . I urge you, as aliens and strangers in the world, to abstain from sinful desires, which war against your soul" (1 Peter 2:9-11, NIV).

Christians become citizens of God's kingdom the moment they come to Christ. At that very time they turn into aliens and strangers to Satan's realm of sin and death. But Paul tells us in Romans 6:12 that sin is still a force even though it is no longer supreme.

John Wesley helps us understand the tension. He writes that sin "*remains* in our heart; . . . 'even in them that are regenerate'; although it does no longer *reign*; it has not now dominion over them. It is a conviction of our proneness to evil, of an heart bent to backsliding, of the still continuing tendency of the flesh to lust against the spirit. Sometimes, unless we continually watch and pray, it lusteth to pride, sometimes to anger, sometimes to love of the world, love of ease, love of honour, or love of pleasures more than God." It shows up "in a thousand ways, and under a thousand pretenses" to depart "more or less, from the living God" (Wesley, vol. 6, p. 50). The good news is that "the usurper is dethroned. He remains indeed where he once reigned; but remains *in chains*" (*ibid.*, vol. 5, p. 154).

The Christian's task, Paul tells his readers in Romans 6:12, is not to let the kingdom of sin regain a dominant place in their lives. The next two verses expand his appeal. Verse 13 begins with the imperative command not to "go on presenting the members of your body to sin as instruments of unrighteousness" (NASB). That passage contains two words of special interest in their context. The first is "present" or "yield" (RSV). The word (*parist mi*) can also be translated as to "*put at one's disposal*," to "*offer*," or to "make something available" (Bauer, p. 778; Rogers, p. 327). It is indeed a serious problem when the servants of God make available or offer their bodies to sin and Satan rather than to their God and true sovereign. *Parist mi* also appears in Romans 12:1, 2, in which Paul exhorts the Romans "to present [offer] your bodies as a living sacrifice, holy and acceptable to God, which is your spiritual worship" (RSV). Thus one aspect of Romans 6:13 is an urging of the Roman believers not to get involved in the wrong type of "spiritual worship" by continuing to offer their "bodily parts to sin."

But we find still other nuances inherent in Paul's use of *parist mi* in verses 12-14, since I could just have accurately translated it as "make available." The implications of that appear in another word of special interest in the passage's argument: *hoplon*, generally rendered "instrument" (KJV, RSV, NASB), but which might better be translated in the book of Romans' context of spiritual warfare as "an instrument designed to make ready for military engagement" or "*weapon*" (Bauer, p. 716). "Weapon" is the obvious meaning in John 18:3, in which Judas guides the band of soldiers to arrest Jesus. The same rendering appears in 2 Corinthians 6:6, 7, in which Paul links love and truthful speech to "weapons of righteousness" (RSV).

> ## WHO IS IN CONTROL?
>
> "Both times that Paul writes *instruments (hopla)*, he uses a word that can refer to a tool or a weapon. Our skills, capabilities, and bodies can serve many purposes, good or bad. In sin, every part of our bodies are vulnerable. In Christ, every part can be an instrument for service. It is the one to whom we offer our service that makes the difference. We are like lasers that can burn destructive holes in steel plates or do delicate cataract surgery. Under whose control will we continue to place our lives?" (Barton, p. 122).

The same understanding fits today's text. The underlying picture is one of sin and righteousness as respective rulers in opposing armies. Hence the warning not to offer or make available bodily parts to the rule of unrighteousness. To do so would not only be false worship of the wrong sovereign (in the offering metaphor) but would also be the action of a traitor (in the making available rendering) to the One who had become our rightful ruler.

Romans 6:13 closes with a final imperative—this time a "to do" rather than a "do not." Christians are to offer or make available both themselves and their "weapons" to righteousness and God. Thus, William Barclay writes, "we are faced with the tremendous alternative of making ourselves the weapons in the hand of God, or the weapons in the hand of sin" (Barclay, *Romans*, p. 88).

Those alternatives, Barclay points out, may overwhelm some people. "A man," he suggests, "may well answer: 'Such a choice is too much for me. I am bound to fail.' Paul's answer is: 'Don't be discouraged and don't be despairing; sin will not lord it over you' [Rom. 6:14]" (*ibid.*).

Why? Because Christians "are not under law but under grace," the apostle asserts in Romans 6:14. Here we find an interesting use of grace. Whereas we usually define the word as "God's unmerited favor toward the undeserving," Paul presents it as "a power" (see Boice, vol. 2, p. 634) that enables Christians to conquer.

Grace won the victory over the lordship of sin at the cross, when Christ triumphed over Satan. Because of that victory, sin is not our "lord" or ruler (Rom. 6:14a). We are "dead to sin but alive to God in Christ Jesus" (verse 11). A change in lordship has already transpired in believers' lives. In the assurance of victory won they can go forth confidently to wage war against sin. Christians don't walk in their own strength, but in that of their new Lord, Jesus Christ.

It is at that juncture that the law and grace issue becomes important. Paul makes it quite explicit that believers aren't under the dominion of sin, *because* they are under grace rather than the law.

The contrast between law and grace was a new thought to both Jews and Jewish Christians. They had traditionally seen the law as a gift of grace. "For them the law was given by grace precisely to prevent sin" (Dunn, *Romans*, vol. 1, p. 351). But here the apostle puts law and grace in an adversarial relationship.

He sets forth law and grace as two alternatives. Thus those who are under one are not under the other. Why does Paul place them in opposition? He did so in this case because he had to combat those of his Jewish contemporaries who sought to use the law as a way of salvation, as a method of gaining God's favor.

The apostle has argued forcefully throughout Romans that God never gave the law for deliverance, but to provide knowledge of sin (Rom. 3:20), to increase the amount of sin and wrath (5:20; 4:15), and so on. Those seeking salvation by the law will find that its condemning function will silence every mouth and make the "whole world . . . accountable to God" (3:19, RSV).

The law has its purposes, but Paul never ceases to hammer home that it is not to rescue us from the rulership of sin. That, he can't seem to say often enough, is the role of grace. It is because of grace that sin is no longer our master (Rom. 6:14). James Denney puts it nicely when he notes that it "is not restraint" of the law, but grace that "liberates from sin: not Mount Sinai but Mount Calvary which makes saints" (Denney, "Romans," p. 635).

26. Two Ways of Life

Romans 6:15-19
  15What then? Shall we sin because we are not under law but under grace? May it never be! 16Don't you know that to whoever you offer yourselves as slaves for obedience, you are slaves of the one you obey, either of sin resulting in death or of obedience resulting in righteousness? 17But thanks be to God that while you used to be slaves of sin, you became obedient from the heart to that type of teaching to which you were committed, 18and having been freed from sin, you have become slaves to righteousness. 19I am speaking in human terms because of the weakness of your flesh. For just as you offered your bodily parts as slaves to impurity and to lawlessness, which resulted in even more lawlessness, so now offer your bodily parts as slaves of righteousness, which will result in sanctification.

What then?" Paul's question sounds very much like the "What then shall we say" of Romans 6:1, in which he pictures his detractors as saying "should we continue in sin that grace may increase?"

Paul smashed that question flat in verses 2-14. But now he sees a new question looming on the horizon. He has just finished declaring in verse 14 that believers are not under law but under grace. That statement has always down through church history raised questions in the minds of two types of people. Emile Brunner notes that as soon as some hear "Free from the Law, the sinful flesh scents the morning breeze." Such individuals see in grace the opportunity to dump the law and to do what they want.

On the other hand, Brunner points out, "legal Pharisaism gets ready to draw dangerous conclusions from the doctrine of grace in order to destroy it" (Brunner, *Romans*, p. 53).

As a result, the "hostile brothers" of lawlessness and legalism always surround the doctrine of grace. Both sides, albeit for quite different purposes, shout out "Freedom from the law means a free and open path to sin."

Paul confronts the hostile brothers head-on in Romans 6:15-23. He will in his usual thorough fashion nail shut the door that suggests "If it is grace that saves, it doesn't matter how we live. Sin doesn't matter, since God has a superabundance of grace and will forgive us 70 times seven." The apostle comes down hard on such a perverse understanding of salvation by grace.

"May it never be!" or "By no means!" (RSV) is Paul's response to the thought that anyone could even think that they could use grace as an excuse for sinning. As in Romans 6:2, he stands aghast at the very idea.

The apostle in verse 16 extends his argument in his astute claim that people are never really free. God made them for obedience. The only question is whether they will be obedient to sin or to righteousness, to God's principles or to Satan's. Freedom in the abstract is an illusion.

Thus freedom from the law does not mean absolute freedom. And for Christians, freedom from the law as a way of salvation, as Brunner notes, "does not mean freedom *from* God but freedom *for* God" (Brunner, *Romans*, p. 53, italics supplied). Faith is just the opposite of being loosed from God. It is an intimate relationship with Him. As Paul so often says, a Christian is one who is "*in*" Christ." Persons of faith know that they belong to God. For Paul, obedience is faith's natural result. As we noted earlier, the expression "the obedience of faith" frames the entire book of Romans (Rom. 1:5; 16:26). Paul cannot even begin to imagine genuine faith that does not lead to obedience.

But in Romans 6:16 he suggests a provocative thought when he claims that individuals offer themselves as slaves to either sin or righteousness. Now offering oneself to slavery is quite foreign to the twenty-first century mind. But the apostle's first readers understood the situation from their everyday experiences. After all, in the Roman world "people in dire poverty could offer themselves as slaves to someone simply in order to be fed and housed" (Zeisler, p. 167). And they also knew "full well that someone who sells himself or herself into slavery owes strict obedience to his or her lord" (Stuhlmacher, *Romans*, pp. 94, 95).

In verse 16 Paul took that earthly reality and transposed it to spiritual events. Thus people could choose to offer themselves to be slaves of sin or of obedience. But those are the only two options. Everyone must serve either Satan or God.

It is in the context of the two obediences that Paul talks about the two destinations of the two possible paths. One leads to death, and we would expect him to say that the other path has life as its goal. But he doesn't. Rather, he says obedience to God leads to "righteousness."

Wait a minute! Has the great apostle gotten confused? Is he saying after all his talk of righteousness by faith without works of law that people can achieve righteousness by obedience?

By no means! But he is telling us that obedience is an important part of a life lived in grace. The grace-empowered obedience of the born-again Christian leads to righteousness in the sense that it motivates conduct pleasing to God, in harmony with the principles of His kingdom.

Romans 6:17 finds Paul excited and thankful for what God has done for the Roman Christians—they have changed masters. That verse also tells us more about their faith. A faith that had responded to the apostolic teaching, it had led them to "enslave" themselves to a new ruler or lord. Paul, like Jesus in the Sermon on the Mount, was absolutely convinced that "no one can serve two masters" (Matt. 6:24, RSV). The Christians in Rome had realized the fruitlessness of serving their first master (sin) and had voluntarily linked up as did Paul (Rom. 1:1) to become slaves of God.

Verse 17 also tells us that the Roman Christians "became obedient from the heart." Paul nowhere else uses that expression. But it is full of meaning. In the ancient word the "heart" was the mind, the reason, the entire personality or character. Thus obedience came from all that a person was. Their obedience wasn't just a casual thing, not a passing fad. It came "from the heart." The verb form used indicates an action taken in a point of time. It points to the decisive act of obedience when they turned away from sin and toward God. The phrase "became obedient from the heart" expresses a deeply felt experience, one that, as Charles Hodge points out, was "voluntary and sincere" (Hodge, p. 207). They had chosen to become slaves of godliness.

One of the great teachings of the last half of Romans 6 is that faith and obedience are inseparable. As one author puts it, "There is no saving faith in God apart from obedience to God, and there can be no godly obedience without godly faith" (MacArthur, p. 346).

Emancipation from sin, Romans 6:18 informs us, does not lead to total freedom. While Christ's followers have been delivered from the dominion and condemning power of sin, Paul was not naïve enough to suggest that they would be absolutely free. He knew that freedom from the reign of sin did not release people to wander in an aimless moral vacuum. To the contrary, the apostle recognized that freedom from sin meant enslavement to Christ and the right.

In order to understand the full implications of what Paul is saying, we need to grasp the status of a slave in his society. Servants in modern cultures owe their time at work to the boss, but after work hours are theirs to do what they please. But not so with a slave. They literally had no time of their own. All of it belonged to the one who owned them. Thus they did not have time to do as they liked. It was impossible for them to serve two masters (their owner and themselves) because all their time belonged to one master.

> ## All or Nothing Kind of Belonging
>
> With God it is all or nothing. Persons who keep some little corner of life to themselves are not really Christians. Christians have surrendered complete control of their lives to Christ and His principles of life. They hold nothing back. And, as Barclay points out, "no man who has done that can ever think of using grace as an excuse for sin" (Barclay, *Romans,* p. 91).

That picture is in Paul's mind. As William Barclay puts it: "At one time you were the slave of sin. Sin had exclusive possession of you. At that time you could not talk of anything else but sinning. But now you have taken God as your master. God has exclusive possession of you. And now you cannot even talk about sinning: you must talk about nothing but holiness" (Barclay, *Romans*, p. 90).

Romans 6:19 finds Paul apologizing for using the slavery illustration since "he did not like to compare the Christian life to any kind of slavery" (*ibid.*, p. 90). When he says that he is "speaking in human terms because of the weakness of your flesh," he is referring "to the frailty of human nature, which cannot grasp profound truth unless it is presented in human analogies" (Barrett, p. 132).

The second half of verse 19 makes it plain that the two life paths related to the two slaveries are both dynamic and progressive in their results. Thus serving sin leads to "greater and greater iniquity" (verse 19, RSV), while serving righteousness "will result in sanctification." Here, in parallel with the dynamic of evil, sanctification means more than merely being "'set apart' from the world for the service of the Lord." But "as Christians give themselves in slavery to righteousness, they will progress further and further on the path of becoming different from the world and closer to the Lord's own holiness" (Moo, "Romans," p. 39).

27. Two Eternal Destinations

Romans 6:20-23

> [20]*For when you were slaves of sin, you were free in regard to righteousness. *[21]*Therefore what profit did you have then from the things of which you are now ashamed? For the result of those things is death. *[22]*But now having been freed from sin and having been enslaved to God, you have profit resulting in sanctification and its outcome, eternal life. *[23]*For the wages of sin is death, but the free gift of God is eternal life in Christ Jesus our Lord.*

Beginning in Romans 6:16 Paul began a discussion of two quite different paths that leads to his conclusion regarding two radically distinct destinations in verse 23. Verses 16-19 treated two slaveries (i.e., sin versus righteousness) related to two lords. Then verses 20 and 22 continue in terms of two freedoms. Paul speaks of it here in terms of sinners being free from righteousness (verse 20), and Christians being free from sin (verse 22).

Underlying the presentation is what we might call the doctrine of human freedom. Not pawns in the hands of an all controlling force, we do have choices in life. God gives each of us freedom to sin if we so desire, or freedom to walk in the path of holiness. Through the gift of the Spirit we have genuine choices.

God forces no one. But neither does He protect us from the consequences of our actions. As a Christian I have the liberty to lie down on the Interstate freeway at rush hour if I choose. But God won't create a miracle to keep me safe. The same applies to substance abuse. I am free to smoke 10 packs of cigarettes a day if I have the time and inclination, but God won't intervene to protect me from lung cancer or emphysema. We live in a moral universe in which people harvest what they sow.

The harvest we eventually reap depends on the type of seeds we plant and nourish throughout life. Those who sow seeds of destruction will eventually see the result (Rom. 6:21). The same goes for those who focus on seeds of love and caring (verse 22).

The good news is that people can alter the orientation and direction of their freedoms. That is where the "but now" of verse 22 comes in. Christians are those who have changed their lords, their enslavements, their life paths, their freedoms, and their destinations. As a result, "nobody but a Christian can say 'but now. . . .' The life of the other man is always the same, there is no difference, no change. He changes his pleasures, he changes his company, changes his sin, but his life is the same. But the Christian is not the same; he

> ### The Paradox of Freedom
>
> In Romans 6 "each slavery is also a kind of freedom, although the one is authentic and the other spurious. Similarly, each freedom is a kind of slavery, although the one is degrading and the other ennobling" (Stott, p. 185).

has left his old life, and now he has something entirely new, something quite different" (Lloyd-Jones, *Chapter 6*, p. 287).

The apostle tells us in Romans 6:22 that God has set Christians free from their enslavement to sin. But just as they were once totally dedicated to sin, now, Paul notes, they will be just as committed to God and His ways—they will be "enslaved to God."

Paul goes on in verses 22 and 23 to spell out the advantages the Christian gets from serving God. The first is "sanctification." That word in Romans 6, as we noted in our discussion of verse 19, means not only to be set apart for holy use but to walk progressively closer to God as through His grace we trod the path of holiness.

D. Martyn Lloyd-Jones caught the contrast inherent in the two freedoms when he wrote: "As you go on living this righteous life, and practising it with all your might and energy, and all your time . . . you will find that the process that went on before, in which you went from bad to worse and became viler and viler, is entirely reversed. You will become cleaner and cleaner, and purer and purer, and holier and holier, and more and more confirmed unto the image of the Son of God" (*ibid.*, pp. 268, 269).

"Eternal life" is the second advantage of being "enslaved to God" (Rom. 6:22). Verse 23 treats that topic more fully, along with outlining the destination of those who elect to remain under the lordship of sin.

"The wages of sin is death." That is about as blunt as one can get. The text then goes on to note that "the free gift of God is eternal life in Christ Jesus our Lord."

Paul in Romans 6 is explicit in his argument that the two paths, the two enslavements, and the two freedoms lead to two quite different destinations. God is not arbitrary. All persons, in the face of the knowledge they possess (Romans 1 and 2), choose the path they want to walk through life, but each path has a specific destination. Every choice, every action in life takes us somewhere. And God in His wisdom and greatness allows people to select the route that they will individually follow.

In Romans 6:23 Paul warns us that the end of the line for the path of sin is death. And, you may be thinking, what does he mean by death? It can't be physical death, because everybody, all the way from the most sincere Christians to the most unrepentant sinners, dies physically.

The clue to the apostle's meaning appears in the last half of verse 23, in which he contrasts death with the reward of the righteous—"eternal life." He does not have earthly life and death in mind here, but eternal life and death.

The Bible consistently speaks of the final end of the wicked as "death" rather than a life of continual suffering in an eternally burning hell. Thus

Scripture describes them as "consumed" (RSV) by the lake of fire at the end of time (Rev. 20:9). That passage goes on to refer to that event as the "second death" (verse 14). In a similar manner, Malachi says that hellfire at the end of time will "burn them up" (Mal. 4:1, RSV).

God is not an infinite Hitler who tortures people who have misused their freedom throughout the ceaseless ages of eternity. But neither does He deny them freedom to choose the addictive and destructive sins so much in today's headlines. Rather, in His wisdom, He allows individuals the freedom to become what they have chosen. And since His loving character can't let the destructive consequences of their lives go on forever and ever, He does the best thing in a bad situation. At the end of time He makes them as if they had never been. That is what Paul and John are speaking of when they refer to the second or eternal death.

In contrast to those who will eventually reap eternal death, "the free gift of God is eternal life in Christ Jesus our Lord" (Rom. 6:23). We should note several things about that promise. First, that eternal "life is not for everyone who belongs to the community [i.e., church], every hearer of the word, and every recipient of baptism," but as the context in Romans 6:1-22 makes clear, only "for those who do his will" (Schlatter, p. 152). That conclusion lines up with the teaching of Jesus in Matthew 7:21-23.

A second thing that we must recognize about Paul's statement regarding eternal life is that it is a free gift. Of course, that is no surprise to those who have followed Paul's argument in Romans:

1. Romans 1:18-3:20 demonstrated why it had to be a gift, since sinners had no way to earn it.
2. Then Romans 3:21-5:21 set forth and expounded upon the gracious gift itself.
3. And in Romans 6:1-22 Paul has been reflecting upon the effects of the gift in human lives, telling his readers that those who have accepted it enter a new life in which their highest desire is to walk with God in the principles of His kingdom.
4. Romans 6:23 merely reinforces the fact that those who receive God's gift and have chosen to walk in the way of holiness rather than in the path of sin will live with God throughout eternity.

A third point we should acknowledge is that eternal life is not something completely new but rather a continuation of what believers have begun with Christ here on earth. That is clear from John, who writes that "he who believes in the Son has eternal life" (John 3:36, RSV). Again, Jesus promised that "whoever hears my word and believes him who sent me has eternal life and will not be condemned; he has crossed over from death to life" (John 5:24, NIV). Part of the good news is that Christians already have eternal life through Jesus Christ.

In Romans 6 even though salvation is a free gift, those who receive it demonstrate their reception of it by accepting the lordship of Christ in their lives and by a Christ-like life. Again, there are two paths and two slaveries in life, and there are two destinations. Romans 6 makes it plain that those who will be in the heavenly kingdom will be those who have so internalized the great principles of God's character that they will be happy to be with God throughout the ceaseless ages of eternity. God forces no one to be what they aren't. The two freedoms lead to the two paths and the two masters and eventually to the two quite diverse destinations.

28. Dead to the Law and Alive to Christ

Romans 7:1-6
> *¹Or are you ignorant, brothers (for I am speaking to those who know the law), that the law rules over a person as long as he lives? ²For the married woman is bound by law to her husband as long as he lives; but if the husband dies she is released from the law concerning her husband. ³So then, if while her husband lives she is married to a different man, she will be called an adulteress. But if her husband dies, she is free from the law and is not an adulteress if she marries a different man.*
>
> *⁴Likewise, my brothers, you also died to the law through the body of Christ, so that you might be married to a different one, to the One who was raised from the dead, so that we might bear fruit to God. ⁵For while we were in the flesh, the sinful passions were working through the law in our bodily parts to bear fruit unto death. ⁶But now we have been released from the law, having died to that which held us so that we serve in newness of Spirit and not in oldness of the letter.*

This is certainly not the easiest passage in Romans to understand. At first glance it appears that it will take the skills of a first-century Jewish lawyer to clarify its meaning. But a study of the passage in its context will help us grasp Paul's intent.

The apostle has been at work on the topic of law and grace ever since Romans 5:20, in which he noted that "law came in to increase the transgression, but where sin increased grace abounded even more." In Romans 6:1-4 he set forth the place of obedience in the lives of those who had been saved by grace, noting that Christians would live in harmony with God's will and would not let sin reign in their lives. He concluded with the dictum that they were "not under law but under grace" (verse 14).

That conclusion raised several questions that Paul begins to face in Romans 6:15. In the rest of the chapter he demonstrated that believers are not under the rule of sin.

Then, in Romans 7:1-6 he argues that they are not under the rule of law either. That insight was important for his Jewish readers, as well as for others who might be tempted to put law in the wrong place in their Christian life. In order to grasp the importance of the illustration regarding marriage that Paul utilizes in Romans 7:1-6 we need to remember that keeping the law was the way that pious Jews expected to gain salvation. The rich young man who told Jesus that he had observed all the commandments was quite sincere in his desire for salvation (Matt. 19:16-22) and when Paul writes that as a Pharisee he had been blameless regarding the law (Phil. 3:6), he was speaking in terms of sober fact as far as the Pharisaic mind perceived things. Yet in Christ he found a new life, new power, new joy, and new peace that he had never known before. But those blessings, he has repeatedly pointed out in the first six chapters of Romans, came through the gift of God's grace rather than through the law.

The apostle uses the marriage relationship in Romans 7:1-3 as an analogy of a person's relationship to the law. Paul lays the foundation for his presentation by stating that "the law rules over a person as long as he lives" (verse 1). Then in verses 2 and 3 he makes three essential points:

1. a woman is married to a man and is legally bound to him during his lifetime,
2. the man dies, releasing her from her obligation to him, and
3. she is now free to marry another husband.

Paul's analogous argument is complex, but his meaning is clear.

F. F. Bruce notes that "as death breaks the bond between a husband and wife, so death—the believer's death-with-Christ [see Rom. 6:2, 3]—breaks the bond which formerly yoked him to the law, and now he is free to enter into union with Christ" (Bruce, p. 137). The law proved to be fruitless as a way of salvation and righteousness. Union with the law resulted in sin and death, but union with Christ brings life eternal as people accept His gift of grace into their existence.

Romans 7:4 finds the apostle applying his analogy to Christian experience, but with a shift of characters. The illustration of verses 1-3 had the death of the husband freeing the wife from the law. But in the application of verse 4-6 the death of the sinful self releases believers from the condemnation and dominion of the law and allows them to join Christ.

As in the marriage analogy of verses 1-3, the application in verses 4-6 has three essential elements in the flow of its argument.

1. The readers had had a binding relationship to the law.
2. But they had died to the law.
3. They were now free to be married to another—Jesus.

A careful reader will note that the parallel between the three-point illustration in verses 1-3 and the three-point application in verses 4-6 breaks down at the second point. In the illustration it is the husband's death that frees the spouse. One would expect the application to argue that the law's death performed the same function. But Paul nowhere states that the law dies. Rather, it is the believer who has "died to the law" through Christ (verse 4).

And how is it that Christians have "died to the law"? That death took place when they allowed their old selves to be "crucified" with Christ as they entered the watery grave of baptism (see Romans 6:3-6). The believer's death with Christ is a death to the law as a way of salvation. Trusting to the grace of God means putting to death any confidence in the law as the road to salvation.

Christians are those who know that they have nothing good in themselves, that God did not give the law to save people, and that faith in Jesus is the only way to life eternal. They have died to all forms of self-sufficiency and lawkeeping as the road to life.

At this point we need to be careful as we read Paul's statement about death in Romans 7:4. It is the believer who died, not the law. The law is still alive and well, and, as Paul will point out a little further in the chapter, the law is holy, just, good, and spiritual (verses 12, 14). But God never gave it so that people could save themselves by keeping it.

The law is not dead. As John Calvin, the great Reformer, notes, "we ought carefully to remember that this is not a release from the righteousness which is taught in the law" (Calvin, p. 246). The law still stands as God's great standard of righteousness, it still condemns the sin of those who break it, and it still pushes men and women to the foot of the cross for cleansing from guilt and sin. But it has no cleansing or saving power in itself. When people become dead to the law as a way of salvation, they can then be resurrected and remarried to God's true plan of salvation in Christ. And in that new union they will produce the fruit of holiness for God's kingdom (Rom. 7:4; cf. 6:22).

But before they died to the law their "fruit" was "unto death" (7:5). And why? Paul takes up that topic in Romans 7:5, in which he writes that "while we were in the flesh, the sinful passions were working through the law in our bodily parts to bear fruit unto death."

We need to stress several points about that verse. First, we should not equate "in the flesh" with living in an earthly body. Rather, Paul is speaking of people's lower nature or "sinful nature" (NIV). Part of that sinful nature, in the context of Romans 7, is to seek to gain salvation through the law. Thus one of the "sinful passions" of verse 5 is the self-sufficiency that puts human ability in a place where it views the law as an avenue to salvation. The only fruit of such an approach is "fruit unto death," since the function of the law is to identify sin (Rom. 3:20) and magnify it (4:15; 5:20; 7:7) rather than to save people from it and its penalty when broken. It is in that context that Paul's dictum that Christians are under grace rather than law (6:14) finds its importance.

Romans 7:6 functions as a contrast to verse 5. Believers "have been released from the law" by dying to it (verse 4) as a way of salvation. And having been released from it they are free now from its condemning dominion over them (what 2 Corinthians 3:7 labeled its "ministry of death" [NASB]). Furthermore, they are now free to live in "newness of Spirit." And that new life in the Holy Spirit, made possible by grace rather than by law, was Paul's emphasis in chapter 6 and will be the focus of chapter 8. Those married to Christ not only have been saved by grace (Rom. 5:21; 6:14), but their Spirit-empowered lives will continually bear fruit that witnesses to the reality that they have died to the old way of life (6:2) and have been resurrected to a new way of life (6:4) in which they walk with God (6:4-6), are slaves of righteousness (6:18), and "bear fruit to God" in their daily lives (7:4). Christians are those who have died to both sin (6:1-11) and the law (7:4). Truly they are "not under law but under grace" (6:14).

29. The Depth of God's "Good" Law

Romans 7:7-12

> [7]*What then shall we say? Is the law sin? May it never be! To the contrary, I would never have known sin except through the law. For I would not have known covetousness except the law said, "You shall not covet."* [8]*But sin, taking opportunity through the commandment, produced every kind of covetousness in me. Apart from the law sin is dead.* [9]*I was once alive apart from the law, but the commandment came and sin revived and I died.* [10]*And I discovered that the very commandment that was intended for life brought death.* [11]*For sin, taking opportunity through the commandment, deceived me and through it killed me.* [12]*So the law is holy and the commandment is holy, righteous, and good.*

What then shall we say?" For the third time Paul uses this literary technique. It forms part of a dialogue triggered by his adversaries' claim that if sin increased it would multiply grace (Rom. 6:1). Therefore sin might be a good thing.

The apostle's first "What then" showed up in Romans 6:1, in which he pictured his detractors as saying, "Shall we go on sinning so that grace may increase?" (NIV). Violently rejecting the idea, he demonstrated that no true Christian could ever think that way, because they had died to sin and been resurrected to a new life in Christ (Rom. 6:1-4).

His second "What then" came in verse 15, in which he pictured his adversaries asking whether sin was appropriate because Christians were not under law but under grace. Once again he aggressively dismissed that suggestion by showing how grace leads to the obedience of faith (verses 15-23) and that even though Christians have died to law as a way of salvation they still serve God in the new and deeper way of the Spirit (Rom. 7:1-6).

In the process of his explanation, Paul has said some pretty unflattering things about the law: that it "was added so that the trespass might increase" (Rom. 5:20, NIV); that it "brings wrath" (4:15, NIV); and that it utilized "sinful passions" (7:5).

He fears that some will conclude from what he has said that the law is evil in and of itself. Once again he vigorously reacts to such a suggestion, using the same Greek words as Romans 6:2 and 6:15, translated as "may it never be!" The rest of chapter 7 Paul will spend defending the goodness, holiness, and spirituality of the law and helping his readers to see that it is not the law that is the problem but sinful humanity's misuse of it.

> Romans 7 provides us with one of Paul's most significant discussions of the role of the law in the lives of Christians. One of the most important things we need to understand is the law's true place in our walk with God.

Paul here walks a tightrope in his discussion of the law. On the one hand, he desires to help his readers see that it is a disaster when employed as a way of salvation. On the other hand, he wants people to recognize that the law is a good gift from God and, if rightly used, is of great importance in the life of believers.

Romans 7:7 argues that far from the law being sin, it actually defines sin. Whereas Romans 1:20 and 2:14, 15 point out that even those without the revealed law have a sense of right and wrong, "it takes the law to show wrongdoing to be sin" (Morris, *Romans*, p. 279).

Paul illustrates his claim that he would never have known sin without the law by referring to the tenth commandment. That is an interesting and insightful choice because it is the only one of the Ten Commandments that explicitly moves beyond outward actions to the inward root that undergirds sinful acts. That is, worshipping an idol, stealing, and so on, are all external behaviors. Because of that, most people, including many Pharisees of Paul's day, identify sin as a behavior.

By deliberately selecting the tenth commandment, Paul goes behind the behavior to the lusting motivation that undergirds it. In other words, he is saying that sin is much deeper than outward acts. Jesus did the same thing in the Sermon on the Mount when He illustrated the depth of sin in His discussion of murder and adultery in the heart (Matt. 5:21, 22, 27, 28). Again He raised the same point in Matthew 15:18, 19, in which He claimed that sinful actions proceed out of a corrupt heart.

The apostle's selection of the tenth commandment is an extremely important contribution to our understanding of the law and sin precisely because it goes beneath the surface and relates them to that sinful self-centeredness that leads people to commit acts of sin in the sense of the other nine commandments.

Romans 7:8 finds Paul personifying sin as a military aggressor. The word used for "opportunity" originally meant a "starting point or base of operations for an expedition," especially a military campaign (Bauer, p. 158; Thayer, p. 90). Thus he depicts sin as an enemy force determined to lead people astray.

And how does sin accomplish its task? Surprisingly, Paul suggests that sin uses the commandment for its evil purpose. Then he once again employs the tenth commandment to illustrate his point: "Sin, taking opportunity through the commandment, produced every kind of covetousness in me."

How, we need to ask, can evil use God's "good" commandment (Rom. 7:12) to trigger sin? The answer is that the very command not to covet awakens in people thoughts about actually doing so. Thus even though the commandments are good, sin drives the unrenewed person to see them as a limitation on freedom, and thus a cause of resentment and opposition. Without something to rebel against there are no rebels. Mark Twain was on target when he noted that "like a mule, a person will do the opposite of what they are told 'just for the sake of meanness'" (in Osborne, p. 176).

The real culprit, however, is not the law but sin, which is hostile to the law (Rom. 8:7). Sin always twists the function of the law from exposing sin to that of provoking it.

Paul tells us in Romans 7:9 that he was "once alive apart from the law." To read that statement at face value is problematic since there were no Jewish boys without a knowledge of the law, let alone one who had been trained to be a Pharisee.

But taken in its context, Paul's words do not mean that he had no awareness of the law, but rather that he had not realized the full force and full depth of the law's demands and therefore lacked personal conviction of his sin. But when "the commandment came," "sin revived." When Paul finally felt the full meaning of the law with its motivational aspects, the law jumped to life for him and he realized that he was indeed a sinner, albeit not one who actually "did" evil things.

Sin, of course, had always been there, but in the full light of the commandment not to covet he could recognize it for the first time for what it was. Because he had come to see the full depth of the commandment he also had begun to realize that he was indeed a sinner, in spite of his "good life" and his sinful pride in his righteousness.

The result? He died. That death is not the Christian's death to sin that he spoke of in Romans 6:2, but death to his spiritual pride, self-confidence, and self-reliance. He realized his hopelessness—that the law, when he really understood it, left him destitute.

Thus "the very commandment that was intended for life brought death" to Paul (Rom. 7:10). He is quite correct when he says that the commandment promised life. God created it as a standard of righteousness and a guide to the good life. But it's purpose shifted after the entrance of sin, when it added the role of helping less than perfect people to identify where they had gone wrong.

An added complication arose with the Fall in that sinful people could no longer keep the law in their own strength. And that is where the deceptiveness of sin entered, suggesting that sinners could become good enough to atone for their wrongs, or righteous through obeying the law. With that line of thought in mind, Paul writes that "sin, taking opportunity through the commandment, deceived me and through it killed me" (Rom. 7:11). The lie that Paul had swallowed in his Pharisaic days was that he could become righteous by keeping the law. But that deception blinded his eyes to the fact that in a sinful world no one "will be justified . . . by works of the law, since through the law comes knowledge of sin" (Rom. 3:20, RSV). Paul's argument in Romans 7:11 is that since the law appears to be the way to life, when it actually isn't, sin utilizes the misunderstanding to bring about condemnation and death.

But that conclusion does not mean that the law is bad. To the contrary, Romans 7:12 declares that "the law is holy, and the commandment is holy, righteous, and good." Here the apostle has come full circle in the argument that he has been presenting since verse 7, in which he pictures his opponents asking if the law is sin.

Sin may have abused the law and sinners may have put it to wrong use, as Paul emphasized in Romans 7:8–11, but that is no reflection on the law itself. The apostle lets his readers know that it is sin that is the culprit and that the law itself is as good as things get. In fact, for the rest of the chapter he continues to uplift the law, calling it "spiritual" in verse 14 and "good" in verse 16, while claiming that his "inner man" delights in it in verse 22.

30. Remaining Sin and Tension in Christian Living

Romans 7:13–20

¹³Then did that which is good become a cause of death to me? May it never be! But sin, that it might be shown to be sin, working death to me through that which is good—through the commandment—might become exceedingly sinful. ¹⁴For we know that the law is spiritual, but I am of the flesh [carnal], sold under sin. ¹⁵For what I do I do not understand; for I do not do what I want, but I do that which I hate. ¹⁶Now if I do that which I do not want to do, I agree that the law is good. ¹⁷But it is no longer I who do it, but sin dwelling in me. ¹⁸For I know that nothing good dwells in me, that is in my flesh. For to will is present in me, but to do good is not. ¹⁹For I do not do the good that I want, but I practice the evil that I do not want to do. ²⁰But if I do that which I do not want to do, it is no longer I who do it but sin dwelling in me.

Paul concluded his previous paragraph by declaring that God's law is "holy, righteous, and good" (Rom. 7:12). He has absolutely no doubt about its goodness. But as he did in Romans 6:1, 6:15, and 7:7, he moves his presentation forward by anticipating an argument from his detractors. This time we could phrase the question as follows: Did that good law become a cause of death? (Rom. 7:13). As with the other three questions, he rigorously rejects the idea with an aggressive "never!" or "may it never be!"

It was not the law that caused death, but sin. And how did sin accomplish that task? Paul's answer is that it used the good commandment to bring about condemnation. And how did the law perform that function? It identified sin for what it was (cf. Rom. 3:20; 4:15; 5:20; 7:7). Thus the law has the good and healthy function of pointing out the wrong and should not be blamed for the crime itself. All blame belongs to sin, which motivated the wrong actions.

But Romans 7:13 doesn't stop with the identifying function of the good law. It goes on to express its magnifying role—the idea that in the light of the law sin is shown to be "exceedingly sinful." Sin not only brings death, but it makes a mess out of human existence.

Paul's conclusion is as clear as can be in verse 13. The good law did not bring death. Rather it was sin that used the law for evil purposes.

But how could the law do such a thing? Answering that question begins in verse 14 with the word "for," which signals the beginning of an explanation. Paul's first point is a highlighting of the tension between the law which is spiritual and human beings who are sinful (Rom. 7:14). He uses human experience as an illustration of that struggle.

And with that we arrive at one of the most controversial parts of the book of Romans. Most of the debate concerning Romans 7:14-25 centers on who the "I" is—whether it is Paul and/or whether it is referring to people before they become Christians or after they have done so. Unfortunately for that ongoing debate, that is not Paul's concern. His interest focuses on the "good" law and how sin uses it to cause death.

Having recognized the apostle's true interests, however, doesn't release us from the necessity of interpreting his words in terms of what they imply about human nature. That wouldn't be so bad, but he appears in Romans 7:14-25 to make statements that apply both to the converted and the unconverted. Thus he can use the "I" in verse 22 to describe someone who delights in God's law and in verse 14 to picture a carnal person. The one fact that we can be certain of is that whoever the "I" is, it represents a person caught between good and evil.

The most adequate solution is to see the "I" in the passage as a true Christian when he or she has fallen into sin. That condition, we must emphasize, is not the full picture of their Christian life, since Romans 6 declares Christians not to be slaves of sin and the victory aspect of the Christian life is clear in chapter 8. But here in chapter 7 we find individuals who know the good but cry out in anguish about their wretchedness when they don't do what they should.

Nearly all of the heat generated by the "I" problem of Romans 7 stems from the fact that people bring to their reading of the text their own theological agenda of how they can use the text to prove this point or that. Yet it is one thing to argue at the level of theological theory but quite another to read the text from the perspective of human experience. After all, the text does accurately reflect every Christian life in the real world. No believer is completely without sin. We are all caught in the tension. Thus the "I" reflects a universal experience among believers, which Paul illustrates from his own life. It is best to read the text for what it actually says without using it to support ideas that are not central to the passage's obvious purpose as indicated by the flow of chapter 7, especially verse 13.

> **A Useless Argument**
>
> The ongoing discussion about human nature in Romans 7 is not only not Paul's topic, but it is merely academic and beside the point, since there are no Christians without sin in the real world of everyday life.

To understand Paul's expressions we need to recall how we feel when we fall into doing what we know is wrong in spite of what we would like to be. I don't know about you, but my cry is "O wretched man that I am!" (Rom. 7:24, KJV). I feel like kicking myself.

Remember that the apostle is not describing the entirety of a Christian's life. But even if that life is generally victorious and Christians have the peace and joy of their faith, at other times they still identify with Isaiah, who declared "Woe is me! . . . For I am a man of unclean lips" (Isa. 6:5, RSV), and with Peter, who in the midst of a crisis fell at Jesus' feet, exclaiming "Depart from me, for I am a sinful man, O Lord" (Luke 5:8, RSV).

Paul advances his argument related to how come the "good" law is not responsible for death (verse 13) in two stages in Romans 7:14-25. After introducing the tension in verse 14, the argument moves from the fact that

1. *he does that which is evil*, in spite of his good intentions (verses 15-17), to the further fact that

2. *he cannot do that which is good*, in spite of his desire to do so (verses 18-20).

For *each* of those two steps he arrives at the same conclusion, that the entity causing the problem is not the law but "sin dwelling in me" (verse 17). He repeats the same idea in verse 20 with the *exact* Greek words. Meanwhile, he reiterates that the law is "good" in verse 16.

His conclusion is certain. Paul has nailed it down from both directions. He does evil and fails to do good for the same reason—the sin that dwells within him. Thus he has exonerated the law from all guilt and successfully defended the proposition set forth in verse 12 that "the law is holy and the commandment is holy, righteous, and good." And he has answered the question of verse 13: "Did that which is good become a cause of death to me?" He has moved beyond the mere declaration of that fact ("May it never be!") to a demonstration of his claim that it was sin working through the law that was the culprit (verse 13).

Now that he has clearly stipulated the problem, Paul will advance to the next stage of his argument in verses 21-25, in which he cries out, "Who will deliver me from this body of death?" (verse 24, RSV). He provides the answer in Romans 8.

Before moving away from our discussion of verses 13-20, we need to note that sin is not the only problem they highlight. The other is that humans—even converted Christians, who love God's law (verse 22)—are not beyond the realm of sin. Paul brings that thought out by two words found in verse 14. The first is slavery, alluded to by the words "sold under sin" in verse 14. James Denney points out that slavery is the only way to explain the situation, since "a slave" is one who is "the instrument of another's will" (Denney, "Romans," p. 641).

But we need to be careful here. After all Romans 6 plainly taught that Christians are not slaves of sin but of righteousness (verse 18) and that sin is not to reign in their lives (verse 12). That is true, but, as Paul has demonstrated and as each of our lives indicates, believers have a difficult time staying totally surrendered in spite of the fact that they now as Christians hate evil and love good. Even though they want to do good and avoid evil they still fall back under the problem of sin from time to time, even as they hate their very actions and repent of them. Thus, as Leon Morris notes, sin is no longer the "honored guest" it used to be before conversion, but a "'squatter,' not legitimately there, but very difficult to eject" (Morris, *Romans*, p. 293). John Wesley, as we saw earlier, said much the same thing in dealing with sin in a Christian's life when he noted that sin no longer reigns even though it remains (see Wesley, vol. 5, p. 151).

And on what basis does it remain? Here we come to Paul's second key word as he deals with the problem of sin in believers. In Romans 7:14 he points out that it is the flesh (*sarx*) that is connected to sin slavery. "Flesh" in Paul's writings does not refer to bodily tissues, but to a person's lower nature. Thus "flesh is," Ernst Käsemann correctly notes, "terminologically, the workshop of sin" (Käsemann, p. 205). And, as each of us recognizes, the devil is an expert in knowing how to manipulate that particular "workshop."

It is absolutely imperative when reading Romans 7:14-20 to realize that those verses are not talking about the better times in Christian living. Paul is not saying that Christians never do right or that they do evil habitually, but rather that they aren't as free from error as they would like to be. By using the slavery metaphor, he expresses the thought that he still finds sin to be a powerful force and that he hasn't managed to resist it every moment. That thought lines up with the biblical understanding that sanctification is the process of a lifetime.

The good news is that in our daily lives we need not become discouraged. Sure we have our ups and downs. And when the down times come we feel that we are absolutely worthless, that there is nothing good in us. But when that happens we can take courage. The same overwhelming discouragement came to Paul, Peter, and David. They had their times of praise, joy, and peace. But when they failed they knew that their only hope was in God's grace and power, a topic that Paul will take up in Romans 8.

31. Who Can Rescue Us?

Romans 7:21-25
> [21]*I find then the principle that even though I want to do good, evil is present in me.* [22]*For I delight in the law of God in my inner self,* [23]*but I see a different law in my bodily parts, warring against the law of my mind and making me a prisoner of the law of sin which is in my bodily parts.* [24]*Wretched man that I am! Who will rescue me from this body of death?* [25]*Thanks be to God through Jesus Christ our Lord! So then, I myself on the one hand serve the law of God with my mind, but on the other serve the law of sin with my flesh.*

Romans 7: 21-25 emphasizes five important ideas. The first is that evil is always close at hand. It is even "present" in Christians who desire to do good (verse 21). Whether we like it or not and whether it is our fault or not, both our environment and our minds, through what we choose to expose them to and through what we can't avoid, are full of images of evil that the "flesh" (sinful nature) finds quite attractive (tempting), despite the fact that a Christian knows the difference between sin and righteousness and desires the good.

Believers need to realize that being baptized and imbibing new loves and desires does not imply a miraculous physical brain transplant. No, the same old "hunk of meat" is still between our ears, and we started our Christian life with a full computer bank of alluring images stored in our memories. As Paul puts it, "evil is present" in us.

Christians may have those old images lodged in their minds, but because they have had a transforming experience with Jesus (Rom. 6:3-11) they also know that they should not encourage those images because of their destructive consequences. Thus their desire to be countercultural in their approach to such things as entertainment and the media.

The message of Romans 7:21 is that because of their conversion Christians desire to do right, but that because evil is so close at hand (even being "present in" us) it can make the "flesh twitch" without a person even having to think about it.

Principle number two in Romans 7:21-25 has to do with the mark of the converted person. "I delight in the law of God in my inner self," the apostle declares (verse 22). The truly converted person delights in God's law. A stronger expression than "to agree with" or to claim goodness for, "delight" indicates a rejoicing in God's law that those in opposition to God don't have.

Here we find the real Paul, the man of God who "delights," rejoices, and finds pleasure in God's law. Here is the Paul who stands over against that other Paul who is tempted and falls. Here is the preoccupation of Paul's "inner self" as opposed to the frailty of Paul's flesh. And here is part of Paul's proof that sin no longer reigns as his master, that God has indeed redeemed him. He delights in God's law.

That same delight will be found in all individuals who have given their hearts to God and have been born from above. God's law is no more an enemy of them than it was to Paul. They will love the law of love with all their heart and mind and soul. Such is the mark of the converted person.

Principle number three in Romans 7:21-25 is the Christian's profound sense of spiritual realism. Paul signals that realism with the word "*but*" in verse 23. He may have loved God's law, *but* he found another law warring against his good desires.

Paul, in short, is not a naïve believer who sees the victory won once and for all. To the contrary, using military imagery he views the Christian life as being locked in deadly combat with the forces of evil. But his realism goes beyond the realm of mere warfare. He recognizes that in spite of his best intentions he is a "prisoner of the law of sin" which especially focuses on his "bodily parts."

Yet even though he is facing serious challenges, it is significant that Paul hasn't surrendered to evil. The lesson is clear: the devil never gives up, and neither should Christians, even though they may have disappointed themselves and fallen short (again).

Four Statements of Foundational Realism Related to Romans 7:14-25

"When God called us to be Christian people he called us to lifetime struggles against sin." Such warfare is not easy, since it is waged against the residue of sin that resides in even converted men and women. "Realism calls for rigorous preparation, constant alertness, dogged determination, and moment-by-moment trust in him who alone who can give us victory."

"Although we are called to a lifetime struggle against sin, we are nevertheless never going to achieve victory by ourselves."

"Even when we triumph over sin by the power of the Holy Spirit, which should be often, we are still unprofitable servants," since even a Christian's victories come only through the power of God's grace.

"We are to go on fighting and struggling against sin, and we are to do so with the tools made available to us, chiefly prayer, Bible study, Christian fellowship, [and] service to others." The same apostle commanded us in Ephesians 6 to "be strong in the Lord and in his mighty power" (verse 10, NIV) and to "put on the full armor of God so that you can take your stand against the devil's schemes" (verse 11, NIV)—(Boice, vol. 2, pp. 766-769).

As Paul has repeatedly mentioned since Romans 7:14, his life hadn't been everything that he would have liked it to be, but he hasn't thrown his hands up in defeat. On the other hand, he has come to a sense of realism that seems to escape some modern Christians. The realism has to do with our willingness to face some problematic truths about ourselves.

Principle number 4 in Romans 7:21-25 is the mark of the repentant sinner. "Wretched man that I am!" (verse 24). Many students of Romans 7 claim that Christians could never say such a thing about themselves. After all, they point out, the Christian life is one of joy, peace, and victory.

Really? Have you never fallen? Have you never disappointed yourself, God, and others by an unloving action or a hasty word? Some people, of course, think that they are beyond sin and thereby deceive themselves and make God into a liar (1 John 1:8, 10). How wretched can you get? Some of those better-than-thou individuals are meaner than the devil in defending their doctrinal or lifestyle issues.

The mark of converted Christians is that they see their shortcomings, repent of them, and cry to God, "O wretched man that I am!" (KJV). That was certainly Paul's experience, even though, as we pointed out earlier, he is talking in Romans 7 about those times when he fell rather than about the general trend of his life which he sets forth in Romans 8.

David, a person whom God claimed was a man after His own heart, shared Paul's experience. Listen to his wretchedness in the face of his sin:
"My iniquities have gone over my head;
    They weigh like a burden too heavy for me. . . .
I confess my iniquity,
    I am sorry for my sin" (Ps. 38:4, 18, RSV).

That is the cry of a converted person, an individual who knows God and how wretched it is to disappoint Him.

Principle number five in Romans 7:21-25 is the joyful shout of those rescued from their terrible state by God through Jesus (verse 25). "Thanks be to God" is the exuberant cry of believers delivered by Christ from their wretchedness and the ongoing tensions created by sin.

The ecstatic shout of Romans 7:25 will provide the subject matter for chapter 8. Dealing with Christian victory, it is in many ways the high point of the book of Romans. But before moving to the victorious themes of chapter 8, Paul adds a bit more balance at the end of chapter

7. His concluding words are "I myself on the one hand serve the law of God with my mind, but on the other serve the law of sin with my flesh" (verse 25).

Some have found that to be a strange thing for Paul to declare after the victory of the first part of Romans 7:25 and just before the tremendous statement of Christian assurance in Romans 8:1. Several interpreters, such as James Moffatt's translation of the New Testament, even go so far as to treat the placement of the last part of verse 25 as a mistake and attach it to verse 23, which has the same theme.

But it is no mistake. Paul may know that Christ is the victory, but he is still a realist. Thus the ending of verse 25 is a reminder that "the war is not over and the battle will continue, but with the certainty of victory instead of the inevitability of defeat" (Briscoe, p. 150).

The good news is that even though the ongoing tensions between the spirit and the flesh remain, the Christian does not fight the battle alone. Christ is on the side of each believer. And through the Holy Spirit (a major topic of Romans 8) the victory will be won. Paul told the Philippians something quite similar: "I am sure that he who began a good work in you will bring it to completion at the day of Jesus Christ" (Phil. 1:6, RSV).

Praise God for all His blessings. Praise God that we do not stand alone. Praise God that He never forsakes us, not even when the going gets tough.

32. "No Condemnation": Christ's Accomplishment for Christians

Romans 8:1-4

¹*Consequently there is now no condemnation for those in Christ Jesus.* ²*For the law of the Spirit of life in Christ Jesus has set you free from the law of sin and death.* ³*For what was impossible for the law to accomplish, in that it was weakened by the flesh, God did; having sent His own Son in the likeness of sinful flesh to deal with sin, He condemned sin in the flesh,* ⁴*so that the righteous requirement of the law might be fulfilled in us, who walk not according to the flesh but according to the Spirit.*

With Romans 8 we have arrived at one of the most loved chapters of the Bible. If chapter 7 dealt with tension, frustration, and temporary defeat, chapter 8 is one of victory. One student has pointed out that the chapter opens with "no condemnation" and ends with "no separation," while in between it is characterized by "no defeat" (Thomas, p. 202).

Romans 8:1 has two absolutely central ideas. The first is that there is "no condemnation." That is good news, particularly for those fighting the power and persistence of sin in their lives as brought out in Romans 7. They may endure lives of struggle and even fall but there "is now no condemnation for those in Christ Jesus."

The Victory Chapter

Romans 8 is about victory. But even more than that it is about the assurance of salvation to those who are in Christ. The chapter illustrates the new and wonderful life that opens to those who put their trust in Him.

And why is there no condemnation? That is what Paul has been explaining ever since Romans 3:21. Carefully outlining how salvation by grace works, he has made it clear that it is by grace through faith.

The idea of faith brings us to the second central idea in Romans 8:1. Everybody is not free from condemnation, but only those who are "in Christ Jesus." Paul is clear that a person is either "in Adam" or "in Christ" (1 Cor. 15:22; Rom. 5:12-21). "In Christ" occurs 164 times in Paul's writings. James Stewart points out that "the heart of Paul's religion is union with Christ. This, more than any other conception—more than justification, more than sanctification, more even than reconciliation—is the key which unlocks the secrets of his soul" (Stewart, p. 147). For Paul, those who are "in Christ" are justified, sanctified, and are being progressively sanctified and perfected. And if they stay "in Christ" they have assurance of the kingdom.

But, we need to ask, "how does one get 'in Christ'"? Not by birth. Paul made it clear in Romans 5 that people are born in the way of Adam. For Paul individuals become "in Christ" when they consciously accept Him by faith as Savior and Lord. The argument thus far in Romans is that there is "no condemnation" for those who have that relationship.

The word "for" in Romans 8:2 is important because it connects Romans 8:1 to verse 2 and thus helps explain the reason there is "no condemnation for those in Christ Jesus." Why? For or because "the law of the Spirit of life in Christ Jesus has set you free from the law of sin and death."

Verse 3 takes up the foundation of that freedom. But before moving on to that verse we should note that the Holy Spirit (spoken of in verse 2 in connection with "the law of the Spirit of life") is central throughout Romans 8. The focus on the Spirit signals a major shift in the Epistle, one especially clear in chapters 7 and 8. Romans 7 mentions the law and its synonyms 31 times, but the Holy Spirit only once. Chapter 8, by way of contrast, speaks of the Holy Spirit at least 20 times.

"The essential contrast which Paul paints is between the weakness of the law and the power of the Spirit. For over against indwelling sin, which is the reason the law is unable to help us in our moral struggle (7:17, 20), Paul now sets the indwelling Spirit, who is both our liberator now from 'the law of sin and death' (8:2) and the guarantee of resurrection and eternal glory in the end (8:11, 17, 23)" (Stott, p. 216).

Romans 8 depicts Christian existence as life in the Holy Spirit. Verse 2 claims that the Spirit through "the law of the Spirit of life in Christ Jesus" (that is, the gospel) sets us "free from the law of sin and death" (that is, the condemnation of the broken law). Thus believers not only are free from condemnation (verse 1), but are liberated. That release, however, is not from the law itself (which is good, holy, just, and spiritual—Rom. 7:12, 14), but from both bondage to sin and from the law's condemnation.

The word "for" in Romans 8:3 is just as important as it was in verse 2. Here it functions as a connector between verse 3 and the first two verses. That is, Christians have "no condemnation" and have been "set free from the law of sin and death" because of what Christ accomplished. It is His life and death that made salvation not only possible but a reality.

But behind Jesus stands God the Father, who "sent His own Son in the likeness of sinful flesh." That phrase is one pregnant with meaning about Jesus the God-man. First, He was God's "own" Son. In a sense we could describe every Christian as a son (or daughter) of God. But as A. M. Hunter put it, Christ is "the Son by nature" and "we are sons by grace" (Hunter, p. 78). Christ is not exactly one of us. He is the Son of God. That is why the angel called Him "that holy thing" in speaking to Mary (Luke 1:35, KJV). The Bible says that of no other child, because Jesus in a very significant sense was different from other humans. He was God's "own Son" and had the direct heritage of the Holy Spirit as His Father.

On the other hand, Jesus came "in the likeness of sinful flesh" (Rom. 8:3). Please note how careful Paul was here. If he had said "in sinful flesh" he would have created a theological disaster, since he had already argued in chapter 7 that sinful flesh was incapable of overcoming sin. Thus to have spoken of Christ as having "sinful flesh" just like other humans would have logically led to the conclusion that He was a sinner like the rest of humanity. But on the other hand was the need to identify Christ with those He came to save. As a result, Paul very carefully selected the words "in the likeness of sinful flesh." Thus he indicates that Christ participated in humanity without being exactly like other people.

The apostle goes on in Romans 8:3 to state why God sent Christ "in the likeness of sinful flesh." He did it "to deal with sin," to condemn "sin in the flesh." After all, the human race was messed up and unable to help itself out of the pit of sin and condemnation.

Here we need to ask what Paul means when he said that Christ was sent "to deal with sin" or "for sin" (KJV). Some translations, such as the *New American Standard Bible* and the New International Version, build upon the Greek version of the Old Testament's repeated and consistent translation of "for sin" as being "an offering for sin." Hebrews 10:6-8 correctly reflects that translation, but the context of Romans 8:3 seems to demand a broader interpretation.

Romans 8:3 states that the way Jesus dealt with sin was to condemn it "in the flesh." He did so in at least two ways. First, as the One sent "in the likeness of sinful flesh," He lived a life of complete obedience to God and thus as the second Adam overcame where the first Adam had failed. Second, He not only lived in complete harmony with the law, thus becoming the spotless Lamb of God, but He died "in the flesh" a sacrificial death "once for all" (Rom. 6:10, NIV) by becoming our "sin offering" (Rom. 8:3, NIV). What Jesus did "in the flesh" in both His life and His death condemned all sin.

Romans 8:4 shifts the scene of action from Christ's work *for* humanity to His work *in* them. Part of the reason for Christ's life and death was "so that the righteous requirements of the law might be fulfilled in us." Some claim that here Paul is suggesting that since Christ kept the law perfectly, He is passing on His perfect obedience to us. Thus He not only died vicariously for us, but He also lived for us vicariously. From that perspective verse 4 would not be speaking about our personal performance as Christians.

While that reading is a possibility, it contradicts Paul's treatment of the Christian life beginning in Romans 6:4 and does not seem to be what Paul has in mind in Romans 8. He appears to be here referring to what happens to people who are in Christ. In the words of F. F. Bruce, "God's commands have now become God's enablings" for those under the power of the Holy Spirit (Bruce, p. 153).

That implies that the fruits of justification and those of sanctification do not exist separately in the lives of believers. God counts those who are "in Christ" as righteous (justified) and provides them with power through the Holy Spirit to live the principles of the law in their daily lives (sanctification).

That victorious living, however, as we noted in chapter 7, is not without problems. But it does provide for a kind of living that is of a totally different quality from that which people had when they were slaves to sin (Rom. 6:16).

The metaphor "walking" in Romans 8:4 is helpful. Paul speaks of those "who walk not according to the flesh [their own impoverished efforts] but according to the Spirit." Progress in the Christian life for most of us is truly more akin to walking rather than to flying. But while our spiritual growth may not be spectacular on a day-to-day basis, it can be steady.

But even that progressive walk is possible only because of the enabling power of the Holy Spirit. Those who live "according to the Spirit" not only have power for victory, but also have their horizons broadened as to what is important and possible in life. Walking with the Spirit is truly a transforming experience. God not only wants to do something *for* those in Christ, He also intends to do something *in* them.

33. "No Condemnation" Witnessed to by the Resurrection

Romans 8:5-11
⁵For those who live according to the flesh set their minds on the things of the flesh, but those who live according to the Spirit set their minds on

the things of the Spirit. ⁶For the mind set on the flesh is death, but the mind set on the Spirit is life and peace, ⁷because the mind set on the flesh is hostile toward God, for it does not subject itself to the law of God, neither can it do so, ⁸and those who live in the flesh are not able to please God. ⁹But you are not in the flesh but in the Spirit, if indeed the Spirit of God dwells in you. But if anyone does not have the Spirit of Christ, he does not belong to Him. ¹⁰But if on the one hand Christ is in you, although the body is dead because of sin, on the other hand the spirit is alive because of righteousness. ¹¹And if the Spirit of the One who raised Jesus from the dead dwells in you, the One who raised Christ from the dead will also make alive your mortal bodies through His Spirit dwelling in you.

We need to be careful not to separate Romans 8:5-11 from verse 4, in which Paul indicated that believers would fulfill "the righteous requirements of the law" because they had the Holy Spirit and did not live according to the flesh. Thomas Schreiner's insight is helpful when he notes that "verses 5-11 do not constitute an exhortation to live according to the Spirit or to fulfill the law. Rather, they describe what is necessarily the case for one who has the Spirit. . . . The fulfillment of the law by believers is the result of the Spirit's work in their heart." As a result, "obedience is rooted in the transforming work of the Spirit, and thus is not a burden imposed from without but a delight embraced from within" (Schreiner, p. 409).

According to verse 5, there is an intimate connection between the orientation of one's mind and the direction of one's life. And the mind in this context is much broader than merely the thoughts and understanding that we moderns think of as the mental processes. To the contrary, "it includes the affections, the emotions, the desires and the objects of pursuit. . . . It is a comprehensive term." Thus "'to mind earthly things' ['things of the flesh'] not only means that non-Christians think about them occasionally, but that these are the things which they think of most of all; these are the things of which they think habitually, the trend or the bent of their thinking is toward them. 'Earthly things' are the things that please them most of all, . . . the things which they seek after most of all" (Lloyd-Jones, *Chapter 8:5-17*, p. 5).

Jesus made the same essential point when He said that "where your treasure is, there will your heart [mind] be also" (Matt. 6:21, RSV), and that thoughts determine the direction of a person's life (Matt. 15:19). Also closely tied to Paul's presentation in Romans 8:5-11 is the dictum of Jesus that "no one can serve two masters" (Matt. 6:24, RSV).

Thus it is that "those who live according to the flesh" do so because they have "set their minds on the things of the flesh" (Rom. 8:5). That is, the realm of this world is their true home—it is what they live for. As a result, they cannot really fulfill God's law because their hearts and minds belong to a different kingdom (verse 4). The opposite, Paul tells us, is true of those whose lives are oriented toward God.

Romans 5:6 continues the discussion of those directed toward either the flesh or the Spirit, but with an insightful twist. It doesn't say that "the mind set on the flesh *leads to* death," but that it "is death." Another way of putting it is that unsaved people, those not "in Christ," are already spiritually dead.

That truth has some interesting consequences. After all, if that is the case, how can anyone ever come to Christ? Here we find an important aspect of God's grace. The truth is that sinners don't go to God—He comes to them. That was so with the fallen Adam, whom God searched for in the garden (Gen. 3:8-10), it was true of the lost coin (Luke 15:8, 9), of Zacchaeus (Luke 19:10), and of every other person in history. God through His Holy Spirit speaks to the hearts of every person to wake them up to their need. John Wesley called it "prevenient grace," or the grace of God that goes before saving grace. Before people can accept God's gift in Christ they need to be aroused from their state of spiritual death.

In the opposite camp from those whose minds are set on the flesh are those whose minds are focused on "the things of the Spirit." Once again such a mind-set does not *lead to* life and peace. Rather, "life and peace" is what born again Christians already have. As we noted earlier, those who are "in Christ" already have eternal life (John 3:36) and peace with God (Rom. 5:1).

Before moving away from Romans 5:6 we should note that Paul's teaching regarding those who have their minds set on the things of the Spirit is not to be equated with church membership. There are, unfortunately, church members and even ministers whose minds are in the realm of the flesh rather than in the realm of the Spirit. But God's prevenient grace is still active in their cases. God is always out to wake up the dead to the joys of true life and peace.

Romans 5:7 pushes Paul's line of thought a bit further and tells us that "the mind set on the flesh"—that is, centered on the things of this world—

"is hostile toward God." Now "hostile" does not mean slightly uncooperative. Those with such an orientation are actually God's enemies, a topic Paul has already raised in Romans 5:10. Hostility to God expresses a deepseated animosity. John Stott remarks that "it is antagonistic to his name, kingdom and will, to his day, his people and his word, to his Son, his Spirit and his glory," and especially "his moral standards" (Stott, p. 224).

The fleshly mind not only "does not subject itself to the law of God" but it cannot (Rom. 8:7). That is why the Bible describes a person's becoming a Christian as getting a new mind and heart (Ezek. 18:31; 2 Cor. 5:17), as being born again (John 3:3-6), and as a death and resurrection symbolized by baptism through immersion (Rom. 6:2-4).

Thus becoming a Christian is not just another step in becoming better. No! It is a radical discontinuity with the old way of thinking and living—a new life altogether. It is a life "in Christ," as opposed to one "in Adam" (Rom. 5:18, 19).

Romans 5:9 picks up on that new life with a forceful "but." "But you are not in the flesh but in the Spirit, if indeed the Spirit of God dwells in you." We find an extremely important truth about the Holy Spirit in this verse. That is, every Christian (rather than every church member) has the gift of the Holy Spirit. It is exactly what Jesus taught during His evening meeting with Nicodemus: "Truly, truly, I say to you, unless one is born of water *and the Spirit*, he cannot enter the kingdom of God. That which is born of the flesh is flesh, and that which is born of the Spirit is spirit" (John 3:5, 6, RSV). One of the unfortunate aspects of church life is that too many members are merely "water" Christians. They have joined an organization but are dead to the things of God (Rom. 8:6), "hostile" to His principles" (verse 7), and do not "belong to Him" (verse 9).

Thus it is that both Paul and Jesus present the Holy Spirit as the key to the Christian's life. The Spirit is God's gift to every Christian. Of course, beyond the gift of the Spirit to all Christians are those special gifts or talents bestowed upon individuals for specialized ministries (Rom. 12:4-8; 1 Cor. 12:27-31; Eph. 4:8-11). But we must not confuse them with the Spirit's indwelling in every person who has faith in Christ.

With Romans 8:10 we have arrived at a tension between a dead body and a live spirit that doesn't find resolution until verse 11, in which Paul speaks of the resurrection and the joining of our living spirit with a living body. The dead body of verse 10 is probably a reference to the physical body, which is mortal, subject to death, and will eventually pass away.

Be that as it may, the apostle's primary interest is life rather than death. Verse 11 is a mighty promise of bodily resurrection to those who have let God's Spirit into their lives and already have life eternal (verse 6). The resurrection of those who are "in Christ" through the Spirit, Paul tells us, is predicated on the historical resurrection of Christ. The apostle treats the same topic in 1 Corinthians 15, in which he hammers home repeatedly the fact that Christ's resurrection *guarantees* the resurrection of those who follow Him on earth. In the great resurrection event at the Second Advent those "in Christ" will not only be blessed with "imperishable" bodies but also with "immortality" (1 Cor. 15:51-54). Never again will they be subject to death or bodily degeneracy. Like Christ, they will also live "evermore" (Rev. 1:18, KJV).

With the promise of resurrection in Romans 8:11 one cycle in Romans 8 has come to completion. That future resurrection is an evidence of the first magnitude of the fact that "there is now no condemnation for those in Christ Jesus" (verse 1). After all, as Martyn Lloyd-Jones points out, the object of the entire chapter of Romans 8 is to prove the "contention of verse 1 . . . that 'There is therefore now no condemnation to them which are in Christ Jesus'" (Lloyd-Jones, *Chapter 8:5-17*, p. 1). Resurrection, in fact, is the polar opposite of condemnation.

34. "No Condemnation" Witnessed to by the Spirit and Adoption

Romans 8:12-17

[12]So then, brothers, we are debtors, not to the flesh, to live according to the flesh—[13]for if you live according to the flesh you are destined to die, but if by the Spirit you put to death the deeds of the body you will live. [14]For as many as are led by the Spirit of God, these are sons of God. [15]For you did not receive a spirit of slavery leading to fear again, but you received a spirit of adoption as sons by which we cry out, "Abba! Father!" [16]The Spirit Himself confirms with our spirit that we are children of God, [17]and

if children, also heirs, heirs of God and fellow heirs with Christ, if indeed we suffer with Him so that we may also be glorified with Him.

So then" or "therefore" (NIV) links verse 12 with the previous 11 verses of Romans 8. And what did they tell us?

1. That believers are no longer under condemnation (verse 1).
2. That they have been set free from the law of sin and death (verse 2).
3. That they are no longer under sin's dominion (verse 2).
4. That they walk by the Spirit (verse 4).
5. That their minds are set on the Spirit (verse 5).
6. That they have life and peace through the Spirit (verse 6).
7. That God's Spirit dwells in them (verse 9).
8. That their spirits have been made alive (verse 10).
9. That the resurrection of their bodies is guaranteed (verse 11).

That's quite a list to be thankful for. Paul tells the Romans in verse 12 that they are "debtors" because of all of God's gifts to them. Their obligation in the face of that debt in the flow of the argument since the beginning of Romans 6 is to live according to God's principles. After all, if the indwelling Spirit has given them life (Rom. 8:10), how can they continue in the way of death? They cannot be both dead and alive simultaneously. Having been rescued from death, they are obligated to live the principles of life through the power of the Holy Spirit.

At this point, following the logic of the book of Romans, it is absolutely crucial to recognize that we are not in God's debt unless He has already rescued us. First comes salvation, then follows the response of faith empowered by the Spirit. That order of events is of the utmost importance. Christians keep God's law not to be saved but because they have already been saved by God's grace. We find that same pattern of events in the Ten Commandments. First comes grace: "I am the Lord your God, who brought you out of the land of Egypt, out of the house of bondage" (Ex. 20:2, RSV). Then follows the law. First comes salvation and then the response. Law from a Christian perspective must always be seen from the viewpoint of grace.

Romans 8:13 sets forth a pair of options that we have become quite familiar with in the book of Romans: The way of the flesh leads to death, while the way of the Spirit leads to life. But verse 13 sets forth a new nuance: the putting to death or mortification (KJV) of the deeds of the body.

Mortification, John Stott points out, "is neither masochism (taking pleasure in self-inflicted pain), nor asceticism (resenting and rejecting the fact that we have bodies and natural bodily appetites)." Rather, it is a recognition of evil as evil, leading "to such a decisive and radical repudiation of it that no imagery can do it justice except 'putting to death'" (Stott, p. 228).

But putting to death is not something that Christians can do on their own, a fact readily attested to in Romans 7. Rather the Holy Spirit is the effective agent, as verse 13 makes clear. Part of the Spirit's role is to give individuals the desire, determination, and discipline to reject evil. Their part is to hand over their will to the will of God. The result is life itself (Rom. 8:13).

The reason that those who let the Spirit "put to death" their fleshly deeds will live is not only because the Spirit leads them but because they have become "sons of God" (verse 14). Yet isn't everyone a child of God, Christian or not? queries J. I. Packer. "Emphatically no!" he replies. "The idea that all men are children of God is not found in the Bible anywhere. The Old Testament shows God as the Father, not of all men, but of His own people, the seed of Abraham." And the New Testament plainly states that we are of Abraham's seed if we have accepted Christ (Gal. 3:26-29). "Sonship to God is not, therefore, a universal status upon which everyone enters by natural birth, but a supernatural gift which one receives through receiving Jesus" (Packer, p. 181). That conclusion rings true to Jesus' discussion of the new birth in John 3:3-6 and John's declaration that "to all who received him, who believed in his name, he gave power to become children of God; who were born, not of blood nor of the will of the flesh nor of the will of man, but of God" (John 1:12, 13, RSV).

Thus sonship and daughterhood is a gift of grace, conferred when a person accepts Jesus as Savior by faith. And it comes when people through the power of God's Spirit decide to give up their "in Adam" status in which they were born and to accept the "in Christ" status made possible by Jesus on Calvary. Those who accept Christ by faith, Paul claims, "receive adoption" (Gal. 4:5; Eph. 1:5, RSV).

Being adopted into God's family, of course, changes every aspect of people's lives. Not only will they continue to live in the Spirit, but it heals their relationship with other members of God's family. After all, it is impossible to love the Father without loving His other children. Or, as Ralph Earle describes true Christians, "they not only belong to the family but act like it!" (Earle, p. 178).

Romans 8:15 highlights the freedom from fear that Christians have after being adopted into God's family. With Jesus, they can now address God both as "Father" and "Abba," a term suggesting intimacy. "Abba" reflects God's closeness to each Christian. He is not merely somewhere out there, but with us and willing to help us in our times of need.

> **A Thought on "Adoption"**
>
> "The word indicates a total break w[ith] the old family and a new family relation with all its rights, privileges, and responsibilities" (Rogers, p. 330).

Verses 15 and 16 mark the high-point of Romans 8:12-17 in relation to the chapter's theme of demonstrating that "there is now no condemnation for those in Christ Jesus" (verse 1). Not only have Christians been adopted into the family of God (verse 15), but "the Spirit Himself confirms with our spirit that we are children of God" (verse 16).

That confirmation has two aspects. The first is the objective element. Christians have read their Bible, understood the plan of salvation, have accepted it, and have agreed to live a life in accord with God's principles. Intellectually they know the truth of what it means to be a Christian. And, of course, they believe that the Holy Spirit has guided them to their understanding and commitment. That understanding provides them with a basis for testing the more subjective aspects of Christianity.

The second aspect of confirmation of the Spirit's "bearing witness with our spirit" (RSV) is the subjective. Here we are talking about something intensely personal that takes place just between the Holy Spirit and the believer. There is such a thing as a genuine spiritual experience of the Spirit in a person's heart. Such individuals have an overwhelming awareness of God's presence or sense that God has come upon them in a special way. They have no doubt that what they are experiencing is from Him.

While such special occurrences do happen in a Christian's life, there is, however, still a real danger that a subjective experience may be false. Thus we need to test the spirits (1 Thess. 5:19-21). But God does want to guide our lives personally. That is why we pray. Do we listen for His answers?

And at times in our lives the Spirit bears witness with our spirit regarding our duty or the course of action that we should follow. After all, He is close to us. He is our Abba.

The Spirit's confirmation to us that we are indeed adopted into God's family means that we are heirs of God (Rom. 8:17). Now that is an interesting thought since we conventionally use the word "heir" to refer to those who receive property when another dies. But God doesn't die.

The Bible does not always employ words in the same sense that we do. "Heir" implies that as Christians we have a special relationship to God as His "children." Because of that relationship, we discover in Romans 8:17, we already possess the Father's blessing, and are assured of further blessing at the end of time in glorification, that is, our transformation at the Second Coming.

Verse 17 notes that Christians receive their blessing on two conditions. First, "if" we are His children. That "if" does not mean possibility but fact. Thus we should not interpret the "if" as "we might be," but rather "because we are His children." As a result of that certainty Christians will receive the blessing of heirship without fail.

Second, "if indeed we suffer with Him." Once again, the "if" means "because." No one ever said, least of all Christ and the apostles, that the Christian walk would be an easy one. Christians have opted for a Lord and a set of principles contrary to those of the "ruler of this world" (John 12:31, RSV). Thus they can expect the same sorts of conflict that caused Christ and the apostles so much difficulty. But trouble isn't an end in itself. Those who "suffer with Him" will also "be glorified with Him" (Rom. 8:17).

35. "No Condemnation" Witnessed to by the Certainty of Hope

Romans 8:18-25
18For I consider that the sufferings of the present time are not worth comparing with the coming glory to be revealed to us. 19For the creation waits expectantly in eager anticipation for the revealing of the sons of God.

> *[20]For the creation was subjected to futility, not willingly, but because of the One who subjected it, in hope [21]that even the creation itself will be freed from its slavery to deterioration into the freedom of the glory of the children of God. [22]For we know that all the creation groans and is suffering in birth pain until now. [23]And not only this, but also we ourselves, having the firstfruits of the Spirit, even we ourselves groan within ourselves, eagerly awaiting adoption as sons, the redemption of our body. [24]For in this hope we have been saved, but hope that is seen is not hope, for who hopes for what he sees? [25]But if we hope for what we do not see, with patience we eagerly await it.*

This powerful paragraph on the Second Advent hope has its origin in Romans 8:17, in which Paul stated that those who suffered with Christ would "be glorified with Him." Two words jump out of that verse: "suffering" and "glorification." Verses 18-25 pick up both of them and provide us with one of his most insightful passages on the current state of the earth and the two-step process of salvation for God's people.

The first point that the apostle highlights is that present sufferings are absolutely minimal when compared to what God has prepared for the future (Rom. 8:18). In line with Jewish thinking, Paul characterized history as being divided into two periods: the present age and the age to come. For him two words—"suffering" and "glory"—depict the two ages.

He wastes no time moving into the suffering theme. Verses 19-23 highlight the fact that not only humanity but all creation bears the effects of sin. The creation not only suffers from "slavery to deterioration" (verse 21) but "all the creation groans and is suffering in birth pain until now" (verse 22).

Here we need to ask, What does Paul mean by "creation"? John Murray, after pointing out that we must interpret the word in the context of Romans 8:20-23, notes that good "*angels* are not included because they were not subjected to vanity and to the bondage of corruption. *Satan* and the *demons* are not included because they cannot be regarded as longing for the manifestation of the sons of God and they will not share in the liberty of the glory of the children of God. The *children of God* themselves are not included because they are distinguished from 'the creation' (vss. 19, 21, 23). . . . [And] *unbelieving* . . . mankind cannot be included because the earnest expectation does not characterize them" (Murray, vol. 1, pp. 301, 302).

Thus creation in Romans 8 denotes "subhuman" creation (the world apart from human beings), which Romans 8:19 pictures as "eagerly waiting" (Jerusalem) or standing "on tiptoe" (Phillips) for God to reveal His children. Then like the psalmist and the prophets who picture the earth mourning and hills, pastures, and valleys that "shout and sing together for joy" (Isa. 24:4; Ps. 65:12, 13, RSV), Paul personifies creation in order to convey to his readers "a sense of the cosmic significance of both humanity's fall into sin and believers' restoration to glory" (Moo, *Epistle*, p. 514).

And what is it that the subhuman portion of creation is waiting for in Romans 8:19? The disclosure of God's children. Paul made it clear in verses 14-17 that Christians are already God's children. "But," as Douglas Moo points out, "experiencing suffering (v. 18) and weakness (v. 26) like all other people, Christians do not in this life 'appear' much like sons of God. The last day will publicly manifest our real status" (*ibid.*, p. 515).

Sin, as Romans 8 makes clearer than perhaps anywhere else in the Bible, has affected all creation. Thus it is more than just a human problem. We see that insight reflected upon in verses 20-22, with verse 21 treating the deterioration of the present order of the natural world and verse 22 describing it's groaning and pain.

The Old Testament passage undergirding Paul's treatment of non-human creation is undoubtedly Genesis 3:17-19, in which the curse following Adam's sin not only fell on him and Eve and their offspring, but upon the natural world. As God told Adam, "Cursed is the ground because of you" (Gen. 3:17, RSV).

Romans 8:20-22 picks up and expands on that curse, capturing nature's travail in terms of its past, present, and future. In the past nature found itself subjected to "futility" or "frustration" (Rom. 8:20, NIV), a term that means emptiness, purposelessness, or transitoriness.

Then in verse 21 Paul projects nature into the future, with the idea that it will be "freed from its slavery to deterioration." Meanwhile, in verse 22 the apostle treats the present status of nature, observing that "all the creation groans and is suffering in birth pain until now." But the good news is that those groans are not meaningless, since they are "birth pains" or "the pains of childbirth" (NIV).

That very allusion points to the coming of a new order in which all "the former things are passed away" and there will be no more "groaning" or crying or pain (Rev. 21:4, 5, KJV). Jesus presented a similar word picture in Matthew 24 when He spoke of wars, famines, and earthquakes as "the beginning of the birth-pangs" of the end of the age (Matt. 24:8, RSV).

Romans 8:23 transitions from the non-human creation to groaning humanity as it eagerly waits its "adoption" as children of God. The word "adoption" cries out for explanation, since Paul had told the Romans back in verses 14-16 that they had already been adopted when they accepted Christ. How can it be that they are still awaiting adoption in verse 23?

The answer lies in the texts themselves and goes back to what we might call being "half saved." When we come to God in faith, we receive justification, He sets us apart for service (sanctification), and He gives us a new heart and mind. Those are all parts of our salvation. And they are things already accomplished.

> **Hope in Spite of it All**
>
> Paul has painted a picture of hope in spite of our world's troubles, in spite of the groanings of the non-human part of creation, in spite of the omnipresence of decay and deterioration. The pains of childbirth point to the end of the Genesis curse; they anticipate the new earth; they announce Christ's return and the fulfillment of all God's promises in their completeness.

But as chapter 7 so graphically illustrated, our new minds and hearts are still housed in the same old bodies, with all of their "twitches" toward temptation (Rom. 7:18, 24). Thus we are adopted into the family of God at our conversion but do not receive its full benefits until "the redemption of our body" (Rom. 8:23). Paul places that event at the second coming of Christ, when those who have died in Christ God now resurrects with bodies that are both immortal and incorruptible (1 Cor. 15:51-54). At that point, according to Romans 8:23, our adoption will be complete.

Romans 8:24 continues the saved but not fully saved tension of verse 23, noting that Christians have already "been saved." But that salvation was in the "hope" that more good things were yet to come.

Then verse 25, in Hebrews 11 fashion, claims that believers await in faith for that which they do not and cannot see. It is on that note of patiently waiting that Paul closes off his treatment of the Second Advent that arose after his mention of believers suffering with Christ until glorification in Romans 8:17.

Thus waiting patiently has been a key concept in Romans 8 since verse 17.

- Waiting patiently for the end of bondage to decay (verse 21).
- Waiting patiently through labor pains for the birth of a new world (verse 22).
- Waiting patiently for glorification and the end of suffering (verse 23).
- Waiting patiently for the hope that is not yet seen (verse 25).

As they wait patiently for the advent of their Lord in the clouds of heaven, Christians know that they have a hope worth the anticipation.

Interestingly enough, the word that Paul uses for "patience" in Romans 8:25 also appears in the third angel's message of Revelation 14:12: "Here is the patience of the saints: here are they that keep the commandments of God, and the faith of Jesus" (KJV). Immediately following that text in verses 14-20 Revelation pictures the great Second Advent harvest.

The *New American Standard Bible* translates the "patience" of Romans 8:25 and Revelation 14:12 as "perseverance." That rendering is helpful, since the context in both passages deals with suffering. The Greek word that Paul uses indicates "the capacity to hold out or bear up in the face of difficulty" (Bauer, p. 1039). It denotes positive and even aggressive endurance more than it does "a quiet acceptance. . . . It is the attitude of the soldier who in the thick of the battle is not dismayed but fights on stoutly whatever the difficulties" (Morris, *Romans*, p. 325).

Those with that kind of patient endurance know the nature of their hope and goal, and in the case of Romans 8 they realize that victory is certain. Thus they not only wait for it, but wait for it "eagerly" (verse 25). What are sufferings, deprivations, and discomforts in the face of such a hope? It is a hope beyond comparison with any possible sacrifice on our part (verse 18).

36. "No Condemnation" Witnessed to by Providence

Romans 8:26-30
>   [26]*In the same way the Spirit also helps us in our weakness; for we do not know how we should pray as we should, but the Spirit Himself intercedes on our behalf with sighs too deep for words.* [27]*And the One who*

searches the hearts knows what the mind of the Spirit is, because He intercedes on behalf of the saints according to the will of God.

[28]And we know that to those who love God, to those being called according to His purpose, He works everything together for good. [29]Because those whom He foreknew He also predestined to be made into the image of His Son, in order that He might be the firstborn among many brothers. [30]And those whom He predestined He also called, and those whom He called He also justified, and those whom He justified He also glorified.

Present suffering (Rom. 8:17, 18) and the groanings of an imperfect world (verse 22) are not the most pleasant facts, even for those no longer under condemnation because they are "in Christ Jesus." While it is true that Christians have hope for the future, it is just as certain that in their present existence they face dreary days and bad experiences.

It is in that context that Paul sets forth two short paragraphs on present hope as he highlights God's providential care for His children. The first, verses 26 and 27, has to do with prayer. The good news is that we are not alone when we pray. One of the Holy Spirit's functions is to guide Christians in their prayer life. And we most certainly need help. Romans 8:26 tells us that we don't even know what we should pray for. Moses and Paul illustrated that weakness—Moses when he vainly prayed for God to allow him to enter the Promised Land (Deut. 3:25, 26), and Paul when he prayed three times for the removal of his "thorn in the flesh," only to have God tell him that His strength "is made perfect in weakness" (2 Cor. 12:7-9, RSV). The real problem is that our deepest needs go far beyond our knowledge of what is best for us, and our power of speech is totally inadequate to express them.

For that reason God has sent the Holy Spirit. The Spirit not only encourages us while we await the consummation of redemption (Rom. 8:23), but He helps us in prayer because of our weakness and ignorance. God leaves no stone unturned in seeking to empower those who have accepted Him by faith and have become a part of His great family.

"The Spirit Himself," verse 26 tells us, "intercedes on our behalf with sighs too deep for words." What exactly is the Spirit doing for us? When we lack words to express our deepest needs, the Spirit takes our confused and stumbling thoughts and desires and makes them into effective intercession.

What a great God we have. Not only is salvation all of God. Not only is our faith a gift from Him. But even meaningful prayer is the Spirit working in spite of our manifold weaknesses.

Romans 8:27 informs us that we are not alone in our prayer life, because when we pray we are in a multiperson operation. Prayer involves at least three individuals—an interesting fact, since most of us tend to think of only two. Verses 26 and 27 set forth those three as:

1. We Christians, who in our weakness don't really know what to pray for,
2. the indwelling Spirit, who intercedes for us with inexpressible groans, and
3. God the Father (who knows our minds and hearts and also the mind of the Spirit), who hears and answers.

Perhaps we should add a fourth person as we think of the ministry of prayer. That is Christ, who is "at the right hand of God . . . interceding for us" (Rom. 8:34, NIV). When we pray we are never alone, no matter how discouraged and isolated we may feel. The Bible tells us that we are in contact with the entire Trinity. Prayer is as awesome as it is important.

Two points are of special interest in the Spirit's intercessory work. First, amazingly, the Spirit is said to "groan" (verse 26, NASB) for God's children as He prays with us. Thus the Spirit's groaning or sighing joins that of the creation (verse 22) and the church (verse 23). The thought seems to be that the Spirit identifies with our attempts to express our frustration, our groaning and sighing in prayer. He does the same with the pain of the world and the church, and, like true Christians, He longs for the final consummation of all things. Thus we and the Spirit groan and sigh together.

The second point of special interest in Romans 8:26, 27 is that the Spirit intercedes for us "according to the will of God." In other words, the Spirit transposes our often misguided and self-centered prayers into the spirit of the prayer of Christ in Gethsemane, who three times prayed, "Not as I will, but as thou wilt" (Matt. 26:39, 42, 44, RSV).

We can be thankful as Christians that we are never alone, even in our darkest hours when we truly feel discouraged and isolated. Through His providential care God has sent His Spirit to translate our "worthless" prayers into the currency of heaven.

But God's providence in a Christian's daily life does not stop with prayer. Romans 8:28 tells us that "we know" that He will guide the events of our daily lives for our best good. Building on the Christian doctrine of assurance that Paul raised in verses 12-17, verses 28-39 push its implications to a thundering climax.

That comforting passage begins with five firm convictions in verse 28.

1. "We know" that God is active in our lives. He is not indifferent to what happens to us, but is ceaselessly and energetically and purposefully involved in the life of each believer.

2. "We know" that God is not merely at work for His people, but that He seeks their good. Of course, the highest good—the one that the book of Romans is primarily concerned with—is their final salvation, to which all else is subsidiary.

3. "We know" that God is not merely guiding *some* things for good, but *all things*. "Paul does not mean that all things serve the comfort or convenience or worldly interests of believers," but that they assist their salvation (Cranfield, *Shorter Commentary*, p. 204). As a result, even the sufferings of verse 17 and the groanings of verse 23 have a positive impact as they force believers to realize their own weaknesses and turn to their only source of help. "Thus all that is negative in this life is seen to have a positive purpose in the execution of God's eternal plan" (Nygren, p. 338).

4. "We know" that the beneficiaries of God's working for good in all things are those who love Him.

5. "We know" that God has called us "according to His purpose"— our salvation.

Romans 8:28 is truly one of the Bible's great passages of comfort to each believer. While we don't always understand why some particular thing is happening to us, we can still trust God that He knows what He is doing and will actively use events in our lives to His glory and our salvation.

That thought brings us to Romans 8:29, 30, in which many think they have discovered the key text teaching the unconditional predestination of some individuals (i.e., the "called") to salvation. But William Barclay is quite correct in his assertion that "this is a passage which has been very seriously misused. If we are ever to understand this passage we must grasp the basic fact that Paul never meant it to be the expression of theology or philosophy" (Barclay, *Romans*, p. 119).

To the contrary, the purpose of Romans 8:29, 30 in its context is pastoral and practical. Paul is continuing to comfort those "suffering" (verse 17) and "groaning" or "sighing" (verse 23, 26) in their half-saved condition (verses 11, 17, 23–25). The apostle is assuring them that not only is the Spirit with them (verses 26, 27), that not only is He actively working in their behalf in each of their troubles (verse 28), but that their ultimate destiny rests in His hands (verses 29, 30). Thus the hands of the very One who foreknew them as Father and who predestined or selected them for salvation also cradles their future. They have nothing to fear in spite of what may be foreboding circumstances.

> **The Joseph Experience**
>
> One of the best illustrations of God's providence in individual lives is that of Joseph, who could tell his brothers: "You intended to harm me, but God intended it for good" (Gen. 50:20, NIV).

Romans 8:29 tells the Roman believers that God not only selected them for salvation, but that He also wants them "to be made into the image of His Son." Here Paul is picking up on a theme he began in Romans 6. God desires for each Christian to become more and more like Jesus. Thus it is that the book of Romans, after presenting justification as the beginning of salvation (chapters 3–5), presents growth in holiness as its continuation in each Christian life (chapters 6-8, 12-14).

Romans 8:30 continues Paul's presentation of pastoral comfort that he initiated in verse 18. Taking up where he stopped in verse 29, the apostle tells us that God also called those whom He predestinated. Those who responded in faith to the preaching of the gospel—or what we might think of as the gospel call—God justified or counted as righteous. And those who remain faithful are assured of glorification. Thus Paul concludes his comforting of believers who experience both the internal tensions of Romans 7 and the external tensions of chapter 8. He will now move to a song of triumph in Romans 8:31-39 to tell them in no uncertain terms that nothing can separate those "in Christ" (verse 1) from God's love. Thus it is that verse 30's use of "glorified" in the past tense is quite correct even though the actual event is still future. Romans 8:31-39 trumpets the truth that glorification is an accomplished reality for those who maintain their faith in Christ.

37. "No Condemnation" Witnessed to by God's Advocacy

Romans 8:31-39

[31]What then shall we say to these things? If God is for us, who is against us? [32]He who spared not His own Son, but gave Him up on behalf of us all, will He not also with Him give freely all things to us? [33]Who will bring a legal charge against those chosen of God? God is the one who justifies; [34]who is the one condemning? Is it Christ Jesus who died, who even has been raised, who is even at the right hand of God and who intercedes on our behalf? [35]Who will separate us from the love of Christ? Will tribulation, or distress, or persecution, or famine, or nakedness, or danger, or sword? [36]As it is written,

"For Your sake we are being put to death all the whole day long;
We were considered as sheep for slaughter."

[37]But in all these things we overwhelmingly conquer through the One who loved us. [38]For I am fully convinced that neither death, nor life, nor angels, nor rulers, nor things present, nor things to come, nor powers, [39]nor height, nor depth, nor any other created thing will be able to separate us from the love of God in Christ Jesus our Lord.

What a passage! Romans 8:31-39 form what some have called "the Christian's 'triumph song'" (Morris, Romans, p. 334). Paul has completed the first half of his letter to the Romans. He has demonstrated the universality of sin (Rom. 1:18-3:20) and has set forth God's plan of salvation in terms of justification (Rom. 3:21-5:21), sanctification, and glorification (Rom. 6:1-8:30). But before he moves on, he decides to give the trumpet of assurance a blast of certainty in Romans 8:31-39.

Building on the themes of adoption (verses 14-17, 23) and glorification (verses 11, 17) for those who remain in the family of God, the apostle asks five questions for which there are no answers. As John Stott frames it, "he hurls" his questions "into space, as it were, in a spirit of bold defiance. He challenges anybody and everybody, in heaven, earth or hell, to answer them and to deny the truth which they contain. But there is no answer" (Stott, p. 254).

The first question asks, "If God is for us, who is against us?" (verse 31). The force of the assertion lies in the claim that *God is for us.* That is one of the most important truths that we can ever understand. The reality that *God is for us* is the entire basis of the gospel as presented by the New Testament. The Lord so loved the world that He sent His Son to die in our place while we were still His enemies (John 3:16; Rom. 5:10, 6). More specifically to Romans is that "God's being 'for us' . . . sums up the thrust of the whole argument since 3:21" (Keck, p. 219). He is a "for us" kind of Diety.

God not only sent Jesus, but He justifies those who by faith accept Christ's sacrifice for them, dispatches the Holy Spirit to empower their sanctification, and guarantees their glorification if they choose to remain in a faith relationship to Him. Truly He is *God for us.*

"If God is for us," then "who is against us?" "He means that with God 'for us' it makes not the slightest particle of difference who is against us" (Morris, *Romans*, p. 335).

But that doesn't mean that Christians don't face opposition. Paul's whole biography is one of persecution and resistance to his message. Also, as we noted in Romans 7, indwelling sin is an ongoing, powerful adversary. And death is still an enemy, defeated but not yet destroyed. Yet, while it is a fact that Christians still have forces against them, it is a greater truth that nothing can defeat them because the "for us" God is on their side.

> That "God is for us" is the distilled essence of the gospel. That realization will give us courage to continue day by day.

Romans 8:31-39 second unanswerable question is "Will He not also with Him give freely all things to us?" (verse 32). The key word in that question is "also." Paul is arguing from the greater to the lesser. That is, since He has already given the greatest gift imaginable (His own Son), "how can he fail to lavish every other gift upon us?" (Rom. 8:32, REB). In the Son He gave everything. The cross is the guarantee of the continuing generosity of a God totally dedicated to completing what He has begun in the gift of salvation through Jesus Christ.

Paul's third question takes us in our imagination into a court of law. The question "Who will bring a legal charge against those chosen of God?" (verse 33) might have been phrased "Who can make a charge stick against God's elect?" After all, they are justified or counted as righteous by God (verse 33b). Acquitted at the highest level, Christians are safe in Christ. They have nothing to fear.

The fourth question: "Who is the one condemning?" (verse 34) is closely related to that of verse 33. It certainly isn't Christ. Why? Because He

1. died for them,
2. was raised from the dead,
3. is sitting on the right hand of God, and
4. is presently interceding for Christians as their heavenly high priest (verse 34).

Let's look at each of those four reasons. First, Christ died for the very same sins that would otherwise condemn Christians. As Paul noted to the Corinthians, He was made "to be sin who knew no sin, so that in him we might become the righteousness of God" (2 Cor. 5:21, RSV). Because Christ gave His life for the sins of His followers, "there is now no condemnation for those in Christ Jesus" (Rom. 8:1). He will not turn around and pronounce judgment against His followers for the very sins that He died for. He absorbed the penalty for those "in Him."

Second, Christ not only died for Christians, but also "has been raised." Note that "has been raised" is a passive verb, symbolizing not only that He rose, but that the Father resurrected Him as a demonstration of the acceptability of His sacrifice.

Third, Christ is "at the right hand of God," the place of honor in the heavenly realm. And fourth, Christ intercedes for us as our heavenly high priest, "able . . . to save them to the uttermost that come unto God by him, seeing he ever liveth to make intercession for them" (Heb. 7:25, KJV; cf. 1 John 1:9, 2:1, 2). If Christ the judge (see John 5:22) is on our side there is no way that we can come under condemnation. We are safe in Jesus.

"Who will separate us from the love of Christ?" (Rom. 8:35) is the fifth of Paul's unanswerable questions. The first half of the triumph song that began in verse 31 demonstrated the impossibility of any charge against the believer being sustained before God. With verse 35 we move into five verses that deal with the impossibility of a Christian's being separated from Christ's love.

With his fifth unanswerable question the apostle suggests seven candidates that might possibly create such a gulf—three denoting the pressures and distresses produced by Christians simply living in an ungodly and hostile world, two representing material needs, and two dealing with physical threats to well-being.

Needless to say, the apostle's seven candidates were hardly of merely academic interest to his first readers. Paul had endured the first six himself, and would in the not too distant future suffer from the sword when the Roman authorities put him to death for his faith.

Paul's argument is not that Christians will be trouble free, but rather that even the severest of troubles can in no way separate them from Christ's love or the salvation they have in Him through faith. In short, they have assurance of salvation in spite of the fact that they will share with Him in suffering (Rom. 8:17).

The apostle, however, did leave unmentioned the one candidate that can indeed come between a Christian and salvation. That is a persistent rejection of faith in Christ as Savior and an unwillingness to walk with Him in God's principles. But Paul didn't have to mention it since his understanding of the faith relationship at the center of salvation had been the theme and thesis of his first 8 chapters in Romans. Even then, though, a rejection of God's love in Christ and His salvation would still not isolate us from His love.

The quotation in Romans 8:36 from Psalms 44:22 is a picture of persecution not because of unfaithfulness on the part of God's people, but persecution because they had been faithful. The cost of following God has historically been high (see 2 Tim. 3:12). According to Hebrews 11, some were tortured, while others were mocked, beaten, stoned, imprisoned, and ill-treated (Heb. 11:35-37).

Yet none of those things were able to separate them from the love of Christ. That lesson was important for the Roman Christians because of the times in which they lived. It is also vital to those alive in the period before the Second Advent. But we, like the Romans of old, can rest in full assurance that even though troubles will come, *nothing* can tear us away from God's love.

To the contrary, "in all of these things we are more than conquerors through him that loved us" (Rom. 8:37, KJV). "More than conquerors" or as I rendered the passage, "we overwhelmingly conquer," is the key phrase as Romans 8 nears its crescendoing climax. *Hypernik men* might be translated as "supervictors" (Fitzmyer, p. 534). It suggests "a lopsided victory in which the enemy or opponent is completely routed" (Rogers, p. 332) or "*a most glorious victory*" (Bauer, p. 1034).

God takes no halfway measures when it comes to His people. Romans 8:38, 39 demonstrate that nothing external to personal faith choices can divorce a Christian from God's salvation in Christ. Romans 8 is the great assurance chapter. It starts with the proclamation that there is "no condemnation for those in Christ Jesus" (verse 1), and it ends up with the declaration that absolutely nothing can come between those "in Christ" and the love of the God who provided the free gift of salvation that Paul expounded upon in Romans' first seven chapters. What more could he have said? In Romans 8 he has hammered home, pounded down, and fully exhibited one of the great teachings of the Bible—that those who choose to maintain a faith relationship with God through Jesus cannot lose. That is powerful. We can praise God from whom all blessings flow.

Part V

Salvation For Everyone

Romans 9:1-11:36

38. Advantages Aren't Always Helpful

Romans 9:1-5

> ¹*I am speaking truth in Christ, I am not lying; my conscience testifies with me in the Holy Spirit, ²that I have great sorrow and unceasing pain in my heart. ³For I could even wish that I myself were accursed, cut off from Christ for the sake of my brothers, my relatives according to the flesh, ⁴who are Israelites to whom belong the adoption of sonship, and the glory, and the covenants, and the giving of the law, and the temple service, and the promises; ⁵to whom belong the fathers and from whom came the Christ according to the flesh, the One who is over all, God blessed forever. Amen.*

Romans 9:1 signals a major shift in Paul's presentation. So far he has set forth four aspects of his argument.

1. In Romans 1:1-17 we met Paul and the Roman Christians and he highlighted his themes for the letter.
2. Next in Romans 1:18-3:20 the apostle introduced us to the problem of sin and its universality among both Jews and Gentiles.
3. Then Romans 3:21-5:21 revealed how God's gracious gift of justification dealt with the sin problem for those willing to accept it by faith.
4. Finally, in Romans 6:1-8:39 Paul helped us see that those who were in a faith relationship with Jesus would walk with Him in the principles of God. The apostle climaxed his treatment with a great hymn of victory and assurance (Rom. 8:31-39).

Paul is now ready to present the fifth segment of his exposition. In this one he will help the Jews see how they fit into God's plan. Some authorities view chapters 9-11 as "a kind of postscript" to the plan of salvation set forth in the first eight chapters (see, e.g., Lloyd-Jones, *Romans 8:17-39*, p. 367), but we should see it as an integral part of that presentation. After all, in the keynote of Romans in 1:16 Paul noted that the gospel "is the power of God unto salvation to everyone who believes, to the Jew first and also to the Greek." He is now ready to show what the gospel means for the Jewish people.

The "Jewish question" is a big one for Paul. The Jews had been God's chosen people, but now a largely Gentile church had seemed to have displaced them. If the Jews are the "elect," why are most of them outside the Christian community? What part do they have to play in the plan of salvation?

It is to such issues that Paul now turns. But he starts out his three chapters on the topic in a strange way. Three times in Romans 9:1 he emphasizes the truthfulness and sincerity of what follows: (1) "I am speaking truth in Christ," (2) "I am not lying," and (3) "my conscience testifies with me in the Holy Spirit."

The apostle feels that some of his readers will have grave doubts about various points of his presentation. He wants them to know that he is speaking with the utmost heartfelt sincerity. All of us can find a lesson here, because all of us face difficult situations in which we may be mistrusted or misunderstood. In such situations we need to bend over backward in reaching people if we hope to communicate with them effectively.

Romans 9:2, 3 expresses Paul's deep concern for Israel, since the vast majority of them had not accepted the gospel that he believed provided the only means of salvation. His anguish reaches the point that he claims that he "could even wish" that he himself might become a sacrifice for them if that would mean their salvation.

That desire reminds us of Moses. After Israel sinned in worshipping the golden calf, he prayed to God for them, saying: "Alas, this people have sinned a great sin; they have made for themselves gods of gold. But now, if thou wilt forgive their sin—and if not, blot me, I pray thee, out of thy book" (Ex. 32:31, 32, RSV).

Thus Paul in wrestling with his fellow Israelites selects a forceful illustration from the nation's history. Yet his "could even wish" represents what Everett Harrison refers to as an "impossible wish" (Harrison, p. 147). After all, Moses had not been able to fulfill his request. God told him: "Whoever has sinned against me, him will I blot out of my book. But now go, lead the people" (Ex. 32:33, 34).

Paul had a parallel concern with Moses for his people. But, as James Denney points out, their concerns were not exactly the same. Moses in his identification with the Jews was willing to die *with* them, but Paul suggested that he would die *for* them. Thus, as Denney phrases it, he was reflecting "a spark from the fire of Christ's substitutionary love" (Denney, "Romans," p. 657). The apostle, of course, knew that his wish was impossible. After all, he had just finished writing about the fact that nothing except unfaith can separate us from God's love (Romans 8:38, 39). And Paul was expressing anything but unfaith.

Martin Luther, the great Reformer, caught the essence of the apostle's anguish when he pointed out that the whole context of Romans 9:2, 3 indicates his deep desire for the salvation of the Jews. "He wants to bring Christ to them. . . . He appealed to them with a sacred oath, because it seems unbelievable that a man should want to be damned in order that the damned might be saved" (Luther, *Lectures*, p. 261).

Romans 9:4, 5 find Paul setting forth Israel's privileged place and special role in salvation history. In the process, he lists eight of the very blessings that should have prepared them to receive Christ.

First, is "the adoption of sonship." The Old Testament repeatedly presents Israel as God's "first-born son" (see, e.g., Ex. 4:22). In a similar manner it proclaims that God is the nation's father (Jer. 31:9). But Romans 9:4 is the only place that speaks of Israel as being adopted, a term that highlights God's grace in electing the nation as His special people.

Second, Israel had "the glory," a term indicating God's "personal presence with his people" (Schreiner, p. 484) represented by the Shekinah that typified God's splendor and filled the Most Holy Place of the wilderness tabernacle and later the Temple. That glory symbolized God as being "enthroned between the cherubim that are on the ark" (2 Sam. 6:2, NIV).

Third, Israel had been the recipient of the covenants that God had made through Abraham, Moses, and David. Those covenants became the vehicle through which Israel entered into a singular relationship to God as a people of both unique privilege and special responsibility.

Fourth, Israel was the custodian of God's law. The Jews prided themselves in having God's special revelation of His will. Paul agreed with them that their possession of the law had indeed put them in a unique position (cf. Rom. 3:1, 2).

Beyond those blessings, the Jews had both the Temple services and the promises. The promises, in particular, related to the coming of the Messiah (the Christ) as God's prophet, priest, and king. And the Temple worship should have helped them see the role of the Christ as the sacrificial lamb of God (Lev. 17:11; Isa. 53; John 1:29).

The seventh blessing of Israel was that they had "the fathers" or "the patriarchs" (NIV). It was through Abraham, Isaac, and Jacob that God's blessing came to the world.

The last blessing is that the Israelite nation was the channel for the Messiah. All the way from the first hint of Him in Genesis 3:15 through the promises to David the hope of the nation focused on God's special Anointed One, who would save His people. For that reason Matthew in his first chapter goes to great lengths to demonstrate that Jesus of Nazareth had the proper Jewish lineage and ancestry to qualify as the predicted Messiah.

> Superb spiritual blessings save no one. They may help prepare people's hearts, but without the personal choice to accept Christ they are meaningless.

Eight great blessings. Yet they did not save the nation. Many individual Jews, of course, had come to Christ, but not the bulk of them. We find a lesson here: superb spiritual blessings save no one. They may help prepare people's hearts, but without the personal choice to accept Christ they are meaningless.

Paul had experienced that truth himself. In Philippians he tells us of his own advantaged background. He had been circumcised on the eighth day, belonged to the people of Israel, was a Hebrew of the Hebrews (had a clear bloodline), was a member of the exclusive Pharisaic party, had demonstrated his zeal for God, and was "blameless" in terms of law righteousness (Phil. 3:4-6).

A young man with everything going for him, Paul had all the advantages. Yet they did not save him. That happened when he encountered Jesus on the road to Damascus (Acts 9:1-9). At that point he concluded that his privileges were not enough. When he met Jesus he realized what true righteousness was, and that all his prerogatives were as "dung." Instantly he traded in all his human advantages and achievements for the righteousness of Christ (Phil. 3:7-9).

Paul wants the same thing for his fellow Israelites in Romans 9-11. And he holds out the same for you and me. He longs for us to trade in all our advantages, all our achievements, even all of our selves, for salvation in Christ Jesus.

39. God Calls the Shots

Romans 9:6-13

>[6]*But it is not as though the word of God has failed. For not all those who descended from Israel belong to Israel;* [7]*nor are they all the seed of Abraham because they are his children, but "through Isaac shall your seed be called."* [8]*That is, it is not the children of the flesh who are children of God but the children of the promise who are regarded as seed.* [9]*For this is the word of promise, "At this time I will come and to Sarah there will be a son."* [10]*And not only that, but also Rebecca conceived [twins] by one man, Isaac our father—*[11]*for though they were not yet born and had not done anything good or bad, in order that God's purpose according to His choice might remain,* [12]*not because of works but because of His calling. It was said to her, "The older one will serve the younger."* [13]*Even as it has been written, "Jacob I loved, but Esau I hated."*

It is of crucial importance to read Romans 9:6-13 in its context. In Romans 8:28-30 Paul set forth the thesis that God cares for those whom He has called. Romans 8:31-39 continues that thought, emphasizing that nothing can separate God's children from His love. Then Romans 9:1-5 raises the problem of why so many of the Jewish nation stood outside of the Christian faith in spite of the fact that they had received God's blessing. And we need to read all of Romans 8:28-9:5 in the context of the first eight chapters of Romans in which Paul taught the universality of human sin (1:18-3:20), that people could be right with God only through faith in Christ (3:21-5:21), and that those who had such faith would live in harmony with God's principles (6:1-8:27).

Thus it is that the preceding teachings in both Romans 1:16-8:27 and particularly in Romans 8:28-9:5 set Paul up for the issue that he needed to raise in Romans 9:6-13. In reading those verses we need to remember that the problem being addressed is the calling of God and why there were so many Gentiles who had accepted the gospel but so few Jews. It is in that framework that Paul deals with the question of whether "the word of God has failed" (Rom. 9:6).

Not so, the apostle asserts. The problem resided in the recipients of the promises. More specifically, "not all those who descended from Israel belong to Israel" (verse 6). Paul had earlier raised this issue when he noted that real Jews are not those who are outwardly so, but those whose circumcision was a matter of the heart and therefore spiritual (Rom. 2:25-29).

Thus the problem is not in the promises of God. He was still calling all Israel to true faith. But they had not been responding to the extent they should have. As a result, they were by their own choices placing themselves outside of the family.

Romans 9:7-9 continues the idea that not all those descended from Israel actually belong to Israel by illustrating it from Abraham's family. Paul writes that not all of Abraham's children were true descendents of Abraham in the sense that they were included in the promises. In the process he quotes Genesis 21:12: "It is through Isaac that your offspring will be reckoned" (NIV). In other words, the promise came through Isaac's line and did not include Ishmael and the sons of Keturah (Abraham's wife after Sarah's death). On that point all of Paul's Jewish readers would have agreed with him. They were quite proud of their religious and family pedigree.

The apostle is not declaring that God did not care for and love Abraham's other children and their descendants, but rather that *God was free to choose* Isaac and reject Esau as the line through which He would bless the world by His special revelation and through whom He would send the Messiah.

The Lord's continuing ability to choose those to whom He will give His blessing is crucial to Paul's presentation since he has already argued in Romans 3:21-4:25 that individuals can only become a part of God's true covenant people as children of Abraham by faith in Christ. That is exactly where the problem is. Not all who were born into the Jewish nation had selected that faith. Thus they were not truly Abraham's children (cf. Gal.

3:26-29). It was not God's promises that were at fault, but the people (Rom. 9:6). God had promised to bless all nations through Abraham (Gen. 22:18), but most of those of Jewish birth had not opted for the faith of Abraham (Rom. 4) and thus could not be considered his spiritual descendants (Rom. 2:28, 29).

But their unfaithfulness had not affected God's ability to make choices regarding the composition of who would be the bearers of His covenant blessings. Just as at one time He had selected Isaac over Ishmael, so now He could elect those who had the patriarch's faith.

If God's prerogative to apply His promises to whom He will is illustrated in His choice of Isaac in preference to Ishmael (Rom. 9:7-9), Paul strengthens the argument in verses 10-13 by his use of the example of God's choosing Jacob over Esau.

Remember that the topic is God's sovereign right to pick those who are to bear His covenant blessing. Thus not all Israel belongs to God's true Israel because they are not opting for God's choices as set forth in the first eight chapters of Romans.

The words "and not only that" (Rom. 9:10) signal an "even stronger proof or example" of God's ability to choose than that found in verses 7-9 (Sanday, p. 243). After all, one could argue, there is an objection to the previous example in that "Ishmael's mother was Egyptian, and thus there are no ethnic grounds for considering him to be part of Abraham's authentic seed." Thus "Paul closes this loophole by offering the case of Rebekah and Isaac and the birth of their twins" (Schreiner, p. 492). In this case they not only have the same mother and father (both of the flesh of Abraham), but they shared the same pregnancy. Yet God selected Jacob rather than Esau even before they could do good or evil—even before they were born—"in order that God's purpose according to His choice might remain" (Rom. 9:11). Thus Paul has demonstrated that God's promises have not failed (verse 6). Rather "God's word stands precisely because it is not based on human actions and choices" (Schreiner, p. 492), but upon God's.

Romans 9:6-13 has also demonstrated that ethnic descent alone does not make a person a part of the people of God. We can garner two lessons from that fact. First, that God's true people need to line up with His choices and can not rely on religious pedigree or family birth. Second, that God is always God and it is He who sets the stage in terms of the plan of salvation. We need to view that thought from the perspective of the argument in Romans that all are guilty (both Jews and Gentiles) and that no one has an exclusive claim on grace. Therefore, if God extends His grace to someone, even to those outside of a given circle, its members have no ground to protest, because the only reason they are inside is past grace—that is true for both Jews and Gentiles. God elects whom He will. But that in itself is good news because Christ died for everybody and wants to save all (Rom. 11:32). Both Jews and Gentiles.

Before leaving Romans 9:6-13, we need to reflect upon the meaning of "Jacob I loved, but Esau I hated" (verse 13). Some have misused that text (cited from Mal. 1:2, 3) to teach the doctrine of double predestination, in which God has predetermined people before their birth either for heaven or hell. We need to ask what the verse is really teaching in its context in Romans.

The first thing we must remember is that the Bible doesn't always use words in the same way that we do. For example, Jesus claimed that we must "hate" our father and mother and wife if we are to be His followers (Luke 14:26). How can we line up that injunction with the fifth commandment, which tells us that we must honor our parents? The obvious implication is that we are not to hate our parents in the modern sense of the term but to choose to put Christ first in our life.

The same applies to Jesus' saying that His followers should "hate" their own life if they wanted life eternal (John 12:25). Franz Leenhardt is quite correct when he writes that "the contrast of 'love:hate' has not in the mind of the Biblical authors the emotional character which we lend to it" (Leenhardt, p. 250). As in the case of Jacob's relationship to Rachel, whom he loved, and Leah, whom he "hated" (Gen. 29:30, 31), Scripture often employed the term to express a preference for one thing or person over another, both of whom one could feel affection for.

The plain fact is that God *chose* the nation (both passages dealing with loving Jacob and hating Esau refer not to individuals but nations) flowing from Jacob (Israel) over the nation issuing from Esau (Edom). It was His choice to send the Messiah through one and not the other.

In the same way, when Jacob's offspring (the Jews of Christ's day) rejected Jesus, God felt compelled to broaden Israel's blessing to another nation—the church composed of all those (both Jews and Gentiles) who were willing to put their faith in Christ (Matt. 21:31-43). Thus Paul states in Romans 9:1-13 that God hasn't changed. He still operates on the principle He did when He selected Jacob instead of Esau. The Lord is not captive to any religious group. His promises have not failed. But because of Israel's rejection of Jesus, He has extended the selection process to a new faith-based people to carry out His mission on earth. But, Paul will emphasize in Romans 11:17-24, God has made provision for Israelites of faith to "be grafted back into their own olive tree" (verse 24, RSV).

40. Mercy Is Everything

Romans 9:14-18

14What shall we say then? Surely there is no unrighteousness with God, . is there? May it never be! 15For He says to Moses, "I will have mercy on whomever I have mercy, and I will have compassion on whomever I have compassion." 16So then, it depends not on the one who wills or the one who runs, but on God who has mercy. 17For the Scripture says to Pharaoh, "For this very purpose I raised you up, so that I might demonstrate My power in you and so that My name might be proclaimed in all the earth." 18So then, He has mercy upon whomever He wills, and He hardens whomever He wills.

Romans 9:6-13 asserted that it was not a failure in the divine promises that had resulted in so few of Paul's fellow Jews being in the church. The focal point of those verses had been on God's unquestionable right to summon whomsoever He would, a call rooted in His sovereign grace. Thus it was with His election of the children of Abraham through the line that flowed through Isaac and Jacob. That calling had nothing to do with human worthiness, but only came through God's decision.

But, the logic of the book of Romans runs, God could choose Gentiles also to be His people if He so desired. And that is exactly what He had done through Christ. Thus the problem of a lack of Jewish response was not a failure on the part of God's promises (Rom. 9:6), but rather of the Jewish people who had not responded in the faith of Abraham their father. Thus, in effect, Paul is arguing in the flow of the book of Romans that "his doctrine of justification is not in contradiction of the Old Testament position that marks out the Jews as God's chosen people. He is saying that the Jews of his day were in error in seeing themselves as the only people acceptable before God" (Morris, *Romans*, p. 358), since He always works on the principle of gracious election (Rom. 9:6-13).

But that answer raises a second question that the apostle answers in verses 14-18. Is God acting unjustly or unrighteously in changing the rules on who the elect are?

Absolutely not! is Paul's reply. Why? Because the question is incorrectly framed. God does not base His selection (or election or predestination or choice) upon justice but mercy. The apostle proves his point by quoting Exodus 33:19: "I will have mercy on whom I will have mercy, and I will have compassion on whom I will have compassion" (NIV). Paul's Jewish detractors might argue with him, but they won't contradict Scripture, which says that God's election is always according to mercy.

And that is a crucial point for us to understand. After all, if God had given the ancient Israelites what they deserved (justice), they would have been obliterated. The same applies to the Jews of Paul's day, or even to Christians living in the twenty-first century. We are totally dependent on God's mercy.

Given the nature of justice, John Stott points out that "the wonder is not that some are saved and others not, but that anybody is saved at all" (Stott, p. 269). If God, therefore, chooses to have mercy on some who are not of "our group," who are we to challenge Him? Paul's point in Romans 9 is that God is so merciful that He elects not only Jews for salvation but also Gentiles, and He is not unjust in doing so, because His salvation is based on His choice (verses 6-13) and His mercy (verses 14-18).

> ### Human Freedom: A Topic Not Discussed in Romans 9
>
> As we read chapter 9 it is important to remember that Paul is not answering *our* questions about free will. He doesn't even address the issue in Romans 9. Rather, He is arguing for God's absolute freedom to have mercy on whomsoever He will. It is unfortunate that so many people have based so much theology on a topic that chapter 9 does not even broach.

"So then," we read in Romans 9:16, "it depends not on the one who wills or the one who runs, but on God who has mercy." "Mercy" is the key word in Romans 9-11. In fact, the entire section climaxes with the idea that "God has consigned all men to disobedience, that he may have mercy upon all" (Rom. 11:32, RSV). Mercy in relation to God appears nine times in these three chapters, but only twice in the rest of Romans.

But even though Romans 1-8 does not contain the word "mercy," the idea itself undergirds those chapters. After all, Paul has demonstrated that all human beings had sinned (Rom. 3:23) and deserved to die (6:23). Yet God opened up for them the plan of righteousness by faith (3:21-5:21), if they would only accept it.

Thus at the very foundation of the concepts of grace and justification lies the bedrock of God's mercy. It is because God is merciful that salvation is possible. He chose to treat men and women with mercy. As a result, as Paul demonstrated in Romans 9:6-13, not only is God free to elect or predestinate, but He has chosen to predestinate to salvation on the basis of mercy. Everything involved in God's mission and the plan of salvation directly derives from His mercy.

Romans 9:16 is especially clear on the centrality of mercy. It is not human running or willing that counts, but divine mercy. And "'willing' and 'running' together sum up the totality of man's capacity" (Dunn, *Romans 9-16*, p. 553). The Greek word he selected for "running" highlights that point. It was a term used of foot races in a stadium, and implies extending *"oneself to the limit of one's powers in an attempt to . . . advance"* (Bauer, p. 1015). But, Paul reminds us, all our effort—even our most strenuous effort—cannot free us from condemnation. Everything depends on God's choosing to be merciful to those who have sinned. Even, in the context of Romans 9:6-13, God's dealings with Abraham, Isaac, and Jacob must be seen in terms of His mercy, since each of them was a sinner.

Thus mercy is not only the central word of Romans 9 through 11, but of the entire book and the entire plan of salvation. We can be thankful that the God who revealed Himself to Moses (and Paul) was "a God merciful and gracious, slow to anger, and abounding in steadfast love" (Ex. 34:6, RSV).

That pleasant thought brings us to Romans 9:17, 18 and God's hardening of Pharaoh's heart. Did the Lord really make the Egyptian king resist Him just so that He could demonstrate His power? That is not what the text says if one reads it carefully. But that doesn't get God off the hook, because the Old Testament leaves us in no doubt that "the Lord hardened the heart of Pharaoh" (Ex. 9:12, RSV). And that is not an isolated statement. The same thought appears in Exodus 10:1, 20, 27; 11:10; and 14:8.

But that's not the whole story. The Bible also repeatedly asserts that it was Pharaoh who hardened his own heart (see Ex. 8:15, 32; 9:34) after the various plagues. How can it be, we need to ask, that the Bible says both that God hardened Pharaoh's heart and that he hardened his own heart?

To answer, we need to look at what actually happened in Exodus. First God dispatched Moses and Aaron to talk to Pharaoh in an attempt to get freedom for the Israelites. Not having any success along that line, the Lord then sent a series of plagues to wake the king up. But the only response was that Pharaoh resisted and hardened his heart after each one. In other words, Pharaoh's stubbornness resulted from his rebellion against God's divine revelation to him. Paul described such hardening in his first letter to Timothy as a searing of the conscience, as with a hot iron (1 Tim. 4:2). According to Romans 1:24, 26, 28 God leaves those who rebel against Him to the inevitable outworking of their actions. In that sense God is responsible, since, as the apostle put it, God "gave them up" to those consequences. But what happened to them came as a result of their own rebellion and sin. The Lord could have intervened so that the outcome never happened. But he didn't and was thus responsible for them.

It is in that sense that He hardened Pharaoh's heart. Hardened people are those who refuse to repent when God offers them grace. But since He allows them to continue living in their resistant state He does bear some responsibility for their condition, whether that hardening took place in ancient Egypt or in the twenty-first century. God does not rescue us from our choices.

But the good news of Romans 9:18 is not that God allows us to harden our hearts, but that "He has mercy upon whomever He wills." The option is up to us just as it was to Pharaoh. In the face of God's grace we can either choose hardening or mercy. It is the primary choice of our lives. The message of Romans 9:17, 18 is that God not only offers mercy, but that He is also capable of withholding it. He forces it upon no one—not even His covenant people.

41. Faith Versus the Stumbling Stone

Romans 9:19-33

[19]You will say to me then, "Why does He still find fault? For who can resist His will?" [20]On the contrary, O man, who are you to talk back to God? Certainly the thing molded will not say to the one who molded it, "Why did you make me so?" [21]Or has not the potter the right over the clay to make out of the same lump this vessel for honorable use and that for dishonorable? [22]But what if God, desiring to demonstrate His wrath and to make known His power, has endured with much patience vessels of wrath made for destruction [23]so that He might make known the riches of His glory for vessels of mercy, which He made beforehand for glory, [24]even us whom He also called, not only from Jews but also from Gentiles? [25]As He says also in Hosea,

> *"I will call those not My people, 'My people,'*
> *And the one not loved, 'beloved.'"*

[26]"And it will be that in the place where it was said to them, 'You are not My people,'

> *There they will be called sons of the living God."*

[27]And Isaiah cries on behalf of Israel, "Though the number of the sons of Israel be as the sand of the sea, only the remnant of them will be saved; [28]for the Lord will execute His sentence upon the earth, bringing it to an end with dispatch." [29]And as Isaiah predicted,

> *"Unless the Lord of hosts had left to us descendants,*
> *We would have become like Sodom, and we would have been made like Gomorrah."*

[30]What then shall we say? That Gentiles, who did not pursue righteousness, attained righteousness, even a righteousness by faith; [31]but Israel, pursuing a righteousness by law, did not succeed in fulfilling that law. [32]Why? Because it was not by faith but by works. They stumbled at the stumbling stone, [33]just as it has been written,

> *"Behold I place in Zion a stone of stumbling and a rock of offense,*
> *And the one who believes on Him will not be put to shame."*

To say the least, Romans 9:19-33 is a complex passage. The best way to come at it is to remember that "all of chapter 9 is a unit, and the single issue is how to understand (in light of God's promise to Israel) that so many in Israel have not found salvation" (Osborne, p. 253). That sad fact, of course, must be seen in the context of the massive influx of Gentiles into Christianity.

In answering the problem, Paul's major premise is that the fault is not in the divine promises (Rom. 9:6). But certainly, he argues in verses 6-13, we need to understand those promises better. Along that line he makes two points. First, that not every Israelite is a true descendant of Abraham (verse 6). And, second, that God's selection of His people is always by His graceful choice alone and does not depend on human actions (verse 11).

But that conclusion raises another issue. Isn't God's arbitrary choice of His covenant people unjust? Not so, Paul argues in verses 14-18, because God can have mercy on whoever He chooses, and He can harden (see explanation in chapter 40) those who refuse His merciful offer (verse 18).

But even that leads to yet another problem that Paul will deal with beginning in verse 19: Why does God find fault with people if no one can resist His will? After all, the objection runs, "if God treats men as Paul supposes, they have no moral responsibility; God himself has no business to condemn as a sinner a man whom he himself has hardened" (Barrett, p. 187).

Paul's answer to that assertion divides into three segments. In the first (Rom. 9:20-24), the apostle slams to the ground the idea that frail and finite human beings have any ability or right to "question God's justice and give him direction on how to run the world (v. 20a)" (Schreiner, p. 513). The apostle backs up his response with quotations from Isaiah 29:16 and 45:9, two passages in which the clay questions the right of the potter to do as he wills with it. Those passages are especially appropriate in Paul's context in Romans because they deal with God's formation of Israel as a nation and His unquestionable authority to treat that nation as He deems best.

God's prerogative to deal with people with perfect freedom and on His own conditions is precisely the issue the apostle has in mind in Romans 9. God is in charge, not Israel or anyone else. He is the potter, they are the clay. If He chooses to have mercy on the Gentiles, that is His business and privilege. No humans, no matter what their religious or racial pedigree, have a monopoly on God or authority over Him. Nor can the Jew or anyone else escape the result of rebellion. If they choose the way of sin, they also can become dishonorable vessels (verse 21). People are not automatically honorable because of their birth as Jews. Nor are they automatically dishonorable because they are Gentiles. God is sovereign, and He sets the rules and conditions.

While God had made it plain in the Hebrew Bible that He would destroy the wicked (verse 22a), the focal point of Paul's argument in verses 22-24 is His patience (verse 22b) and mercy (verse 23), which He has chosen to extend to *both* Jews and Gentiles (verse 24).

Here we have the apostle's point at last. In verse 24 he puts in plain language the issue that has been behind his discussion all through Romans 9: that God can save Gentiles as well as Jews. But that is a point he needs to defend to his Jewish readers.

That takes us to the second major section of verses 19-33. Verses 25-29 find Paul substantiating his claim of mercy to the Gentiles from the Old Testament. His quotations fall into two groups. The first (verses 25, 26) is from Hosea 2:23 and 1:10, which the apostle uses to ground the acceptability of the Gentiles. Thus those who were not God's people could become His people and join the colony of God's beloved. Such acceptance was a crucial part of Paul's presentation, since Gentiles by then formed the majority of the church in Rome.

But that defense, while it succeeded in justifying the inclusion of the Gentiles, said nothing about the dearth of Jewish response. Paul turns to that issue in verses 27-29, in which he utilizes two quotations from Isaiah to demonstrate that even though God had blessed the people with the Abrahamic blessing of being a multitude like "the sand of the sea" (see Gen. 15:5; 22:17), still only a "remnant" of Israel would be saved (Rom. 9:27; Isa. 10:22). Thus the Hebrew Bible had spoken to the problem of the lack of Jews in the church that Paul has been addressing since Romans 9:1. But he doesn't leave his argument about the lack of Jews in the church with the remnant idea. He uses a second quotation in verse 29 from Isaiah 1:9, in which the prophet had stated that if the Lord hadn't left some remnant of Israel, the nation would have become like Sodom and Gomorrah, two cities that had ceased to exist. Thus Paul raised two issues: (1) that there would indeed be a remnant from Israel that would be saved and (2) that that remnant would only be redeemed through God's choice to do so by grace.

Romans 9:25-29 form a crucial segment in Paul's proof that God can call both Jews and Gentiles (verse 24) and that He will have mercy on all, even though all are sinners (Rom. 11:32; 3:23). But having made that point, the apostle needs to be explicit regarding *how* people enter the realm of God's mercy. He begins to undertake that task in Romans 9:30-33.

Verses 30-32 are absolutely crucial for understanding Romans 9, a chapter that has put the emphasis on divine initiative, on predestination, on election, on God's will, and on His choosing people such as Abraham, as well as on His "hardening" of Pharaoh. Many have incorrectly assumed from Paul here that everything is up to God and that humans are so much passive clay in His hands, that even before their birth God has predestined some to heaven and others to hell regardless of any choices they might make in life.

Paul puts all such theorizing to rest in verses 30-32. Here he shows us the human part in God's plan. As Emil Brunner describes it, the answer does not lie "in the mysterious decree of God, who predestines some to salvation and others to damnation," but in the human response to Christ (Brunner, *Romans*, p. 89).

The apostle presents a topsy-turvy picture. On the one hand are the Gentiles who didn't even have any interest in righteousness but who found it in spite of themselves (verse 30). On the other hand are the Jews who earnestly pursued righteousness but failed, in spite of their zeal, to obtain it (verse 31).

"Why?" (verse 32). With that question we have come back to the heart of Paul's argument in Romans 1 through 8. The reason the Gentiles had obtained righteousness was that they had accepted the free gift of God through Jesus by faith (cf. Rom. 3:23-25). And the Jews failed because they had sought to attain it by works of law, but they "did not succeed in fulfilling that law" (Rom. 9:31; cf. 3:20). Worse yet, they had "stumbled at the stumbling stone" (Rom. 9:32). In order to make his point more forceful Paul utilizes four short quotations from Isaiah 28:16 and 8:14.

Paul uses those phrases from Isaiah to affirm that God Himself has laid down a solid rock for His people. That stone he saw as none other than Jesus Christ. As he noted to the Corinthians, "no one can lay any foundation other than the one already laid, which is Jesus Christ" (1 Cor. 3:11, NIV). And Jesus had boldly applied Psalm 118:22 to Himself: "The stone the builders rejected has become the capstone" (Matt. 21:42, NIV).

In Romans 9:32, 33 Paul claims that some would take "offence" at Christ. The word "offence" is the Greek word *skandalon*, from which we get our word "scandal." Paul employs it in 1 Corinthians 1:23 to tell us that it is "Christ crucified" that was a *skandalon* or offence or "stumbling block" (RSV) to the Jews.

The plain fact is that it is the crucified Christ who is the key to salvation. And when people come face to face with His substitutionary sacrifice they either accept it by faith or it becomes an offensive teaching that they end up rejecting. Humans like to do it on their own or at least have a part in their salvation. Attempting that, however, ignores God's clear teaching on grace through faith. But "the one who believes on Him will not be put to shame" (Rom. 9:33)—and that is true for both Jews and Gentiles. God's word has not failed (Rom. 9:6).

42. Christ the Only Way

Romans 10:1-13

¹Brothers, my heart's desire and prayer to God for them is for their salvation. ²For I bear them witness that they have a zeal for God, but not according to knowledge. ³For being ignorant of the righteousness of God and seeking to establish their own righteousness, they did not submit to the righteousness of God. ⁴For Christ is the culmination of the law for righteousness to everyone who believes.

⁵For Moses writes that the man who practices the righteousness of the law shall live by it. ⁶But the righteousness of faith speaks thusly, "Do not say in your heart, 'who will ascend into heaven?' (that is, to bring Christ down), ⁷or 'Who will descend into the underworld?' (that is, to bring Christ up from the dead)." ⁸But what does it say? "The word is near you, in your mouth and in your heart" (that is, the word of faith which we are preaching); ⁹because if you confess with your mouth the Lord Jesus and believe in your heart that God raised Him from the dead, you will be saved. ¹⁰For with the heart one believes, and so is justified, and confesses with the mouth, and so is saved. ¹¹For the Scripture says, "Whoever believes in Him will not be put to shame." ¹²For there is no difference between Jew and Greek, for the same One is Lord of all, rich to all those calling on Him. ¹³For "everyone who calls on the name of the Lord will be saved."

Romans 10 deals with the same problem as chapter 9: Paul's desire to see more people of Jewish descent accept Christ. Both chapters explore the problem of what had gone wrong. From Romans 9:6 through 9:29 the apostle argues that God is not at fault. And in Romans 9:30 through 10:21 he asserts that Israel is to blame. And "what was

Israel's mistake? Misconstruing the Torah [Law], regarding it as requiring not trust but legalistic works. This is why Israel has not received what God has promised her" (Stern, pp. 385, 386).

Romans 9:30-33 highlighted the essence of the Jewish failure, attributing it to an attempt to gain righteousness through law rather than faith. That was a serious problem, but Paul has not written them off. To the contrary, he desired their salvation with all his heart (10:1). We find an important lesson in that verse. After all, the Jewish leaders had plagued the apostle's work practically from the time he had become a Christian. They not only hindered his efforts, but also made sure that he got more than his share of physical pain and imprisonment. Some of them would eventually seek his death. They meant him nothing but harm. Yet Paul never abandoned them or consigned them to hell. Rather, he continued to pray for their eternal salvation. Therein is the kind of love that Jesus said that individuals must have if they are to be perfect as their heavenly Father is perfect (Matt. 5:43-48). It is the same kind of love that God had for us when He sent Jesus to die for us while we were still His enemies (Rom. 5:8, 10). It is the identical love that God commands each of His followers to exhibit.

Romans 10:2 raises the issue of Israel's zeal for God. C. K. Barrett reflects on that point when he writes that "no nation had given itself to God with such devoted and courageous zeal as Israel" (Barrett, p. 196). Rabbi Judah ben Tema nicely phrased that mentality when he said, "Be strong as a leopard, fast as an eagle, fleet as a gazelle, and brave as a lion, to carry out the will of your Father who is in heaven" (M. Abot 5:20). And Paul himself had experienced that zeal in his persecution of Christians (Acts 26:9-11; Gal. 1:13).

But it was a zeal "not according to knowledge" (Rom. 10:2). The sad fact was that the Jews were "ignorant of the righteousness of God" and had sought "to establish their own righteousness." As a result, they "did not submit to the righteousness of God" (verse 3). At that point in his discussion Paul writes that "Christ is the culmination of the law for righteousness to everyone who believes" (verse 4).

That verse has proved to be a controversial one in Christian understanding. What is it that Romans 10:4 is teaching? Before beginning, we should note that whereas nearly all English translators render the verse as Christ is the "end" of the law, I have translated that phrase as "culmination" of the law (cf. Moo, *Epistle*, pp. 641, 642). Good reasons support that rendering. For one thing, even though *telos* can mean "end," that translation has too often led to a misunderstanding related to the idea of the abolition of God's law and that Christians are now free to do as they please. Such an interpretation directly contradicts such passages as Romans 3:31; 7:12, 14; and 13:8-10. For Paul faith "establishes" the law, which is holy, just, and good.

Of course, many have viewed the meaning of verse 4 as Christ being the end or termination of the law as an avenue to righteousness. And that is most certainly true. Paul has repeatedly pounded home the fact that righteousness comes by faith rather than through lawkeeping. Recognition of that fact means the death of all legalisms in genuine Christianity. Thus he noted in Romans 10:3 that Christians gain righteousness by submitting to God's righteousness. There is no other way to achieve righteousness.

While that interpretation is certainly true, it does not capture the full meaning of Romans 10:4. The word *telos* not only means "end" in the sense of termination, but also "*goal*" or "*outcome*" (Bauer, p. 998; cf. Badenas). Thus, notes F. F. Bruce, "Christ is the goal at which the law aimed, in that he embodies the perfect righteousness which it prescribes. . . . Since Christ is the goal of the law, since in him the law has found its perfect fulfillment, a righteous status before God is available to everyone who believes in him, and that implies the termination of the law's function (real or imagined) as a means of acquiring such a righteous status" (Bruce, p. 190). John Ziesler is thinking of Christ as the goal of the law when he writes that Jesus fulfilled "the promises to Abraham" and thus opened "up the people of God to all who had faith in him" (Ziesler, p. 254). Douglas Moo makes the same point when he observes that "as a result of Christ's coming and bringing the law to its culmination, righteousness is now available for everyone who believes" (Moo, *Romans*, p. 331).

> Christ is the *telos* or consummation of all that the law pointed to. And because He is the consummation, salvation flows out of faith in Him.

Romans 10:5-13 contrasts two types of righteousness. The first is righteousness by law. In that regard, "Moses writes that the man who practices the righteousness of the law shall live by it" (verse 5). The quotation from Leviticus 18:5 means to Paul that the person who desires to establish righteousness by keeping the law must live up to all aspects and details of the law. That is, it must be obeyed to the very letter. Anything less than that cannot lead to salvation, since the law can condemn (Rom. 3:20), but contains no inherent grace or mercy. Paul has already headed off that path to righteousness in Romans 1:18-3:20, in which he demonstrated that even at their best the most diligent human beings have been able to produce only imperfect and unacceptable righteousness according to the law. As a result, all stand under condemnation.

That implication brings the apostle to God's solution in "the righteousness of faith" (Rom. 10:6). And how does one get such righteousness? Not by some great act of exertion, such as ascending to heaven or into the grave to find Christ (verses 6, 7), but by accepting that which is near at hand, even the gospel of righteousness through faith that Paul has been preaching (verse 8).

Here we find the apostle exposing an interesting quirk in the human psyche. How it enthralls people to go on religious pilgrimages or to participate in a crusade, or to give all their possessions to achieve a spiritual goal. Tell us to do some great feat of human accomplishment, and we get all excited. That's sacrifice—something to be proud about, something to write a book about. By contrast, merely accepting Christ by faith sounds so pedestrian, so valueless, so void of anything I can brag about. But it is that very unglamorous road to salvation that Paul is telling us is the only way.

The real road to salvation is believing with the heart and confessing with our voices (Rom. 10:13). At the core of that confession and believing is the acceptance of Jesus as the resurrected "Lord" (verse 9). Acknowledging that Jesus is Lord meant a radical break with their past for both Gentile and Jewish converts, because it pointed to His deity. That was extremely clear for Jewish Christians, since the Greek version of the Old Testament (the Septuagint) uses the word "Lord" more than 6,000 times for the name of God. Beyond that, in the Gentile world the word referred to a deity or for the emperor when worshipped as a god. Thus to confess Christ as Lord was to declare Him as God the Son.

The second aspect of the confession, dealing with Christ's resurrection from the dead, Paul also considered extremely important. The Resurrection placed the seal of God's approval on Christ's life and death (see Rom. 1:4). As Leon Morris puts it, "the resurrection is of critical importance. It is at the cross that God did his saving work, but Paul does not believe in a dead martyr but in a living Savior" (Morris, *Romans*, p. 386).

Verses 11-13 find the apostle reiterating his central theme in Romans (see 1:16, 17; 11:32): that "everyone who calls on the name of the Lord will be saved" (verse 13). And that "everyone" includes both Jew and Gentile (verse 12). Racial issues and caste find no place in Christianity since all are humbly rescued by grace through faith at the foot of the cross (Gal. 3:26-29; Eph. 2:18). None of us has anything to boast of (Eph. 2:9), since all are guilty (Rom. 3:23) and stand under condemnation (Rom. 6:23) outside of God's free gift in Christ Jesus our Lord (Rom. 3:23-25).

43. Stubbornness in the Face of Invitation

Romans 10:14-21

[14]*How then will they call on Him in whom they have not believed? And how will they believe in Him of whom they have not heard? And how will they hear without a preacher?* [15]*And how will they preach if they are not sent? As it is written, "How beautiful are the feet of those proclaiming good news of good things!"* [16]*But not all obeyed the good news; for Isaiah says, "Lord, who has believed our report?"* [17]*So faith comes from hearing and hearing through the word of Christ.*

[18]*But I say, did they not hear? Indeed they did,*
"Their voice has gone out into all the earth,
And their words to the ends of the inhabited world."
[19]*But I say, did Israel not know? First, Moses says,*
"I will provoke you to jealousy by those who are not a nation,
By a nation without understanding I will anger you."
[20]*And Isaiah is very bold and says,*
"I was found by those not seeking Me,
I became visible to those not asking for Me."
[21]*But to Israel He says, "All the day I reached out My hands toward a disobedient and contrary people."*

The four questions in Romans 10:14, 15 refer us back to the previous verse, which noted that "everyone who calls on the name of the Lord will be saved." Thus Paul appears to be saying that sinners must call on the Lord if they are to be saved. But that raises a series of questions that the apostle fires off in rapid sequence in verses 14 and 15.

Question 1: "How then will they call on Him in whom they have not believed?" The very act presupposes a knowledge of God.

Question 2: But "how will they believe in Him of whom they have not heard?" People need to hear about God before they can believe in Him.

Question 3: "How will they hear without a preacher?" Before the days of mass media the role of the herald (translated "preacher" above) was vital. In ancient times the major means of transmitting news was the herald's proclamation in the city square or other public place. It is obvious that there could be no hearers without a herald.

Question 4: "How will they preach if they are not sent?" The word "sent" derives from the same word as "apostle." A true herald or preacher is to pass on the message that God has for His people.

John Stott suggests that "the essence of Paul's argument is seen if we put his six verbs in the opposite order: Christ sends heralds; heralds preach; people hear; hearers believe; believers call; and those who call are saved" (Stott, p. 286). With that line of logic the apostle lays the foundation for Christian evangelism and mission.

And who is to be evangelized? Both Jews and Gentiles. But given the context in Romans 9-11, Paul undoubtedly aimed these verses at the Jews, a conclusion reinforced by a string of quotations that he utilizes for the rest of chapter 10.

The first, a loose paraphrase of Isaiah 52:7, notes the beauty of the feet of those who proclaim "good news of good things" (Rom. 10:15). In its original setting that comforting passage refers to the certainty of Israel's return from the Babylonian captivity. Paul now applies it to his gospel of freedom from the captivity of sin. Implied in his usage of the passage is the idea that if people rejoiced at the good news of release from the Babylonian exile, they should do it much more in the light of the gospel message.

A person in a modern culture wonders why it was the feet that were "beautiful." That idea would have stumped no one in Paul's time. Good news traveled by the feet of the messengers themselves.

Romans 10:16, citing Isaiah 53:1, points out the fact that even though good news arrives, not everyone will believe it. That was true in both the ministries of Jesus and Paul. Most of the people they preached to never became followers of Christ.

But rejection does not mean that people should stop telling the gospel story. After all, Paul notes in Romans 10:17, "faith comes from hearing . . . the word of Christ."

But, the apostle asks in verse 18, did the Jews really hear, did they have a fair chance to listen to the gospel message? Perhaps the reason that not many of them accepted it (see verse 18) is that they never really heard it in the first place. Not so, exclaims Paul, quoting Psalm 19:4 to prove his points. "Their voice goes into all the earth, their words to the ends of the world" (NIV). He selected that psalm because it spoke of worldwide witness to God. What he did was to transfer the forceful language about global witness from God's physical creation to the church, viewing the former as symbolic of the latter.

> ### A "Beautiful Feet" Thought
>
> Have you thought much lately about the "feet" that brought you the good news of salvation? Whoever it was, why not return the blessing today? Write them a card or give them a call expressing how much you have appreciated their ministry in your life. Who knows, your card or call may prove to be a blessing to them just when they need it most. Then your feet will be beautiful too.

The plain fact is that the message of the gospel had spread to the far corners of the Jewish world. Jewish pilgrims from all over it filled Jerusalem both at the Passover crucifixion and the day of Pentecost. Certainly a fair percentage of them heard the big news (or the juicy gossip) and took reports home with them. Thus the gospel story had indeed gone "into all the earth, . . . to the ends of the inhabited world" (Rom. 10:18).

"OK," we hear Paul's readers mutter to themselves, "we agree that the Jews had at least heard the gospel. But maybe they didn't understand. Wouldn't that explain the reason for their unbelief?"

Once again Paul rejects the claims of his detractors. In the process, he not only asserts that the Jews understood, but in Romans 10:19, 20 he presents two texts to prove it.

The first comes from Deuteronomy 32:21, in which God says that He will transfer His favor to another people because of Israel's rebellion and disobedience. That will force the Jewish nation to become jealous of a people that was "not a nation" and lacked the understanding possessed by Israel.

The idea in the Deuteronomy passage is that when Israel saw what was happening among the Gentiles it would provoke them into securing some of the blessing for itself. Paul, or course, is implying that if that is true in the political realm, it is also the case in the spiritual realm.

After all, the Jewish people did not lack knowledge. We might describe the Gentiles as "a nation without understanding," but the Jews had the law, the covenant, and a knowledge of God's ways (Rom. 9:4, 5). Given their spiritual advantages, they should have been angry that they were losing their blessing. Paul, of course, was applying that ancient lesson to the Jews in Rome who needed to be aroused to their need as they witnessed disproportionately large numbers of Gentiles flowing into the Christian community in Rome.

Having presented Moses as a witness against the excuse that many Jews hadn't accepted the gospel because they hadn't understood it, Paul summons Isaiah in Romans 10:20, who is even more forceful in making the apostle's point. If Moses had cut off any valid plea for ignorance on the part of the Jews and set the stage for the inclusion of the Gentiles, Isaiah is bolder yet for incorporating them into the covenant promises.

From the first part of Isaiah 65:1, Paul quotes:

"I revealed myself to those who did not ask for me;"

"I was found by those who did not seek me" (NIV).

The context in Isaiah contrasts God's active seeking after the Gentiles to the failure of the Jews to respond to His grace, so much so that they "provoke" Him with their rebellion in religious things (Isa. 65:1b-3).

> **An Important Lesson From Isaiah 65**
>
> God's people in every age can learn much about their present situation by reviewing how God has dealt with His people and His church in its past history.

Paul is telling the Jews that they don't know their own history. If they think that they are the only people that God cares for because they are Abraham's children, then they need to go back and read Isaiah 65.

With Romans 10:21 Paul concludes the issue he raised in verse 16 as to why not all the Jews had accepted the gospel. It wasn't because they hadn't heard (verse 18). Nor was it because they didn't understand (verses 19, 20). Their real problem was that they were "disobedient and contrary" or "obstinate" (NIV). Citing Isaiah 65:2 the apostle demonstrates that God had repeatedly reached out His hands to the Israelites. He had played the part of the parent, "inviting a child to come home, offering a hug and a kiss, and promising a welcome" (Stott, p. 289).

Not only had God taken the initiative in extending His hand to Israel, but He did so "all day long" (Rom. 10:21, NIV), symbolizing the persistent nature of His care for them. But, Isaiah points out, they had been just as determined to reject God's repeated overtures as He had been in caring for them. Thus He defined them as "obstinate" people.

We need to take the passage that we have been studying in Romans 10:14-21 in its context. Romans 1-8 find Paul setting forth his gospel as being for both Jews and Gentiles. But not many Jews had accepted it. That led Paul into a major discussion of why the Jews had failed and, on the other hand, how the Gentiles had found entrance into the covenant promises. Chapter 9 set forth the answer to those issues in terms of God's mercy. He chose to offer mercy to all who would accept it. Chapter 10 then examined the issue in terms of Israel's response to the gospel. By and large, it had not been positive. The apostle will conclude his treatment of the Jewish rejection of the gospel in chapter 11.

44. The Remnant Chosen by Grace

Romans 11:1-10

^{1}I say then, surely God did not reject His people? May it never be! For I also am an Israelite, a descendant of Abraham, of the tribe of Benjamin. ^{2}God did not reject His people whom He foreknew. Or do you not know what the Scripture says about Elijah, how he pleads with God against Israel? ^{3}"Lord, they have killed the prophets, they have torn down Your altars, and I alone am left, and they are seeking my life." ^{4}But what is the divine reply to him? "I have reserved for Myself seven thousand men who have not bowed the knee to Baal." ^{5}So then also in the present time a remnant chosen by grace has come into being. ^{6}But if it is by grace, it is no longer by works, for then grace would no longer be grace.

^{7}What then? What Israel is seeking it has not obtained, but the chosen obtained it, and the rest were hardened. ^{8}As it is written,

> *"God gave to them a spirit of stupor,*
> *Eyes that do not see and ears that do not hear,*
> *Until this very day."*
> *⁹And David says,*
> *"Let their table become a snare and a trap,*
> *And a stumbling block and a retribution to them.*
> *¹⁰Let their eyes be darkened to see not.*
> *And bend their backs always."*

Romans 11:1, 2 picks up the thread that Paul had begun in Romans 9:6, in which he asked if God's promises to Israel had failed in light of the fact that most of the Jewish people and their leaders had not accepted the gospel. He had ended chapter 10 by stating that the problem hadn't been with God, who had stood before them with open arms, but with the people who had rejected Him out of rebellion. Well then, one might ask, if they had spurned Him, perhaps God had done the same for them.

Paul violently rejects that suggestion. "May it never be!" (11:1) is the strongest exclamation that he could use. God does not go back on His promises (cf. Ps. 94:14).

The apostle then offers four pieces of evidence in verses 1-5 to back up his claims. The first is that Paul is himself a Jew and God had not rejected him (verse 1). That is especially significant in his case, since he had been a prominent persecutor of Christians, yet God had still welcomed him with outstretched arms. That is grace. If the Lord hadn't spurned Paul, the way was certainly open for other Jews to follow the path to the gospel that he had traveled.

The apostle's second evidence regarding God's nonrejection of the Jews was that He "foreknew" them (verse 2). To foreknow in the sense that Paul here employs it means to choose (Cranfield, *Romans*, vol. 2, p. 545). God had elected Israel to be His people in a definite way. They had been the recipients of His revelation—the law—and many blessings (Rom. 9:4, 5). Certainly He would not shut them out of the blessings of the gospel.

A historical lesson from the experience of Elijah (11:3, 4) provides Paul's third evidence that He had not rejected the Jews. The Old Testament context of that illustration is the victory Elijah had just gained over the prophets of Baal on Mount Carmel. Immediately afterward he had fled from Queen Jezebel in a state of absolute panic. Eventually he took refuge in a cave on Mount Horeb. God found the prophet there and asked why he was hiding. He replied that Israel had apostatized and that he was the only faithful one left (1 Kings 19:1-18). The Lord then told the prophet that Israel's apostasy had not been complete, that He had a remnant of 7,000 still faithful to Him. He had not rejected His people. To the contrary, He had "reserved" for Himself those who were faithful (Rom. 11:3).

The apostle's fourth evidence that God has not abandoned Israel is that there is "in the present time a remnant chosen by grace" (Rom. 11:5). Just as there had been a faithful remnant of 7,000 in Elijah's day, so there still existed one in Paul's. Such a remnant was neither a figment of his imagination nor wishful thinking. Even though the Jewish leadership and the majority of the Jewish people had not accepted the gospel, James was able to tell Paul during one of his visits to Jerusalem that "many thousands of Jews" had believed. It appears that James was referring to Jews in and around Judea (Acts 21:20, KJV). God had most certainly not rejected His people.

The Elijah Syndrome

It is easy to identify with Elijah as we glimpse the state of society and even the church. "What a mess," we are tempted to think. We can quickly conclude that we are the only one left who is truly faithful to God. But at such times we need to recognize that we don't see the big picture that God does. Just as in Elijah's day, God has a remnant in every situation, even though we might not be able to identify it from our limited and often discouraged situation. The good news is that God is alive and at work in His church in spite of its problems.

One of the more interesting words in Romans 11:5 is "remnant." The Old Testament pictures the remnant of Israel as those Israelites who had remained faithful to God. Thus there was, so to speak, an Israel within Israel. We can say the same of the church down through the ages. There has always been what Martin Luther called the visible and the invisible church. Those who hold membership in the organization represent the visible church. The invisible church consists of those who have a living "by faith" connection with God. It is the invisible church that makes up God's remnant at any given time.

The fact that God's remnant is "chosen by grace" leads the apostle into a short commentary on grace versus works in Romans 11:6 before he returns to the main flow of his argument in verses 7-10. He refuses to allow the slightest misunderstanding on that most important point, even though he had treated it earlier in his letter. Paul wants to highlight the fact that grace and works are mutually exclusive. It has to be one or the other.

Thus if a person is saved by grace, it cannot be by works, or else grace is no longer a free gift but an earned commodity or a bargain. We should note that some Greek manuscripts of lesser reliability add a second part to verse 6: If being a part of God's people is on the basis of works, then grace must be excluded. The King James Version reflects that extended reading. But the meaning is clear in both the shorter and longer readings. Grace and works are totally incompatible.

Paul loved the doctrine of grace because of what it had meant in his personal life. He knew that even though as a Pharisee he thought he was better than most people because of his accomplishments, he had failed to realize that he had a depth of sin that not only made him self-righteous, but ready to kill anybody who disagreed with him on religion. It was the extent of his sin problem that he had had to face on the road to Damascus. Paul knew that he had been saved totally by grace. Thus his emphasis.

By Romans 11:7 Paul has come to the place where he needs to summarize what he has said. What conclusion can we draw about the position of the Jewish people in the light of what he has discussed so far in Romans 9-11? Since God has not rejected His people (11:1), what exactly is their position?

His answer is that the bulk of the nation had not obtained true righteousness. It's not, he notes, that they didn't try. No other people "sought [it] so earnestly" (11:7, NIV). Their lawkeeping was truly a wonder. They had developed hundreds of rules and regulations related to the law. On Sabbathkeeping alone they had formulated some 1,520 rules. By anyone's count that constitutes earnest seeking. They wanted righteousness, Paul argues, but they had chosen the wrong route.

But not all of them, the apostle points out, fell into that pit. Some of them—whom he calls the chosen or elect—found the proper way to righteousness. The chosen were those who, realizing their helplessness in the face of sin, accepted Christ through faith. The others persued righteousness through human effort and failed.

That latter group, Paul tells us, "were hardened" (Rom. 11:7), a word meaning *"to cover with a thick skin, to harden by covering with a callous"* (Thayer, p. 559). How did they get that way? The same way Pharaoh did in Exodus, as Paul reflected upon in Romans 9:17, 18. They had become resistant, not because God had cast them away—which He had not done according to Romans 11:1—but because they did not submit to the righteousness of God. Thus when a person "persistently resists this grace, God, who will not force anyone against his will, . . . leaves man to the natural consequences of his stubborn resistance" (Nichol, vol. 6, p. 606).

One of those results is hardening—they "became callous" (Rom. 11:7, Goodspeed). Paul points to other consequences in Romans 11:8-10, such as unresponsiveness, having their blessings turn into a snare, having their spiritual eyesight dimmed, and having their backs bent under the burden of ceaseless attempts to attain righteousness by the law (see Fitzmyer, p. 607). In the light of such outcomes, it is little wonder that Paul ceaselessly offers grace not only to the Jews but to all.

45. Hope for the Jews

Romans 11:11-24

[11]*I say then, have they stumbled so as to fall? May it never be! But by their transgression salvation came to the Gentiles, so as to provoke them to jealousy.* [12]*Now if their transgression means riches for the world and their failure means riches for the Gentiles, how much more their fullness!*

[13]*Now I am speaking to you Gentiles. Inasmuch then as I am an apostle of Gentiles, I glorify my ministry,* [14]*if somehow I might provoke to jealousy those of my flesh and might save some of them.* [15]*For if their rejection brings the reconciliation of the world, what will their acceptance mean but life from the dead?* [16]*Now if the firstfruit of the dough is holy, the lump is also. And if the root is holy, the branches are also.*

[17]*But if some of the branches were broken off, and you, being a wild olive shoot, were grafted in among them and became a partaker of the rich root of the olive tree,* [18]*do not boast toward the branches. But if you do boast, remember that you do not support the root, but the root supports you.* [19]*You will say then, "Branches were broken off so that I might be*

grafted in." [20]You say well. They were broken off because of unbelief, but you stand by faith. Do not be conceited, but fear. [21]For if God did not spare the natural branches, neither will he spare you. [22]Behold then the kindness and severity of God; severity toward those who have fallen, but God's kindness toward you, if you continue in His kindness. Otherwise you also will be cut off. [23]And they also, if they do not continue in unbelief, will be grafted in, for God is able to graft them in again. [24]For if you have been cut from what is by nature a wild olive tree, and were grafted in against nature into a cultivated olive tree, how much more will these who are natural branches be grafted into their own olive tree?

It is imperative that we read Romans 11:11-24 against the problematic tensions between the Jewish and Gentile believers of the Roman church we discussed in the section of the "Introduction" titled "Founding and History of the Church at Rome." That situation is important for understanding the entire letter, but especially so for the middle verses of chapter 11. Both racial groups apparently believed that they somehow had a superior standing with God. Both were somewhat disdainful of the other. And both were united in their disunity if in nothing else. Paul has been addressing the problem since Romans 1:16, 17, leveling the field by demonstrating that no one has any room for boasting, since all have been saved in the same way—by faith in God's saving grace in Christ.

Whereas Romans 9 argued that God had a perfect right to include the Gentiles in the gospel, and chapter 10 put forward the thesis that the rejection of the Jews was not His fault but their own, Romans 11 tells us that God will save a remnant from Israel and that Israel's future salvation is a reality for those of them who believe. Thus Paul can climax his extensive treatment in chapters 9-11 with the declaration that God "may have mercy upon all" (11:32, RSV).

With Romans 11:11 the apostle raises a new question, the second one in Romans 11. In verse 1 he had asked whether God had rejected Israel. His answer was that God hadn't cast off the Jews but that most had been hardened through their persistent rebuff of His grace. Of course, not all had let themselves be spiritually calloused—a remnant had accepted the gospel (verse 5).

But the hardened condition of the majority of the Jews suggests a new question in Paul's mind: "Did they stumble so as to fall beyond recovery?"

(11:11, NIV). His answer is an explosive "No!" He will demonstrate in the rest of Romans 11 that hope still remains for his fellow Jews.

His first evidence is what we might call the chain of blessing. The God who makes all things work together for good to those who love Him (Rom. 8:28) has caused something good to come out of the Jewish refusal to accept the gospel. Because of their failure, the gospel went to the Gentiles, who accepted it more readily (11:11).

The book of Acts repeatedly reflects that fact. There the apostles first preached to the Jews in new locations. But when the Jews rejected Paul's message he went to the Gentiles, who often accepted it. That of course stirred up the Jews. Paul's hope in verse 11 is that they will stay stirred up ("provoked"), look into the blessings the Gentiles have found in the gospel, and in turn accept it themselves.

And what a blessing it would be if they did. "For if [Israel's] failure has so enriched the world, and their defection proved such a benefit to the gentiles, think what tremendous advantages their fulfilling of God's plan could mean" (11:12, Phillips). Their inclusion would mean an even greater blessing to the world than if the Gentiles alone accepted it. Thus Paul sees even greater days for the spread of the gospel message if the Jews would participate in the evangelistic outreach of the Christian community.

Romans 11:13-16 continue on the chain of blessing argument with its "holy envy" aspects, concluding with the assertion that "if the firstfruit of the dough is holy, the lump is also. And if the root is holy, the branches are also." The first illustration in verse 16 originates in Numbers 15:17-21. Paul notes that when people offer flour as a holy firstfruit offering from their grain crop, the bread made from that holy flour will also be sacred. The second illustration comes from agriculture and compares Israel to a tree. If the tree's root is holy, then so will be any shoots from that tree. In both examples he appears to be referring to the patriarchs, especially Abraham. If they were holy, that would have an effect on the latest branches in the Jewish line of descent.

In Romans 11:17-24 Paul expands on the metaphor of the holy tree of verse 16. Here, however, he identifies it as an olive tree. The olive tree was not only one of the most common and most useful trees in the Near East, but the Old Testament had repeatedly employed it as a symbol of Israel. Jeremiah 11:16, for example, notes that God had once called Israel "a green olive tree, fair with goodly fruit" (RSV). For the purpose of Paul's illustration in Romans 11, it is of interest that the Jeremiah passage goes on to predict that God would send a great tempest and set fire to that tree, "and its branches will be consumed" (RSV).

Parallel with Jeremiah, some of the branches in Paul's tree were "broken off." But all was not lost, since many Gentiles had been grafted in (Rom. 11:17). But that blessing could become problematic if the branches foreign to the tree developed an arrogant attitude toward the original Jewish branches (verse 18). The Gentiles needed to remember that they had nothing to boast about since their faith was in actuality rooted in Judaism. Or as William Barclay points out, *"there would have been no such thing as Christianity unless there had been Judaism first"* (Barclay, *Romans*, p. 161).

Romans 11:19, 20 hits at the heart of Paul's presentation, since it deals with who can belong to the olive tree of the kingdom and who cannot. It is meaningful that no article appears before the word "branches" in verse 19, signifying that not all of the Israelites had been broken off but just some of them so that some Gentiles might be grafted in.

But the crucial questions are: On what basis are some Israelites broken off while others remain in the tree? And on what basis are some Gentiles grafted in while others continue in their natural state?

The answers to those questions take us to the heart of Paul's gospel and to the very secret for the revival of Israel as being like a resurrection from the dead (verse 15) that the apostle so fervently hopes for in Romans 11. Paul comes right to the point. According to verse 20, those on the olive tree (whether they be Jews or Gentiles) are those who have faith. Those not on the tree, either because they have not been grafted in (Gentiles) or because they were broken off (Jews), Paul characterized as having "unbelief."

Thus he pushes home the same lesson that he did in the first few chapters of Romans. That is, there is only one way to be saved—to have faith in Jesus Christ as Savior and Lord.

That thought brings us to the last word of verse 20—"fear." "Fear what?" we might ask. Fear the result of spiritual pride and arrogance (verse 18) because we Gentiles have been saved but the Jews have not (verse 21). Those individuals who maintain that type of racial prejudice will find that the "kind" God can also be "severe" enough to prune them from the tree of salvation (verse 22).

Paul is far from teaching the doctrine of once saved always saved. C. E. B. Cranfield suggests that the clause about being cut off "is a warning against a false and unevangelical sense of security" (Cranfield, *Romans*, vol. 2, p. 570).

But if he is not teaching once saved always saved, neither is he proposing once lost always lost. The apostle makes that clear in verse 23, in which he notes that if Jews come to Him in faith "God is able to graft them in again." And if that happens, there is every evidence that they will flourish second to none in the Christian tree (verse 24).

A Lesson on "Holy Fear"

C. K. Barrett writes that "the proper attitude for the Gentile Christian, as indeed for any Christian, is 'reverent fear,' for he must recognize that there is in himself absolutely nothing which can secure his position with God. The moment he begins to grow boastful he ceases to have faith (humble dependence upon God), and therefore himself becomes a candidate for 'cutting off'" (Barrett, p. 218).

46. There's a Wideness in God's Mercy

Romans 11:24-36

[25]*For I do not want you to be ignorant of this mystery, brothers (lest you be wise in human wisdom), that a partial hardening has happened to Israel until the fullness of the Gentiles comes in,* [26]*and so all Israel will be saved; as it is written,*

"The Deliverer will come out of Zion,
He will remove ungodliness from Jacob."
[27]*"And this is My covenant with them,*
When I take away their sins."

[28]*As regards the gospel, they are enemies because of you, but in regard to election they are beloved because of the fathers.* [29]*For the free gifts and the calling of God are irrevocable.* [30]*For just as you once disobeyed God, but now you have received mercy because of their disobedience,* [31]*so also these now have been disobedient in order that, by the mercy shown to you, they also may now receive mercy.* [32]*For God has shut up all in disobedience so that He might show mercy to all.*

> [33] *O the depth of the riches of the wisdom and knowledge of God! How unsearchable His judgments and incomprehensible His ways!*
> [34] *"For who has known the mind of the Lord,*
> *or who has become His counselor?"*
> [35] *"Or who has first given to Him,*
> *that it might be repaid to him?"*
> [36] *Because from Him and through Him and to Him are all things. To Him be the glory forever. Amen.*

When reading these verses we must always keep in mind the tensions between the Jewish and Gentile Christians in Rome. In Romans 11:25 we find Paul still speaking to the Gentiles. Apparently some of them had concluded that the Jews as a people were beyond hope. They had rejected the gospel, and it had passed to the Gentiles. Thus God had abandoned the Jewish people and chosen the Gentiles. That is exactly the kind of boastful pride that Paul now opposes (see, e.g., 11:18).

He is quite straightforward that a part of Israel (actually most of Israel) had become hardened. But that did not mean that God had closed the door to them. Paul personally, in fact, had great hopes for Israel. While it was true that at that time Gentiles were predominant in the church, no one should count the Jewish people out. The apostle went on to say that "all Israel will be saved" (11:26).

That phrase has caused a great deal of discussion. But it does not stand alone in chapter 11, which later notes that God will have mercy on "all" people (verse 32). What did Paul mean by "all" in such places? One thing is certain—God will never force anyone to be saved. Paul has been arguing all the way through Romans that salvation is a choice that requires accepting God's gift of grace, and that it is against God's values to impose His gift on anyone. The apostle is not teaching universalism (i.e., the doctrine that every human being will ultimately be saved).

As to "all Israel" being saved, Paul has already expressed his hope that "some" of the Jewish people might be saved (verse 14). It seems evident that he believed that many would continue to reject all efforts to save them. And in verse 5 Paul had raised the concept of a faithful remnant of Jews from within the nation who had accepted the gospel. Building on the remnant idea and the realization that even though salvation comes from God it still needs a faith response, all those Jews who will have accepted Christ throughout the Christian Era will constitute the "all Israel" who will be saved. That conclusion lines up with similar Jewish uses of "all" in the *Mishna*. Thus Sanhedrin 10:1 declares that "all Israelites have a share in the world to come," but then goes on to exclude Sadducees, heretics, and others.

Romans 11:28 notes that even though the majority of the Jewish nation were enemies of the gospel in part because of its Gentile adherents, they were still a nation loved of God because of His covenant beginning with the patriarchs. Just because the bulk of the Jewish nation had spurned the gospel offer through Jesus does not mean that God had rejected them (Rom. 11:1). Those Jews who had rebuffed His offer of grace may have become His enemies, but God still loved them and desired their salvation. He hasn't forgotten the gifts (such as sonship, the covenants, and the law [9:4, 5]) that He gave them, nor His call to make them His special people (11:29). The Lord still offers them mercy on the same basis that He extends it to the Gentiles, in spite of all that they had done to block the spread of the gospel and to destroy it (verses 30-32).

That thought brings us to Romans 11:32: "For God has shut up all in disobedience so that He might show mercy to all." Who are the "all?" Some, as we noted above, have concluded that the "all" implies that every person who has ever lived will eventually be saved. But such an interpretation ignores the context of the New Testament. In Romans itself Paul has taught that there will come a day of "wrath and fury" against the obstinate (Rom. 2:5, 8, 9, RSV). His position is in line with that of Jesus, who repeatedly distinguished between those taken to the kingdom and those left in outer darkness (Matt. 25:31-46; 7:13-27).

As in so many passages, it is the context that supplies the answer to what Paul meant by "all." From Romans 1:16 on he has been arguing that all, both Jew and Gentile, had sinned and that both could be justified by faith in the gospel. Then, beginning in chapter 9, he relates in a highly detailed way how God would have mercy on both groups because of His sovereign choice to do so. Now in Romans 11:30-32 Paul sums up his argument of chapters 9-11. Just as both groups have been disobedient, so both can receive God's mercy. Thus he does not have in mind every individual when he says "all," but rather the sense of both Jew and Gentile. The only way to salvation for either group is through God's mercy and grace.

In painting his picture of mercy for all, the apostle in verse 22 compares disobedience to a dungeon in which all people have been "shut up" or incarcerated. This prison is so secure that "they have no possibility of escape except as God's mercy releases them" (Cranfield, *Romans* vol. 2, p. 587). Such is the magnitude of divine mercy.

> **Thank God for Mercy**
>
> - *Mercy for all* is the central theme of the book of Romans.
> - *Mercy for all* is the triumph of God's grace over the prison house of sin.
> - *Mercy for all* is open to every man, woman, or child who has ever lived.
> - *Mercy for all* is our only hope.

John Brunt helps us envision the breadth of God's gift when he wrote that "God's plan is to save not only all Israel [verse 25], but all, period [verse 32]." While "it is true that God will not violate human freedom and force us to be saved against our will, . . . it is also true that His tenacious commitment to have mercy on *all* goes far beyond our wildest imagination" (Brunt, p. 202). Truly there is a wideness in God's mercy.

With "mercy for all" Paul concludes his unparalleled treatment of the plan of salvation. Step by step for 11 chapters he has guided his readers through the universality of sin (1:18-3:20), God's salvation in justification by faith (3:21-5:21), the way in which Christians should live their lives (6:1-8:39) and how both Jews and Gentiles are on equal ground when it comes to divine mercy (9:1-11:32).

The apostle has covered a great deal of territory. Now he has reached the mountaintop. As the Swiss commentator F. L. Godet notes: "Like a traveler who has reached the summit of an alpine ascent, the apostle turns and contemplates. Depths are at his feet; but waves of light illumine them, and there spreads all around an immense horizon which his eye commands" (Godet, p. 416).

As Paul views the plan of salvation, he sets forth a mighty doxology in Romans 11:33-36. All he can do is praise God for all that He has done. Ordinary speech won't do. The majesty of what God has done leaves the apostle awestruck. "O the depth of the riches of the wisdom and knowledge of God! How unsearchable His judgments and incomprehensible His ways!" (verse 33).

Riches is an important word to Paul. He never ceases his wonder of God's "unsearchable riches" (see Rom. 2:4; 9:23; 10:12; Eph. 2:4; 3:8).

The dominant thought in Paul's theology is that God, who has riches in Christ undreamed of, has chosen to pour out His treasures on human beings who have not the slightest legal claim to them. The wonder of God's generosity never ceases to amaze the apostle. How God could take a miserable persecutor of the church such as himself and shower him with blessings, including that of salvation, left him with nothing but praise, awe, and wonderment.

Romans 11:34 and 35 present quotations from Isaiah 40:13 (LXX) and Job 41:11 emphasizing the profundity and inscrutability of God's wisdom and the fact that humans can never give to God, but only receive His free gifts. And the chapter closes with a statement of why we are dependent upon God ("all comes from him, all lives by him, all ends in him" [verse 36, Moffatt] and an ascription to Him. "To Him be the glory forever. Amen." It is because God is the source of everything (including mercy) that all glory belongs to Him alone.

In short, no room exists for human pride or for some people thinking themselves as better than others. Pride is behaving as if we were God, or, as someone put it, "strutting around the earth as if we owned the place, repudiating our due dependence on God, pretending instead that all things depend on us, and thus abrogating to ourselves the glory which belongs to God alone." Thus pride is the apex of the anti-God approach to life.

With that in mind, it is easy to see why Paul has been so concerned with boasting thus far in Romans: both the wrongness of boasting in our human efforts at salvation (2:17, 23; 3:27; 4:2), and the rightness of boasting in what God has done for us in Christ on the cross (4:20; 5:2).

All glory belongs to God above. That is the theological conclusion that flows out of Romans 1-11. But it is also the devotional conclusion. We praise God because we know the truth of what He has done in us.

Part VI

Living God's Love

Romans 12:1-15:13

47. Transformed Living

Romans 12:1, 2

> *¹Therefore I urge you, brothers, through the mercies of God, to offer your bodies as a living sacrifice, holy and acceptable to God, which is your spiritual worship. ²And do not be conformed to this world, but be transformed by the renewing of your mind, so that you may discern what the will of God is, what is good and acceptable and perfect.*

Therefore" is an important word in Romans 12:1. Here it signals that Paul is not only changing topics but that the new topic is directly related to his previous discussion in the first 11 chapters of Romans.

Thus far in Romans the apostle has covered five topics progressively. Romans 1:1-17 acquainted us with Paul, his mission, and the recipients of his letter. Romans 1:18-3:20 put us into contact with the depth and breadth of the problem of sin. In the process Paul told us that *all*—both Jews and Gentiles—have sinned and are under condemnation. Romans 3:21-5:21 provided a grand tour of God's remedy for the sin problem through the cross of Christ and our acceptance of Christ's righteousness by faith. Romans 6:1-8:39 took us into the way of godliness, what it means to walk with Jesus in the principles of God. And Romans 9:1-11:36 showed us how *all*—both Jews and Gentiles—fit into God's program of "mercy upon all" (11:32).

"Therefore" in Romans 12:1 signals the beginning of the next step in Paul's explanation of what it means to be saved. He has completed setting forth his theology. Now he is ready for its ethical implications in daily life. The "therefore" indicates that the issue of how we live is dependent upon what we believe. First comes salvation, then the response to salvation, a pattern that Paul develops in many of his letters. Those to the Galatians and Ephesians are excellent examples.

While we might correctly think of living the Christian life as an issue of progressive sanctification, Leon Morris provides a provocative idea when he writes that "in a way we can say that here Paul is still concerned with justification by faith, for it is fundamental to him that the justified man does not live in the same way as the unrepentant sinner. 'Faith expressing itself through love' (Gal. 5:6) is the kind of faith of which he has been writing" (Morris, *Romans*, p. 431). The apostle raised that issue in Romans 6-8 as the only possible result of a person's being raised to "newness of life" (Rom. 6:4), but now he is ready to devote three chapters (12:1-15:13) almost exclusively to the topic.

He is now ready to talk about the great sub theme with which he brackets the entire letter: "the obedience that comes from faith" (Rom. 1:5; 16:26, NIV). For Paul, theology always precedes ethics, salvation must go before behavior. People walk with Christ in God's law because they have already been saved. To the apostle, the order is fundamental. All too many seek to obey without being saved first. The end result is legalism, meanness, spiritual pride, and lostness.

> ### Legalism Versus Sanctified Obedience
>
> "The legalist says something like 'Do these things and you will live,' but Paul is saying 'Live and you will do these things'" (Morris, *Romans*, p. 431).

Romans 12:1 contains several key words and phrases pregnant with meaning for Christian living. The first is "brothers" or "brothers and sisters" (NRSV). Paul now moves beyond the distinction of Jews and Gentiles—of natural branches and grafted branches (11:17-24)—that has occupied him for the previous three chapters. He will now address all believers as part of the family of God. All, no matter what their race or ethnic origin, are a part of that family and have the duty of living God's love and of treating one another as brothers and sisters.

The second key word is "mercies," one that takes us back to Romans 1-11 and especially to 11:32. God expects us to live His love because of His mercies that have united us in one faith.

The third word, surprising to some, is "bodies." No Greek would have put it that way. To them the body was a prison to leave behind for a spiritual/mental existence. But not so with Christianity. A Christian's body is important. The temple of the Holy Spirit (1 Cor. 6:19), God will resurrect it at the last day (1 Cor. 15). Holy living includes not only how we live in the mental/spiritual realm (Rom. 12:2), but also how we live as physical beings (verse 1).

The fourth key phrase is "living sacrifice." At first it sounds like a contradiction in terms. After all, a sacrifice was something that people in Paul's day took to a temple to be slain in a ritual manner. To suggest that Christians should be living sacrifices is a vivid piece of imagery.

I have often thought that it might be easier to die for Christ than to live for Him. After all, as difficult as dying might be, it is only necessary to wind up your courage once. Then it's all over. But being a living sacrifice means dedication to Christ every day for the rest of my life. And that, according to Paul and Jesus, means a continuous crucifixion of my willful self (Matt. 16:24, 25; 1 Cor. 15:31). It calls for a ceaseless offering of all that I am and all that I have to God. We must have daily grace to live the life of a living sacrifice.

But that kind of life, Paul hastens to add in a fifth key phrase, is "spiritual worship" or a "spiritual act of worship" (NIV) or "reasonable service" (KJV) or "intelligent worship" (Phillips) and is the only possible response when we realize what God has done for us in Christ. Here Paul utilizes an adjective of "rich complexity" that has several important ideas in it (Leenhardt, p. 303). But William Barclay helps us catch the essence of the phrase when he writes that "when Christ becomes the centre of life then we can offer the real worship, which is the offering of every moment and every action of life to God" (Barclay, *Romans*, p. 171).

"Transformed" is the word that jumps off the page in Romans 12:2. An interesting word, it comes from two Greek words, the first meaning "across" and the second from "form." Thus to be transformed "means to change across from one form to another" (Earle, p. 199). We use the word in English as "metamorphosis."

And what is "metamorphosis"? It is the biological process by which a slug-like caterpillar becomes a butterfly. That is one of the most graphic illustrations of what happens to a person when he or she meets Jesus. God finds us in our self-centered, proud, and self-serving ways, and then totally changes us. God wants to take a slug like me and teach me to fly. The Lord transforms drab crawling creatures and paints them in beautiful hues and gives them wings. Now, that is a miracle! Perhaps it's the greatest of all miracles.

> ## Transformation in Daily Living
>
> "Transformation is no magic change effected whilst men sleep. It is a commandment which we have to brace ourselves to perform, day by day to set ourselves to the task of more completely assimilating ourselves to our Lord. It comes to be a solemn question for each of us whether we can say, 'To-day I am liker Jesus Christ than I was yesterday; to-day the truth which renews the mind has a deeper hold upon me than it ever had before" (MacLaren, p. 236).

And the good news is that God can do it in our lives. He wants to make us like Him in character. Not only does He desire to change us into something we are not, He longs to develop us into new creatures after the image of Jesus.

Paul isn't the only one to speak of transformation. Jesus described it as being born again (John 3:3, 5). Then again, Paul tells us in 2 Corinthians 5:17 that Christians are "new creatures." They are not only transformed but they refused to "be conformed to this world." The word I translated as "world" actually means "age" or "time" in the Greek. But the idea is the same. To be conformed to the age in which we live is to be conformed to the world and its values. But according to the apostle that should never be. God's command is "transformation" rather than "conformation." J. B. Phillips' translation of Romans 12:2 is helpful in catching Paul's meaning: "Don't let the world around you squeeze you into its mould, but let God re-make you so that your whole attitude of mind is changed. Thus you will prove in practice that the will of God" is good.

Karl Barth refers to becoming a Christian as "the great disturbance," since "human behaviour must inevitably be disturbed by the thought of God" (Barth, p. 424). Becoming a Christian changes every aspect of people's lives. The Christian value system opposes that of the world. Thus it is impossible for the Christian to conform to the values and lifestyles of the present age. God has transformed a Christian's mind, and he or she lets that new mind guide each and every activity. It is to the various realms of Christian activity that Paul turns to in Romans 12:3-15:13 as he applies the gospel of transformation to everyday living.

48. Lesson Number 1 in Transformed Living: Using God's Gifts

Romans 12:3-8

³For through the grace given to me I say to everyone among you not to think more highly of himself than he ought to think, but to think so as to be reasonable, each as God has apportioned a measure of faith. ⁴For just as in one body we have many members, and all the members do not have the same function, ⁵so we, though many, are one body in Christ, and individually members of one another. ⁶And we have gifts that differ according to the grace given to us. [Let us use them]: if prophecy, in proportion to faith; ⁷if ministry, in service; if teaching, in instructing; ⁸if encouraging, in providing encouragement; the giver, in generosity; the leader, in diligence; the compassionate, in cheerfulness.

Romans 12, 13, and 14 are intimately connected to the admonition in Romans 12:2 to live the transformed life. The word "for" signals that connection to verses 3-8. As Thomas Schreiner puts it, "the exhortations in verses 3-8 flow out of the call for total commitment to God expressed in verses 1-2 and describe more correctly and practically the nature of that commitment" (Schreiner, p. 650). The same applies to the sections of Romans that follow verses 3-8. All of them deal with lessons in transformed living.

Lesson number one in living the transformed life, the "living sacrifice" (verse 1) kind of life, is that people need to have a correct estimate of themselves in the context of the church and its ministries. And that lesson was crucial for the church at Rome. After all, they were not only split along racial and ethnic lines (Jew and Gentile), but, being a normal human population, they had differences in talent, position, and function that could easily lead to unhealthy attitudes and ways of relating (or not relating) to one another, all to the detriment of the church. Of course, those problems of difference were not unique to the Roman congregations in the first century. They have the same implications for our day.

The real need of the church in Paul's day and ours is not only to recognize our differences, but to put them to use in such a manner that will not only lead to unity in the church but provide a positive blessing. It is in that context that we must examine Paul's discussion of God's gifts in Romans 12:3-8.

The first point that he stresses in these verses is that we should each have a correct estimate of ourselves. Unfortunately, thinking too highly of ourselves seems to come with the baggage of being human. As James Denney notes, everybody in the church requires counsel on this topic because "to himself, every man is in a sense the most important person in the world, and it always needs much grace to see what other people are, and to keep a sense of moral proportion" between ourselves and them (Denney, "Romans," p. 689).

According to Paul in verse 3, Christians can no longer think of themselves in the proud way they did before they came to Christ. They can no longer conform (verse 2) to that worldly pattern, but must let God through His Spirit transform them to a genuine Christian humility. After all, what do we have to be proud about? Paul has already demonstrated that all are sinners and that every one of us is alive and has salvation only because of God's mercy (11:32) extended through the gift of grace. No person in that context has even the slightest pretext for pride in anything.

Yet Christians are still human beings in which sin remains even if it no longer reigns (Rom. 7). They will therefore find themselves tempted to be proud even about the gifts that God has given them despite the fact that they come through no merit of their own. "The danger," Ernest Best points out, "is that they will be so thrilled with [those gifts] that they will become *conceited* and not use them for the good of all, but to gather the admiration of others. So, taking up the idea of the renewal of their 'minds' (verse 2), Paul warns them to *think* soberly about themselves" (Best, p. 141).

A second lesson that Romans 12:3-8 teaches is the need for unity in diversity. "For just as in one body we have many members, and all the members do not have the same function, so we, though many, are one body in Christ, and individually members of one another" (verses 4, 5).

Those verses highlight two aspects of the Christian community. One is unity. Being a Christian means becoming a part of the body of Christ. Thus when people become connected to Christ they also have a relationship to one another. That is why Christians often refer to each other as brother and sister. They have all been adopted into the family of God (Rom. 8:14-17).

The immediate environment in which the "family" operates is the church. Paul in such letters as the one to the Ephesians characterized the church as the body of Christ (Eph. 5:23). From his perspective, the church is a unity that he can describe as a functional body (cf. 1 Cor. 12:12-31).

Romans 12:4, 5 not only emphasizes unity, but also diversity among the various members. Not all members have the same role. The church may be one in purpose, but the various members each make a different contribution, depending on their special gifts.

Thus the plurality of the members leads to the health of the church as a body. Both unity and diversity are important at every level of the church. A church in which everyone had my temperament and talents would be a pretty boring place. It would also be quite ineffective. Part of the message of Romans 12:3-8 is that Christians need to value both the unity that they share with other believers *and* the diversity that makes the church effective. Of course, that unity, if it is to be healthy, must be in Christ.

Unity in diversity was an important message to the Romans. After all, being located at the crossroads of the empire, the church in Rome comprised many ethnicities and races beyond the major Jewish and Gentile categories. The members needed to learn both how to work together and at the same time how to utilize their differences to increase their effectiveness in reaching out to the community around them. The same challenges face the church in the twenty-first century. One of its greatest needs today is to maximize the beneficial effects of both its diversity and unity.

Romans 12:6 notes the fact that God has given different spiritual gifts to various individuals. The only thing that their gifts have in common is that they all are blessings of grace. Thus they do not reflect on the "value" of one person above another. All of us, no matter what our gifts, are equal in God's sight as sinners whom He has saved through no merit of our own. But He has not only saved each Christian through grace, but also gifted each through grace.

Verses 6b–8 go on to list seven gifts. Some, such as prophesying, seem more glamorous than others. Those others may have less prestige but they are equally important. But given the way people get puffed up about who they think they are, it is no wonder that when he discussed the gifts Paul included an admonition for persons not to think more highly than they ought of themselves. As Jesus told us, the sad fact is that people even get proud about giving or how well they think they have prayed (Matt. 6:1-8). The problem of people in the church comparing their gifts with others also came up in 1 Corinthians, in which Paul told them that nothing truly mattered if they didn't have genuine love for one another (1 Cor. 12:12-13:2).

Beyond prophecy, Paul lists six other gifts in Romans 12:3-8: serving, teaching, encouraging, giving, leading, and being compassionate. Most of those gifts find their meaning in the everyday life of the church and its surrounding community. They are not exotic but regular duties.

The great danger is that we as Christians will not utilize the gifts that God has given us. That is why Paul specifically urges the use of each one in verses 6b-8. It is all too easy to be a spectator in the struggles of life and, so to speak, sit on our gifts rather than be a participant. God's command to both the Romans and to us is to get off of our gift and let God use it and ourselves to His glory.

Perhaps it is not an accident that the last word in Paul's list of gifts is "cheerfulness." Nothing is as unappealing as cheerless, dour persons who are just "doing their duty." While the word "cheerfulness" in Romans 12:8 refers specifically to showing mercy, it is important in the use of all the gifts. God wants us to serve Him with a smile on our face.

49. Lesson Number 2 in Transformed Living: Loving One Another

Romans 12:9–16

> *⁹Let your love be without hypocrisy. Despise evil. Cling to the good. ¹⁰Tenderly love one another with brotherly love, outdoing one another in honor. ¹¹Be not lazy in zeal, but fervent in spirit, serving the Lord. ¹²Rejoice in hope, be patient in tribulation, persevere in prayer. ¹³Contribute to the needs of the saints, eagerly pursuing hospitality.*

¹⁴Bless those persecuting you; bless and do not curse. ¹⁵Rejoice with those who rejoice. Weep with those who weep. ¹⁶Be of the same mind toward one another. Do not be haughty in mind, but be willing to associate with the lowly. Do not become conceited.

With verse 9 we have come to Paul's second lesson in transformed living and one of the central words in his vocabulary—love. Just as in 1 Corinthians 12 and 13, Paul moves from the topic of spiritual gifts (Rom. 12:6-8) to that of love. Again, in Galatians 5:22 he put "love" first in his list of the fruit of the Spirit. Beginning with Romans 12:9 Paul begins to spell out what it means to live the life of love. That task will carry him through Romans 15:13.

Up to the present passage in Romans we have seen love demonstrated on the cross (5:8), poured into our hearts (5:5), and persistently refusing to let us go (8:35, 39). But now Paul begins to spell out the meaning of love for Christian discipleship. As John Stott notes, "Romans 12-15 are a sustained exhortation to let love govern and shape all our relationships" (Stott, p. 330).

> "As the new relationship to God can be summed up in the one word faith, so the new relationship to men can be summarized in the one word love" (Brunner, Romans, p. 106).

The first characteristic of love set forth in Romans 12:9 is that it is "without hypocrisy." The Greek word for hypocrites signified play actors who wore masks to cover their true identity. That is, they were not their real selves. But love, as verse 9 points out, is always sincere and transparent. Having been cleansed of it's focus on itself, Christian love aims, as Paul brings out, to give more than it receives.

That transformed love both despises evil and clings to the good (Rom. 12:9). The apostle uses forceful Greek words in that description. "Despises" indicates "a strong feeling of horror" (Sanday, p. 360) while "cling" derives from a word meaning "glue." Thus Christian love is not a moderate love. It hates and is repulsed by those things that destroy the quality of human life (i.e., evil) and is "cemented securely to what is right" (Earle, p. 201). When a life is truly infused with God's love it will not be just partially transformed but totally.

Such a complete change will revolutionize all human relationships. It will, Paul tells us in Romans 12:10, lead us to "tenderly love one another with brotherly love, outdoing one another in honor." That spirit was definitely needed in the Roman church with its major divisions between Jews and Gentiles and with some thinking of themselves as better than others because of their special gifts (verses 3-8).

Paul goes out of his way in verse 10 to utilize family terms to highlight the need of the Romans (and all the rest of us) to truly care for one another. Thus the word he twice uses in that verse to express love (*phile*) highlights both family tenderness and a family connection. Christians, he is telling us, love each other because they belong to one family. They have God as their Father and are thereby brothers and sisters in the Lord. Thus "the Christian Church is not a collection of acquaintances; it is not even a gathering of friends; it is a family in God" (Barclay, *Romans*, p. 177).

That being so, the church's members need to live out their family love, lest they fall into that insincere "love" that Paul spoke of in Romans 12:9. Part of living out that love is "outdoing one another in honor" (verse 10), a phrase translated from an expression meaning to "*consider better*" or "*esteem more highly*" (Bauer, p. 869). Thus the sense of the passage is that Christians should honor and esteem other church members more than themselves. Such a way of relating would have definitely reduced the racial tensions and the feelings of superiority (Rom. 12:3-8) that had led to disharmony in the Roman church. Of course, such an attitude could also help in twenty-first century congregations.

Romans 12:11, 12 goes on to lay out six more descriptions of Christian love. First, it will not lack in zeal. Love is enthusiastic rather than sluggish. That is true of human love. I remember courting my wife. I had a hard time just walking in her direction. I wanted to run and shout and give her a big hug!

Thus, secondly, love is "fervent in spirit." "Fervent" comes from a word meaning to boil, seethe, or bubble. A zealous love boils over and is irrepressible. Christianity is no back-burner affair. The Holy Spirit infuses the human spirit with ardent zeal. The person indwelt by the Spirit of God is one desperately in earnest.

That fervency expresses itself in "serving the Lord," characteristic number 3 of the Christian love Paul describes in verse 11. The word "serve" (actually "slave") takes us back to the second word in the Greek text of Romans, which tells us that Paul was God's slave. And so is every Christian. We are not slaves from fear, but from love, a love that impels us to serve the One who has given everything for us, a love that burns within and is shaped by zeal, a love that flows out to other members in the family of God.

For a Christian, serving Christ is not an irksome duty but a joyful privilege. That thought brings us to Paul's fourth characteristic of love: it rejoices in hope (Rom. 12:12). Hope is a key word in Paul's theology. Not only do Christian's have hope because of their salvation, but they await "the blessed hope" of full redemption at the end of earth's history (Titus 2:13). A hopeless Christian is a contradiction in terms. "Hope-full" (i.e., "full of hope") is the spiritual profile of all those who have met and imbibed the love of God in Jesus.

It means that a genuine Christian can "be patient in tribulation"—a fifth aspect of Christian love in verses 11 and 12. A Christian's relationship to God will buoy him or her up and carry a believer through life's troubles. And troubles there will be. One person has noted that suffering colors all of life. But Christians can choose the color. They encounter tribulation with a patience supported by hope and joy. "A man can meet anything when he meets it with Christ" (Barclay, *Romans*, p. 180).

A final characteristic of genuine love in verses 11 and 12 is that it will "persevere in prayer." Paul sees such prayer not as some duty to perform by rote or mechanical repetition, but as the voice of one lover in conversation with another.

Romans 12:13 continues to expound on the implications of true love as it contributes "to the needs of the saints" or fellow church members, irrespective (in the context of Romans) of considerations of race or social status. It is all too easy not to reach out to others. But what a blessing is in store for us (and our guests) when we do.

Verse 14 moves on from the "normal" aspects of Christian love to the "abnormal." "Bless those persecuting you." The point to note here is that the Greek tense for "persecuting" expresses an ongoing action. This is not some aspect of ancient personal history in which you need to forgive someone for an old but somewhat far-off hurt. No! It is both present and ongoing! Such is the radical nature of Christian love. It is the kind of love that Jesus said that we must have if we would be perfect like our Father in heaven (Matt. 5:43-48). Jesus was not playing mind games when he told His followers to "pray for those who persecute you, so that you may be sons of your Father who is in heaven" (verses 44, 45, RSV). As He hung on the cross Jesus prayed for those in the act of killing Him (Luke 23:34).

Here, I must say, is a challenge to the genuineness of our Christian love. Have we prayed for our enemies lately? If not, why not? Today—right now—is a perfect time to do something that's not normal. It could change your life and theirs, as it did when Stephen prayed for Saul, who was in the act of killing him (Acts 7:60). Augustine had it right when he said, "The Church owes Paul to the prayer of Stephen" (Barclay, *Romans*, p. 182).

Romans 12:15 continues Paul's description of the contours of Christian love, with its command to "rejoice with those who rejoice" and to "weep with those who weep." That is not as easy as it might seem. The problem is that people are generally so caught up in their own selves, their own things, their own achievements, that they find it inconvenient if not downright troublesome to truly rejoice and weep over the triumphs and tragedies of others. And, as strange as it might seem, it is easier for most of us to weep with others than to rejoice with them. After all, it is difficult not to feel sorry for someone when everything has gone wrong. But it is entirely another matter to rejoice with those who have received blessings that we wish were ours or about which we might feel more than a tinge of jealousy. Christian love is love that is not conformed to the patterns of this world but transformed by the principles of God's kingdom (Rom. 12:1, 2).

Being "of the same mind toward one another" (verse 16) probably means in its context to "treat everyone with equal kindness" (Jer). That interpretation lines up with not being haughty, being willing to associate with the lowly, and not being conceited—sentiments that make up the rest of the verse.

What a wonderful place the church would be if all of its members practiced the qualities of genuine love presented in Romans 12:9-16. But the good news is that we as individuals don't have to wait for others to make it that way. We can begin the reformation today in our own congregation as we set out in earnest to live the transformed life of Romans 12:1, 2.

50. Lesson Number 3 in Transformed Living: Overcoming Evil With Good

Romans 12:17-21

[17]Pay back evil for evil to no one. Practice what is right before all men. [18]If possible, as far as it depends on you, live in peace with all men. [19]Beloved, never avenge yourselves, but leave room for God's wrath, for it is written, "Vengeance is Mine. I will repay," says the Lord. [20]"But if your enemy hungers, feed him; if he is thirsty, give him a drink; for in so doing you will heap coals of fire upon his head." [21]Do not be conquered by evil, but conquer the evil with good.

Paul's third lesson on living the transformed life focuses on how Christians deal with those who mistreat them (Rom. 12:17-21). Here is a topic that speaks to every person. After all, given the instinct for self-protection that every individual has, it is only natural that thoughts of revenge surface in every human heart. Paul has already touched on the topic in verse 14, in which he said that Christians are to bless, rather than curse, those who persecute them. But that is easier said than done. As a result, he returns to the topic in verses 17-21.

His first injunction is that Christians should not repay evil for evil. Here the apostle appears to be building upon Christ's teaching in the Sermon on the Mount: "You have heard that it was said, 'An eye for an eye and a tooth for a tooth.' But I say to you, Do not resist one who is evil. But if any one strikes you on the right cheek, turn to him the other also" (Matt. 5:38, 39, RSV). Both Jesus and Paul are setting forth a Christian ethic of non-retaliation that is not only countercultural but counterhuman. After all, in the New Testament world slapping a person on the right cheek was considered a gross insult that must be avenged lest one lose even more honor. One of the great facts of history is that revenge is universal in the human heart. But the core of Christianity centers not only around Christ's death on the cross and salvation by grace through faith, but also living the transformed life (Rom. 12:2) of the new heart and new mind.

Genuine Christianity as Paul pictures it in Romans 12 is intensely practical. It instructs us on how to live in the real world in which people hurt us deeply. Central to that instruction is the command not to retaliate when people have hurt us.

But why? Don't they deserve it? They certainly do. We all know that. And God knows it too and, Paul tells us, He will handle it at the proper time (verse 19). But retribution is not our task. Why? First, because Jesus and Paul have commanded us not to. But, second, if you need a *real* reason, revenge doesn't work. The history of both nations and individuals tells us that one shove merely brings another in return, usually one with a bit more force. Beyond that, retaliation distorts our characters in a way that moves us in the direction of the character of the devil rather than that of God. In other words, revengeful people have ugly characters.

The Root of Revenge

"It is the love of self that destroys our peace. While self is all alive, we stand ready continually to guard it from mortification and insult; but when we are dead and our life is hid with Christ in God, we shall not take neglects or slights to heart. We shall be deaf to reproach and blind to scorn and insult." (White, Mount, p. 16).

But there resides something deeper here. To get at it we need to ask why we seek revenge. The answer is not difficult to find. Someone has hurt our precious self and thus they deserve to be paid back and in kind. That, whether we like it or not, is hardly the sanctified reasoning of one who has been crucified in Christ (Matt. 16:24). When the old self has been crucified and a new self has been resurrected, we will desire to walk in the way of that Christ (Rom. 6:4-8) who prayed for His enemies even as they taunted Him on the cross (Luke 23:34).

And then again who are we as Christians to give other people what they "deserve"? If God gave us what we deserve we wouldn't exist. Rather than giving us our just desserts, He bestows on us what we don't deserve—free grace. That teaching stands at the very foundation of Paul's letter to the Romans, and it not only forms the basis of salvation but also that of Christian ethics or the living of the transformed life.

The second half of Romans 12:17 moves away from the negative injunction regarding revenge to the positive command to "practice what is right before all men." Verses 18-21 explain the meaning of doing what is right. Paul's flow of thought is as follows:

1. A Positive command: "Live in peace with all men" (verse 18).
2. A negative command: "Never avenge yourselves" (verse 19) because that is God's business.
3. A positive command: Care for your enemies in their time of need (verse 20).
4. A negative command: "Do not be conquered by evil" (verse 21a).
5. A positive command: "Conquer the evil with good" (verse 21b).

The positive command of verse 18 to "live in peace with all men" is of interest because it contains two conditions that highlight the realism and practicality of the Bible and the limitations of living the transformed life in a world of sin. The command to live peaceably with everyone raises a question in our minds if we think about it very long: Is it possible? The answer is an obvious "no." That is why Paul adds two conditions in verse 18:

- "if possible"
- "as far as it depends on you."

We might as well face it—in a sinful world cantankerous people can make it impossible to live in peace with them. That is why Paul adds "as far as it depends on you." While we cannot control other people, we are responsible for ourselves as we seek to be peacemakers in whatever situation we find ourselves.

"Beloved, never avenge yourselves" (Rom. 12:19). Easy to say, but hard to do. How quickly we feel that old payback urge. C. S. Lewis caught the point when he wrote that "everyone says forgiveness is a lovely idea, until they have something to forgive" (Lewis, p. 104). It is the having something to forgive that brings the blood to our eyes.

Pastor Martin Niemöller tells of his experience in the Nazi concentration camp at Dachau, while incarcerated as a political prisoner. The gallows stood just outside his window. He saw thousands go to their deaths. Some, he noted, cursed, others whimpered, and some prayed.

"What will happen," Niemöller asked himself, "on the day they lead you there and put you to the test? When they put that rope around your neck, what will be your last words? Will you then cry out, 'You criminals, scum! There's a God in heaven! You'll get yours!'

"What if Jesus had said that," he queried, "if He had taken his last breath to cry out to the soldiers and the Sanhedrin, 'Criminals! Scum! This is My Father's world. You'll get yours!'?

"What would have happened? Nothing! One more poor sinner would have died there, lonely and forgotten, and nothing would have happened."

If Jesus, Stan Mooneyham comments, had cursed His executioners, demanded justice, or pleaded His rights, no one would have been surprised. "He would have died as just one more sorry spectacle of broken, flawed, self-centered humanity. His name would not have been remembered beyond his generation" (Mooneyham, pp. 43, 44).

Jesus understood that vengeance does not belong to us, that it is God's responsibility. He realized that justice in the end would be done in the Lord's good time. At that time, Paul tells us while quoting Deuteronomy 32:35 in verse 19, God will make all things right. Not in the way of senseless vengeance that required a pound of suffering for a pound of sin, but in a manner that will be just to everyone.

Meanwhile we as Christians need to learn the lesson that Jesus practiced and Paul taught. It is not one of the easiest to absorb. After all, as the apostle taught in Romans 7, the residue of sin remains in us even though it no longer reigns.

That thought brings us to Romans 12:20, with its positive command to feed those who have abused us so that their consciences might be wakened, and the negative command of verse 21a not to let evil take control of us.

The crux of Paul's presentation comes in 21b, in which he tells us to "conquer the evil with good." Truly this must be the apex of "abnormal," "transformed" (verse 2) living.

But how does a person conquer evil with good? That question brings me to the story of Harry Orchard, a man with a string of murders for hire on his record, including the death of the governor of Idaho in the official's own front yard in 1905.

How would you feel if you were the late governor's wife? Would you desire "sweet revenge" as your natural right?

We happen to know how she reacted. As a Seventh-day Adventist Christian she prayed *for* Orchard. But she did more than pray for him. She prayed *with* him in prison. In fact she actually went to the prison and pleaded with her husband's killer to give his heart to God.

That caught Harry off guard. He knew how to handle a fist in his face. And he knew how to escalate a fight by retaliation. But he didn't know what to do with love. Eventually, overcome by goodness, he gave his life to God. For the rest of his days he served others for Christ in prison, even refusing an eventual pardon so that he could continue his prison ministry from the "inside."

"Don't allow yourself to be overpowered by evil. Take the offensive—overpower evil with good" (verse 21, Phillips). That is what God has done for us in Christ. He didn't retaliate and give us what we deserve. Rather, He offered us what we don't deserve—grace, forgiveness, life everlasting. And those who value that gift will pass it on to others. In the context of Romans, only those who have been justified freely by God's grace know the power of love, and only they can pass on that love as God uses them to overcome evil with good. And there is no better time to begin that passing on than today.

51. Lesson Number 4 in Transformed Living: Respecting Civil Government

Romans 13:1-7

> *¹Every person is to be subject to the governing authorities. For there is no governing authority except from God, and those that exist have been appointed by God. ²Therefore the one who opposes the authority has opposed the ordinance of God, and those who have opposed will receive condemnation upon themselves. ³For rulers are not a terror to good behavior, but to evil. Do you want to have no fear of authority? Do good and you will have praise from him; ⁴for he is a servant of God for your good. But be fearful if you do evil, for he does not bear the sword in vain, for he is a servant of God, an avenger bringing wrath to the one who practices evil. ⁵Therefore it is necessary to be subject, not only because of wrath, but also because of conscience. ⁶For because of this you also pay taxes, for they are God's public servants to attend continually to this very thing. ⁷Pay to all what is due them, tax to whom tax is due, custom to whom custom is due, fear to whom fear is due, honor to whom honor is due.*

It might seem strange to think of Adolf Hitler as having a favorite Bible passage. He actually had two of them that he was especially fond of. The first was Romans 13:1-7 and the second 1 Peter 2:13, 14: "Be subject for the Lord's sake to every human institution, whether it be to the emperor as supreme, or to governors as sent by him to punish those who do wrong and to praise those who do right" (RSV).

One of those two texts had to be preached every year in every church in the Third Reich. And "observers" made sure that the passages were "interpreted properly." Hitler as God's "servant" or "minister" (13:4, NASB, KJV) is an interesting thought. He wanted all to know that he had authority direct from God to take up the sword, that God had appointed him, and that he was God's agent. Therefore, so the theory went, whatever he did was right.

That may at first sound convincing, but it is not what the text says. Several points undergird any valid interpretation of Romans 13:1-7. A first is that it is none other than God who established civil government. Because of that, Christians are duty-bound to obey such authority. And from this passage it appears that Paul would hold the position that even a bad government is better than none at all.

That very point seems to be a main lesson in the book of Judges. Judges 19 though 21 contains one of the worst stories in the Bible. The tale of a "cleric" gone wrong, it records murder, sexual misconduct, and a vast catalogue of perversions. But the important point is that the words "in those days there was no king in Israel" (Judges 21:25; 19:1, RSV) brackets the passage. Judges 21:25 goes on to add the punch line for the book when, after reporting that Israel had no king, it claims that "every man did what was right in his own eyes" (RSV).

One of the lessons of reading of Romans 13 in the light of Judges is that civil government may not be perfect, but it is better than anarchy. Thus God established civil government (Rom. 13:1) for humanity's own good. Without it life exists only by the law of the jungle. Therefore it is the government's duty to punish those who do evil (verse 4) and Christians should obey the government rather than oppose it (verses 1, 2).

Does that mean that the government is always right and that it is always wrong to oppose it? And if one does oppose it, on what basis? Those are not academic questions. For much of the world's history they have been at the center of daily living for a significant part of the global population. And all of us may face them some day.

Romans 13:3, 4 puts the issue to the front when it tells us that "rulers are not a terror to good behavior, but to evil." Therefore "do good and you will have" the government's "praise," for it is "a servant of God for your good."

Is that really so? Do those who do right never have to fear the civil ruler? Will the government always commend them?

What about Daniel's three friends? They did what was right when they refused to worship Nebuchadnezzar's golden image. And what did the king do? Commend them? No, he threw them into the fiery furnace (Dan. 3:20).

And what about those early Christian martyrs who lost their lives to the Roman emperors Decius and Diocletian? They had commanded Roman citizens to worship them on the pain of death. All that a Christian had to do was to bow down and curse Christ. Such was the direct order of the Roman government. And we should never forget that it is the very government that Paul refers to in Romans 13 that not only crucified Jesus but would eventually take the apostle's own life. That brings us back to the question of how far a Christian is duty bound to obey civil government.

We now come to the second important point in interpreting Romans 13:1-7. What Paul actually says is that *God has appointed* civil authority (verse 1) to be *His* "*servant*" (verse 4). Thus earthly rulers are not supreme but operate under delegated authority. They are God's servants and nothing more, in spite of whatever exalted views they may have of themselves. Heads of state from the Pauline perspective are not free agents. And their function is to bring about good. That "good," of course, must fit God's perspective rather than that of Nebuchadnezzar, Caesar, Hitler, Stalin, or some modern ruler.

Thus Paul in Romans 13 is not seeking to cover every situation involving every government. Rather than speaking to every possibility, he presents the case in which a legitimate authority makes an appropriate demand on its citizens. In healthy times the apostle is correct. The government rewards people for doing right and punishes those who do wrong (verse 3, 4). Thus the Christian to whom Paul is writing should obey the government in its legitimate demands. He is firm that every Christian has a definite responsibility to the government under which he or she lives. Obedience to the state for a Christian is not an option. As T. W. Manson puts it, "resistance to legitimate authority legitimately exercised is wrong" (in Morris, *Romans*, p. 462).

That raises another question. What is legitimate? Who defines what is right or wrong? Those questions take us back to Romans 13:4 and the truth that civil government is God's "servant." From Paul's perspective, it is not the state that is the ultimate authority in such definitions but God who "appointed" the state.

"Therefore, loyalty to the State is prescribed so long as it conforms to its divinely ordained functions and rights" (Wood, p. 38). When the state steps out of its rightful role and seeks to become the supreme authority in the place of God it has departed its legitimate function. Thus when the regulations of the state conflict with loyalty to God, civil disobedience is not only appropriate but demanded by the first commandment of the Decalogue (Ex. 20:3).

Such was the situation early faced by the disciples. After Pentecost their preaching had spread throughout Jerusalem. The Jewish authorities had become so upset that they imprisoned the leading apostles and forbade them to preach. The next day, however, they again proclaimed Christ. Once more they found themselves hauled before the Jewish rulers, who asked them why they continued to cause a disturbance when they had received an explicit command not to do so. Peter's answer was that "we ought to obey God rather than men" (Acts 5:29, KJV). When the government's laws conflict with God's the duty of Christians is plain.

But, then, what is the legitimate function of the government as God's servant? The ruler is God's servant (literally "deacon"), suggests Leon Morris, "to enable God's other servants to get on with the job of doing God's will" (Morris, *Romans*, p. 464). Thus it is incumbent upon rulers to act responsibly. It is in that spirit that Paul writes: "I urge that supplication, prayers, intercessions, and thanksgivings be made for all men, for kings and all who are in high positions, that we may lead a quiet and peaceable life, godly and respectable in every way. This is good, and it is acceptable in the sight of God our Savior, who desires all men to be saved and to come to a knowledge of the truth" (1 Tim. 2:1-4, RSV).

Thus one of the functions of government as God's servant is to establish and maintain law and order so that the gospel might be preached. Paul was respectful of the government that would eventually take his life because he knew that without the *pax Romana* (the Roman peace) the empire of the Mediterranean world would disintegrate into fragments. He knew that it was the stability maintained by Rome that had enabled him and other early Christian missionaries to move freely from one region to another so that within a few decades they had evangelized much of the empire.

Paul had not the slightest doubt that government, though problematic at times, is fundamentally a good thing, and that Christians have a duty to respect civil authority. Thus, following Christ's lead from Matthew 22:17–21, he told the Roman believers to pay their taxes and render to both God and civil rulers honor and respect (Rom. 13:6, 7). As a result, Christians have a responsibility to make a positive contribution wherever possible toward the health of civil government. In short, we need to be responsible citizens of two kingdoms; God's and the one in which we find ourselves here on earth.

> "Wherever and whenever governments have been too weak to carry out this mission of preserving order in society, anarchy has engulfed the citizens of that land" (Martin Scharlemann, in Huegli, p. 33).

Before leaving Romans 13:1-7 we need to ask why Paul placed these particular verses where he did. It was undoubtedly stimulated by the previous verses, in which Paul told his readers that God would eventually avenge injustice (12:19) and that Christians should love their enemies (verse 20). Those thoughts led in the direction of civil government, which is the dispenser of justice on earth at the present time but can be seen as an enemy in its acts of injustice (such as the crucifixion of Christ). The apostle apparently felt that here was an excellent place to discuss living the transformed life in the civil sphere. As Walter Pilgrim points out, "Romans 13 occurs within the wider context of Romans 12-15, where Paul sets forth the transformed life of the believer and love as the shape of the new life. Romans 13 thus spells out the love ethic in the public sphere, an ethic of subjection and respect for those who rule" (Pilgrim, pp. 29, 8).

52. Lesson Number 5 in Transformed Living: Living God's Love

Romans 13:8-10

> [8]*Owe no one anything except to love one another, for the one who loves others has fulfilled the law.* [9]*For the law which says "You shall not commit adultery, You shall not murder, You shall not steal, You shall not covet," and if there is any other commandment, is summed up in this saying: "You shall love your neighbor as yourself."* [10]*Love does no evil to a neighbor; therefore love is the fulfillment of the law.*

Paul's fifth lesson in transformed living has to do with living the law of love. Here he again emphasizes the need for unity in the church that he highlighted in Romans 12:3-8. Along that line, Romans 13:8-10 resumes the discussion of love initiated in 12:9. Whereas Romans 13:1-7 concerned his readers' external relationships to civil authorities, verses 8-10 return to internal relationships in the Christian community in Rome and set the stage for chapters 14 and 15, in which Paul addresses the quarrels between Jews and Gentiles over certain aspects of law observance.

In Romans 13:8-10 we find what we might regard as the very foundation of transformed living. That foundation is the core meaning of God's law—the Christian attribute of love. Romans 12:19, 20 earlier told us to love our enemies and let God handle the vengeance. Here in Romans 13:8-10 Paul moves back to the love theme, but now his emphasis is on loving our neighbors.

The key concept in verse 8 is debt, a topic that has arisen several times in Romans (e.g., 1:14; 8:12; 13:6, 7). From debt to the state in the form of taxes in 13:6, 7, Paul shifts to our debt to our fellow human beings—from official debt to private debt. But the two are different. Taxes are finite. We receive a tax bill, and when we pay, we take care of it in full. On the other hand, the debt of love is infinite. We can never totally repay it. Christians can never stop loving others and say "I have loved enough." They have an ongoing debt "to love one another" (Rom. 13:8).

That makes most of us uncomfortable, because we want to eliminate our debts, so that we can relax and be our real selves. We want to know the limit of love. It would be very nice to know, for example, when we have fulfilled our quota of love to that truly obnoxious person (neighbor, wife, husband, fellow church member) so that we can then let him or her get what they deserve.

Paul's answer to that wish is the same as the one Jesus gave to Peter when he asked when he could quit forgiving his neighbor. The answer is "never" (Matt. 18:21-35). Just as God's love is infinite for me, so must my love and care for those around me be without end. We are to "owe no one anything except to love one another" (Rom. 13:8).

> **A Third-century Insight on Debt**
>
> "The debt of love remains with us permanently and never leaves us; this is a debt which we both discharge every day and for ever owe" (Origen in Barclay, Romans, pp. 190, 191).

The second half of Romans 13:8 is pregnant with meaning. Paul makes the astounding assertion that "the one who loves others has fulfilled the law." Here we find Paul alluding back to Jesus' teaching in Matthew 22:34–40 that the heart of the law is love to God firstly and then love to other people. "On these two commandments," Jesus declared, "depend all the law and the prophets" (verse 40, RSV). Paul makes the connection of his teaching with that of Jesus explicitly clear in Galatians 5:14, in which he writes that "the whole law is fulfilled in one word, 'You shall love your neighbor as yourself'" (Gal. 5:14, RSV).

But in Romans 13:8-10 the apostle takes the issue one step further when he ties the law of loving one's neighbor to the second table of the Decalogue (abbreviated from Deuteronomy 5:17-21). Here is a profound insight. The Ten Commandments do not stand on their own. Undergirding them is a more basic LAW that gives meaning and direction to the various laws set forth in the Decalogue.

Apparently Paul does not address the Great Commandment to love God in Romans 13:8-10 because that was not the problem in the Roman church. Rather, it was in the divided congregation truly loving one another across racial and other barriers. Thus the focus on loving one's neighbor.

"To support the claim that 'the one who loves another has fulfilled the law,' verse 9 selects four commandments from the 'second table' of the Decalogue" (Keck, p. 327). Thus when individuals

(1) abstain from adultery it is proof that they love their neighbor;

(2) refrain from killing others it is proof that they love their neighbor;

(3) choose not to steal it is proof that they love their neighbor, and

(4) opt not to covet their neighbors' position or things it is proof that they love their neighbor.

"The phrase 'and any other commandment' shows that these four are treated as representative" and thus support the premise that "the law prohibits doing wrong to the neighbor" (*ibid.*).

Such thinking was not unique to Jesus and Paul. Rabbi Hillel (first century B.C.) summed up the basic point from a negative perspective when he wrote: "That which you hate do not do to your fellows; this is the whole law; the rest is commentary." And Rabbi Akiba (cir. 50 A.D. - cir. 132 A.D.) identified Leviticus 19:18 ("You shall love your neighbor as yourself," RSV) as "the greatest general principle in the Torah" (see Dunn, *Romans 9-16*, p. 778).

One of the important contributions of Romans 13:8-10 is its explicit linking of the Ten Commandments to Jesus' "great commandments." Paul only made that link with the second great commandment, although he could have just as easily done so with the first. But his point is clear. Living the Christian life is not loving God and one's neighbors *versus* keeping the Ten Commandments, but loving God *through* keeping the various injunctions of the Decalogue. Thus William Barclay is quite correct when he pens that "it is Paul's claim that if a man honestly seeks to discharge this debt of love, he will automatically keep all the commandments" (Barclay, *Romans*, p. 191).

Romans 13:10 repeats the fact that "love is the fulfillment of the law," thereby emphasizing the LAW behind the many laws (cf. verse 8). But the entire block of teaching running from verses 8-10 does something else for us. It makes explicit the spiritual nature of God's law.

Too many church members have missed the law's spiritual nature and have made a mess of things. Let me put it this way: When people have the LAW of God in their hearts it becomes natural and normal to keep God's many laws. But the reverse is not true. One may obey God's many laws and still not be observing God's LAW. That is, a person can have outward obedience but not have God's love in his or her heart. Or to put it another way, one can refrain from theft or breaking God's Sabbath but be as mean as the devil.

The predicament of outward obedience accompanied by a lack of inward Christianity is one of the most spiritually dangerous situations a person can be in. After all, people who are deceived at that point may feel quite satisfied with themselves spiritually because they are doing what is right. Like the prodigal son's older brother, they may never "come to themselves" and see their true condition (Luke 15:17, 25-32). That was the problem with both the Pharisees of old and their modern counterparts—they sincerely keep the laws but break the LAW.

One spiritual implication related to the law in Romans 13:8-10 is that we need to get our priorities right. God wants us to keep His LAW so that we can truly honor His laws. The order is absolutely essential. The correct order keeps us from that legalism which "is 'natural,' and readily finds favour with men" (Walker, *Gospel*, p. 182), one that focuses on self and personal achievements.

> ## Another Third-century Lesson on Love
>
> "If you love somebody, you will not kill him. Nor will you commit adultery, steal from him or bear false witness against him. It is the same with all the other commands of the law: love ensures that they are kept" (Origen in Bray, p. 331).

That is precisely where the teaching of Romans 12:1, 2 comes in. Salvation does not change the law, but transforms a Christian's relation to it. The story of Zacchaeus (Luke 19:1-10) is one of the clearest on a saved person's spiritual law keeping as a response to God's grace. As soon as Zacchaeus was saved, he was out sharing his goods with the poor and restoring fourfold to those people he had defrauded. His new life in its relation to the law was an evidence of salvation. God's saving action reversed Zacchaeus' life from selfishness to serving others. That is transformation and evidence of new birth (John 3:3-7) and adoption into God's family (Rom. 8:14-17). When a person is converted, there develops a natural outflow of love from the heart that expresses itself in channels identified by the various commands in the Decalogue.

ER-9

To put it another way, transformed living means that not only will people's love be refocused from theirselves to God and others, but it means that the wellspring of God's love will undergird their every action. That is what Hebrews 8:10 refers to as the new covenant experience, in which God puts His laws into people's minds and writes them on their hearts. With that in mind, it is little wonder that Jesus identified the acid test of Christianity as love toward others (John 13:35—"By this all men will know that you are my disciples, if you have love for one another" [RSV]). It is that understanding that informs the transformed life. Anything else, no matter how many "commandments" one may keep, is a mere imitation of the real thing.

53. Lesson Number 6 in Transformed Living: Walking in Advent Hope

Romans 13:11-14

[11]And do this, knowing the time, that it is already the hour for you to wake up out of sleep, for now our salvation is nearer than when we became believers. [12]The night has far gone and the day is drawing near. Therefore let us put away the works of darkness, and let us put on the armor of light. [13]As in the day, let us walk decently, not in orgies and drunkenness, not in sexual immorality and debauchery, not in strife and jealousy. [14]But put on the Lord Jesus Christ and give no forethought concerning the flesh, for fulfilling its lusts.

Up to this point in Romans 12 and 13 Paul has been writing about how justified people should live. The Christian should demonstrate the transformed life of a living sacrifice (12:1, 2) in humbly using their gifts for God (12:3-8), in respectful harmony with civil government (13:1-7), and in Christian love (12:9-21; 13:8-10).

But why? First because they have been justified freely by God's grace (Rom. 1-11). Second, because Christ will come again. Phillip's translation of Romans 13:11 brings out that connection nicely: "Why all this stress on behaviour? Because . . . every day brings God's salvation nearer." Lesson number six for the transformed life has to do with living in the hope of the

Second Advent. Thus we might think of Romans 13:11-14 as motivational. We need to wake up, because this life is not all there is.

When Romans speaks of salvation, it does so in three different aspects. One of them, justification, is past. Another, glorification, is future. And the third, sanctification, is a present reality. Whereas people often think of Romans as a book about justification, Paul devotes even more space (chapters 6-8 and 12-15) to sanctification—living the crucified life (6:1-4), the transformed life (12:1, 2).

Sanctified living in Romans takes place on the basis of a person's having been justified and in the certainty of eventual glorification. Emil Brunner phrases it nicely when he writes that "the remembrance of what God's mercy in Jesus Christ has done for us is one powerful impulse of the new life; the other, which is inseparably linked with it, is the sure expectation of what he will do. Where faith in Christ looks at the future, it turns into hope. . . . This future is already in process of happening. . . . Faith is indeed nothing but living in the light of that which is to come" (Brunner, *Romans*, pp. 112, 113).

Thus Christians live between two great events. The first is the beginning of the kingdom of God, which Christ asserted He had inaugurated when He began His earthly ministry (Matt. 4:17). The second is the consummation of the kingdom, when Christ comes again, redeems our bodies (Rom. 8:23), and takes believers home to be with Him. That event, Paul claims in Romans 13:11-14, ought to motivate us to live the transformed life.

Wake up! Paul tells us in Romans 13:11. James Denney notes that "the Christian's life is not a sleep, but a battle" (Denney, "Romans," p. 699). As the apostle Peter puts it: "Be sober, be watchful. Your adversary the devil prowls around like a roaring lion, seeking some one to devour" (1 Peter 5:8, RSV). The apostles realized that our world is in the midst of a battle between good and evil and that each individual's life is the scene of a microcosmic great controversy, an individual manifestation of the macrocosmic struggle between Christ and Satan.

One of the great fears of Christ and Paul was that Christians wouldn't keep awake, but would slumber and sleep and therefore get caught unawares at the Second Advent (Matt. 25:1-13; 1 Thess. 5:1-11).

Romans 13:12 tells believers to do two things:

1. "put away the works of darkness" and
2. "put on the armor of light."

Being ready for the return of Christ, according to Romans 12 and 13, is not being hyped up because we see the "signs of the times" being fulfilled, but rather living a sober and responsible life of Christian love. Christ had the same message for His hearers in Matthew 25. It was those living a Christian life and actually doing God's love who would be saved when He returns in the clouds of heaven. Yet how many church members looking for the Advent get their excitement from the signs of the times rather than from the service of living God's love that Paul talks about in Romans 13 and that Christ repeatedly emphasized in the context of the Second Advent.

Putting off and putting on are the focal point of 13:12. Douglas Moo suggests that "this language was widely used with metaphorical association in the ancient world, and the NT writers adopt it as a vivid way of picturing the change of values that accompanies, and is required by, conversion to Christ" (Moo, *Epistle*, p. 823). While verses 13 and 14 expand upon Paul's meaning related to the "works of darkness," they barely touch on the "armor of light," with the exceptions that verse 13 informs his readers to "walk decently" while verse 14 tells Christians to "put on the Lord Jesus Christ." That relative neglect may be because Paul's extensive treatment of living God's love in Romans 12:9-21 and 13:8-10 focused on the positive aspect of the Christian life.

Before leaving Romans 13:12 it is of interest to note that Paul shifts from "*works*" of darkness to "armor" or "*weapons*" of light, whereas the two words are actually parallel. C.E.B. Cranfield suggests that his use of "weapons" or "armor" "reflects Paul's consciousness that the Christian life is necessarily a warfare" (Cranfield, *Shorter Commentary*, p. 333).

Verse 13 sets forth an interesting contrast between daylight activities, which are presumably visible to everyone, and the activities of the dark night, which one might prefer to hide from the eyes of others. On the one side is walking decently or living "honorably" (Goodspeed), while the other is represented by three unsavory pairs. The first pair, "orgies" and "drunkenness," both point to abuses related to strong drink. *Thayer's Greek-English Lexicon* notes that "orgies" (*kōmos*) was used by "a nocturnal and riotous procession of half-drunken and frolicsome fellows who after supper parade through the streets with torches and music in honor of Bacchus [the god of wine] or some other deity, and sing and play before the houses of their male and female friends; hence used generally of *feasts and drinking-parties that are protracted till late at night and indulge in revelry*" (Thayer, p. 367).

The second pair, "sexual immorality and debauchery," refer to sexual sins. The word that I translated "debauchery" (*aselgeia*), William Barclay points out, "is of the ugliest words in the Greek language" and describes not merely immorality, but the person who is totally lost to shame. Persons characterized by *aselgeia* are beyond hiding their sins in darkness. Such a person "does not care what people think of him. . . . *Aselgeia* is the quality of the man who is so deeply in the grip of sheer lust that he dares publicly to do the things which are unbecoming for any man to do" (Barclay, *Romans*, p. 194).

The third pair, "strife and jealousy," are diseases of the spirit. While average church members might not view those sins as on the same level with the first two pairs, it is significant that Paul clusters them together. He sees all as deeds of darkness. In fact, the "more polite" sins of strife and jealousy may seem to be less harmful, but they are just as serious—perhaps even more so since they are all too often regarded as within the acceptable range by many church members. But it is those very sins that are destroying the unity of the Roman Christians. There is a sense in which "nice sins" are even more destructive than "nasty sins" since they disrupt the social fabric. All six of the vices Paul lists "stem from self-will; they are all the outreach of a determined selfishness that seeks only one's own pleasure" (Morris, *Romans*, p. 473). All of them are a failure in love and transformed living.

"But" is an important word in Romans 13:14. Here we find the alternative to the three sinful twins of verse 13. Paul's solution has two parts. The first is to "put on the Lord Jesus Christ." That injunction reflects back to verse 12, in which the apostle told us to put on the "armor" or "weapons" of light. Any Christian who desires victory must have an intimate union with Christ.

Verse 14 goes on to command that Christians "give no forethought concerning the flesh" or "fulfilling its lusts." The Good News translation gets to the heart of Paul's idea when it says "stop paying attention to your sinful nature and satisfying its desires." That is good counsel whether our besetting sins are of the more nasty type or of the more "vegetarian" variety (i.e., jealousy and strife or just plain self-centeredness). The answer to all of them is a transformed heart and mind that leads to transformed living (Rom. 12:1, 2).

In closing we should note that reading Romans 13:14 led to one of the most significant conversions in Christian history. Augustine of Hippo (354-430) was brilliant intellectually, but he had found it completely impossible to break from his sexual sins. Struggling in the chains of lust, he heard a voice "repeating over and over, 'Take up and read. Take up and read.'" In response he took his Bible and read the first passage his eyes fell on: "Not in rioting and drunkenness, not in chambering and impurities, not in strife and envying; but put you on the Lord Jesus Christ, and make not provision for the flesh in its concupiscences" (Augustine, *Confessions* 8.29). God used those words to bring home to Augustine not only the reality of his sin, but also the reality of salvation through Christ. His conversion changed the face of Christianity as he became its most influential voice for the next 1,000 years. Paul's gospel has a converting power that hasn't ceased in our day.

54. Lesson Number 7 in Transformed Living: Remembering Who We Are

Romans 14:1-12

¹Now accept the one who is weak in the faith, but not for the purpose of quarreling over opinions. ²One believes in eating all things, but another, being weak, eats only vegetables. ³Let not the one who eats despise the one not eating, and let not the one not eating judge the one who eats, for God has accepted him. ⁴Who are you to judge another's servant? To his own master he stands or falls, and he will be upheld, for the Lord is able to make him stand.

⁵One judges one day above another day, but another judges every day the same. Let each person be convinced in his own mind. ⁶The one who regards the day, regards it to the Lord, and the one who eats, eats to the Lord, for he gives thanks to God, and the one not eating does not eat to the Lord, and gives thanks to God. ⁷For not one of us lives to himself and not one dies to himself; ⁸for if we live, we live to the Lord, or if we die, we die to the Lord. Therefore, whether we live or die we are the Lord's. ⁹For to this end Christ died and lived again, that He might be Lord of both the dead and the living.

¹⁰But why do you judge your brother? Or indeed, why do you despise your brother? For all of us will stand before the judgment seat of God.

¹¹For it is written,
    "As I live, says the Lord, every knee will bow to Me.
    And every tongue will give praise to God."
¹²So then each one of us will give an account of himself to God.

With Romans 14:1-15:13 we enter into Paul's longest section of advice on how to live the transformed life (Rom. 12:1, 2), one based on the law of love (13:8-10). The core of that advice is not to be judgmental of others in the church who may not agree with you on various issues not central to the Christian message.

The apostle has been preparing his readers for chapter 14 from the beginning of his letter. In the first chapter he raised the issue of Jews and Gentiles in the church. Then in chapter 2 he condemned one person's censuring of another. Those who passed judgment on others, he noted, actually judge themselves (2:1).

Romans 14 raises an issue of central importance to the church in every age. As Leon Morris points out, "the church was never meant to be a cozy club of like-minded people of one race or social position or intellectual calibre. Christians are not clones, identical in all respects. One of the difficulties the church has always faced is that included in its membership are the rich and the poor, the powerful and the powerless, those from every stratum of society, the old and the young, adults and children, the conservative and the radicals" (Morris, *Romans*, p. 476). And, of course, there are both Jews and Gentiles, a particularly prominent issue in the Roman congregation.

> One of the most natural things is for me to want everyone in the church to believe and act as I do. After all, I'm right and have a text or 10 quotations to prove it. Thus the matter is settled.

One of the most natural things is for me to want everyone in the church to believe and act as I do. After all, I'm right and have a text or 10 quotations to prove it. Thus the matter is settled.

That is just the attitude Paul confronts head-on in Romans 14. From the first verse he argues for mutual acceptance of the "strong" and the "weak" and against "quarreling over opinions." While it is true that he identifies himself with the strong (15:1), it is equally the case that he has a great deal of understanding for those he deems "weak in faith" (14:1, RSV).

Romans 14:1 also makes it clear that not every belief held by church members is of equal importance. Some of them Paul identifies as "opinions" or "disputable matters" (NIV) or "doubtful disputations" (KJV). The problem comes in when we hold that everything that *we* believe is of equal importance and then try to force our concepts on others.

Paul raises his first illustration (a less than central issue) in verse 2, in which he notes that some believers argue that they can eat all things, while others take a vegetarian position. One aspect to note here is that the apostle is not discussing those who eat or do not eat unclean meats. To the contrary, the issue is eating meat versus eating none at all.

A second point of importance is that Paul's main concern here is not diet. Rather, it is the attitude of the church members toward one another. Diet (as days will be in verses 5 and 6) is merely an illustration.

A third thing to note is that the apostle's two illustrations (permissible diet and holy days) directly related to the Jewish/Gentile division in the Romans church.

Those preliminary thoughts bring us to the diet issue of Romans 14:2, 3. He is not condemning health-related vegetarianism but rather those who had given up eating flesh foods for the wrong reason—that is, because they had weak faith. While we do not know exactly what the dietary issue was in Rome, we do know that in Corinth disagreement had raged in the church between those who would not eat meat sacrificed to idols and those who did. In that situation some whom we might regard as the "weak in the faith" refrained from consuming any meat because they could never be positive that someone hadn't offered it to an idol. Paul responded that it really didn't make any difference, since a firmly grounded Christian knew that an idol was nothing (1 Cor. 8:1-13). While the problem in Rome may not have been exactly the same as in Corinth, it was most likely related.

Romans 14:4 finds Paul moving beyond his illustration to his main point: "Who are you to judge another's servant?" After all, God is their Master and Lord and they will stand or fall based on His judgment alone. For church members to judge one another is for them to take upon themselves the prerogative of God. Thus *passing judgment on another Christian is the ultimate sin, because it places ourselves in the role of God.*

Verse 5 brings us to Paul's second illustration related to judging others on peripheral matters of opinion. This time the apostle takes up the fact that some in the Roman congregation believed that certain days should be observed while others took the opposite position.

Paul doesn't explicitly identify the issue, but it was apparently not the weekly Sabbath, since the seventh-day Sabbath is one of the Ten Commandments, and the apostle has already spoken in Romans several times to the importance of the Decalogue in the Christian life (see Rom. 13:8-10; 7:12, 14, 16; 3:31).

The most likely candidates for the dispute were the feast days and yearly Sabbaths. The debate between Jewish and Gentile Christians over issues related to the Jewish ceremonial regulations had already led to a conference between Paul and the leaders of the Jewish Christians in Acts 15. On other occasions we find Paul dealing with the issue of special days and feasts in Galatians 4:10, 11 and Colossians 2:16, 17. In that latter passage, as in the present one, Paul had to deal with church members passing judgment on fellow believers regarding both food and disputed days. But there he explicitly notes that the festivals and Sabbaths in question were "only a shadow of what is to come" (RSV). That language implies the yearly ceremonial Sabbaths (Lev. 23:4-44), symbols pointing forward to Christ. The weekly Sabbath of the Decalogue, by way of contrast, directed attention backward to God's work of creation (see Gen. 2:1–3; Ex. 20:8-11).

With that distinction in mind, even though differences probably existed between the problems in Rome and those in Colosse, Paul tells his Roman readers that those whose faith enabled them to immediately leave behind all ceremonial holy days should not despise others whose faith wasn't as strong. Nor should the latter criticize those who had given up the Jewish feasts when they came to realize that, like the Passover (1 Cor. 5:7), they all pointed forward to Christ.

Beyond the debate over days, Paul sets forth the important lesson in Romans 14:5, 6 that each person must live by their own convictions. God is leading each person who chooses to be led. But all don't have the same background or advance at the same speed. It is important for a Christian to have convictions, but it is equally vital that those convictions come from the Lord.

Verses 7 and 8 highlight the fact that all that a Christian does must be in relationship to God. It is the Christian's connection with God that directs every action in his or her life. The passage, as does Romans as a whole, leaves us in no doubt regarding the fact that Christians are all slaves of their divine Lord (see Rom. 1:1; 6:18). Thus Paul's emphasis in Romans 14 that they are out of their place when they seek to become Lord to their brothers and sisters in the faith—when they want to become mind and conscience for their fellow church members.

Romans 14:10-12 forcefully drives home the major lessons that Paul has been focusing on since verse 1. Namely, that no Christian has the responsibility or right to judge or despise another because each of us will have to stand before the judgment seat of God (verse 10) to give an account of his or her own life and actions (verse 12).

Now that is a thought some people don't like. "Why," they ask, "is there a final judgment for God's people? Didn't Jesus say that Christians have 'passed from death to life,' already have 'eternal life' and will 'not come into judgment' [see John 5:24, RSV]?"

Those things are all true. No person who continues to accept Christ will ever come under judgment in the sense of "condemnation" (John 5:24, KJV, NIV), but Paul makes it abundantly clear in Romans 14:10-12 that there will be a final judgment. Daniel makes that same point. But he is quite straight forward in saying that God's judgment will be "*for* the saints of the Most High" (Dan. 7:22, RSV; cf. Rev. 18:20). The final judgment of Christians is in effect a legal statement to the universe that they have accepted God's grace and thus have a right to immortality. For a Christian the judgment is part of the good news. But it will be bad news for church members who have usurped the prerogative of God and have continued to pass judgment on others. After all, "each one of us will give an account of himself to God" (Rom. 14:12) in that day. In his injunction for us to stop judging others, Paul is absolutely serious. We church members need to take him more seriously—today.

55. A Second Reason Not to Judge

Romans 14:13-23
> [13]*Therefore let us no longer judge one another, but rather determine this— not to put a stumbling block or obstacle in the way of a brother.* [14]*I know*

and am persuaded in the Lord Jesus that nothing is defiled in itself, except to the one who considers it to be defiled, to that man it is defiled. [15]For if because of food your brother is hurt, you are no longer walking according to love. Do not destroy by your food the person for whom Christ died. [16]Therefore do not let your good be spoken against, [17]for the kingdom of God is not eating and drinking, but righteousness and peace and joy in the Holy Spirit. [18]For the one who in this way serves Christ is pleasing to God and approved by men. [19]So then, let us pursue the things of peace and the things that build up one another. [20]Do not destroy the work of God for the sake of food. All things are indeed undefiled, but evil to the man who causes offence by his eating. [21]It is good not to eat flesh or to drink wine or to do anything by which your brother stumbles. [22]The faith which you have, have by yourself before God. Blessed is the one who does not condemn himself by what he approves. [23]But the one who doubts is condemned if he eats, because he is not acting from faith, and everything which is not from faith is sin.

Thus far in Romans 14 Paul has presented one basic reason for not judging our fellow believers—such a prerogative is God's alone. Therefore, people are not accountable to one another but to Him. As a result, to judge another person is to put oneself in God's place.

Romans 14:13-23 supplies us with a second motivation for not judging others—one flowing out of Christian love. Believers who are strong in faith, because of their love, will be considerate of the consciences and scruples of their weaker neighbors in the church, who may not have figured out which are salvational issues and which are not. As a result of their faith and love, Paul emphasizes in Romans 14:13-23 that the "stronger" believers will exercise care not to offend the weaker.

> Part of Paul's "formula" for a healthy church is for Christians to be tolerant with one another on the "nonessentials" of Christianity.

He begins his discussion in verse 13 with an admonition for the various factions in the Roman church (largely aligned along the axis of Jew versus Gentile) to cease judging one another—a problem that was tearing apart the Christian community. Thus their focus should not be on judging but on the determination not to cause another to stumble or fall.

The words that the apostle uses for "stumbling block" are interesting. He uses two of them in verse 13. The first of them also appears in 1 Corinthians

8:9, in which he gives the same warning, again in relation to food. After noting that food offered to idols shouldn't be an issue for Christians, he goes on to add, "Take care lest this liberty of yours [to eat such food] somehow become[s] a stumbling block to the weak" (RSV). The main idea behind the word is to strike one's foot against something and thus stumble.

The second word, which I translated as "obstacle," the Greek-speaking New Testament world used to represent a snare or a trap. Paul employed the term in a way that suggests that a Christian should not do those things that become a hindrance in the sense that they cause others to fall.

Christians, therefore, must live with care. In spite of their liberty, they will avoid those things that will harm a brother or sister. That thought reminds us of the words of Christ, who said that "it would be better" for anyone who hurts the weak ones "to have a great millstone fastened round his neck and be drowned in the depth of the sea" (Matt. 18:5, 6, RSV).

Romans 14:14 reverts to the topic of food, suggesting that nothing is "defiled" ("unclean" in many translations) in itself, even though it may be such in the minds of some believers. Here we need to ask what kind of defiled or unclean foods Paul has in mind. We don't know for sure, but of one thing we can be certain—that he is not referring to the unclean food prohibitions of Deuteronomy 14. How do we know that? From the context. The issue Paul lays out in 14:1, 2 is not between eating unclean and clean meats but rather between eating meat and no meat at all. Thus I have translated *koinon* as "defiled" in order to avoid the confusion inherent in "unclean." Others have translated the Greek as "impure" (NEB, REB, Weymouth) or "intrinsically unholy" (Phillips) or "unhallowed" (Wuest).

The context is all-important in understanding Romans 14:14. Rather than discussing unclean food forbidden to the Jews in Deuteronomy, Paul is referring to foods that had become an issue of conflict in the Roman Christian community. As noted in our discussion of verses 1 and 2, it probably involved foods offered to idols that may have found their way into the marketplace. For Paul, that possibility was not a problem, since an idol was nothing anyway (1 Cor. 8:1-13). Thus, as a "strong" believer, he didn't worry about such things.

But not everyone shared Paul's position. Some definitely held that such food was defiled or impure and was forbidden to eat. The apostle doesn't condemn such people, even though he believes they are wrong. Rather he respects their conscientious convictions.

We find a lesson for us here—the need to respect other people for their convictions, just as we would like them to do the same for us. While we may not always agree, we can still live together in mutual respect.

Romans 14:15-23 moves from the problem of food that was disrupting the church to some general principles of Christian living. The first urges the "strong" not to hurt those who have scruples against certain kinds of foods by what they eat. William Barclay sums up Paul's counsel as "*it is a Christian duty to think of everything, not as it affects ourselves only, but also as it affects others*" (Barclay, *Romans*, p. 207). That thought represents an important aspect of Christian love. After all, we are in a sense the keepers of our brothers and sisters in the faith. What we do has an impact on those around us.

A second principle appears in verse 17: "the kingdom of God is not eating and drinking, but righteousness and peace and joy in the Holy Spirit." That verse used to offend me back in the days when dietary issues stood at the center of my religious experience. Only gradually did I come to see that while diet and good health were instrumental to balanced religion, we should not confuse them with religion itself. They are means to an end rather than the end itself. But great confusion has reigned in the church because of those who have confused ends and means.

Paul is quite clear that the central issues of religion are "righteousness and peace and joy in the Holy Spirit." Righteousness here is not merely related to a Christian's justified standing that brings peace and joy, but "in this context, 'righteousness' refers to that 'faithfulness to the community' which is lived out by the members of the congregation, 'peace' refers to that mutual behavior which is averse to all dissension, while 'joy' refers to the joyful cheerfulness with which afflictions are endured together within the church" as it awaits the Second Advent of its Lord (Stuhlmacher, *Paul's*, p. 228).

That thought emerges again in verse 19, in which the apostle tells us to "pursue the things of peace." The Bible makes it absolutely clear that when we love God we will love our neighbor (Matt. 22:36–39). The person who claims to love God and to be at peace with Him, yet who fails to live out God's love in peaceful relationship with other people—even people who differ from him or her racially, ethnically, or theologically—has something wrong.

Those who have met Jesus will be peacemakers. They will pass on the peace they have found with God (Rom. 5:1). This business of peace presents only two options. Either we will be peacemakers or we will be among those who increase alienation in the world and the church. That alternative brings us to Paul's point in Romans 14:19. Christians should be involved in building up one another. The only other path is to tear down or "destroy the work of God" (verse 20).

> Paul's lessons in Romans 14 are important to us. The church with its various strong-minded people had a difficult time getting along in Paul's day. It still does.

Verses 20b and 21 take us back to the topic of eating what some considered defiled meat. "It is good not to eat flesh or to drink wine or to do anything by which your brother stumbles" (verse 21). Here we need to emphasize again that Paul's main topic in Romans 14 is *not* eating or drinking or any other lifestyle issue. Rather, he is writing about the responsibility of each Christian not to be offensive to other Christians. In verse 21 he illustrates his point with eating, drinking wine, and doing anything else that might harm others. As with the defiled food, the wine drinking here referred to undoubtedly had to do with the fact that some of the Roman Christians found themselves troubled by the realization that some wine sold in the marketplace had been offered to a pagan deity as a libation. Thus Paul is not talking about abstinence, but abstinence for a *wrong* reason.

The entire passage running from Romans 14:13-23 highlights the responsibility Christians have for one another. Verse 21 focuses on the "strong" who should be peacemakers rather than entering into dispute or flaunting their understanding. Those who have a better grasp of the uniqueness of Christ and the gospel of salvation should, as their neighbors' keepers, live in such a way as not to offend others who have a less adequate faith.

But weaker brothers and sisters also have an obligation. They should not make an issue of all their beliefs, but keep their faith on the peripheral, disputed issues to themselves and between themselves and God (verse 22a). That is, they are not to be constantly advocating their particular convictions on this or that lifestyle issue as if it were a matter of salvation.

But even though Paul tells the "weaker" members not to agitate their views, he never downplays their importance to them as individuals in their walk with God. If they truly believe that God has convicted them on these matters, then it is wrong for them to transgress their beliefs. Thus Paul writes that "blessed is the one who does not condemn himself by what he approves. But the one who doubts is condemned if he eats" (14:22b, 23a).

We must not skim over these words lightly. Each of us is accountable to God for living up to our convictions. Even if they are mistaken, we need to be honest to them until God shows us a better way. To do otherwise would make us hypocrites in our own eyes and would be detrimental to our faith. Whenever we act in contradiction to our faith we are sinning (23b).

56. Lesson Number 8 in Transformed Living: Building Up One Another

Romans 15:1-6

¹Now we who are strong ought to bear the weaknesses of those who are not strong, and not to please ourselves. ²Let each one of us please his neighbor for his good, to build him up. ³For even Christ did not please Himself; but as it is written, "The reproaches of those reproaching You fell on Me." ⁴For whatever things were written in the past were written for our instruction, that through patience and through the encouragement of the Scriptures we might have hope. ⁵Now may the God of patience and encouragement give to you the will to think alike among yourselves, according to Christ Jesus, ⁶so that with unity of mind and with one voice you might glorify the God and Father of our Lord Jesus Christ.

Paul's advice in Romans 15:1 goes against the trend of all human history in every culture. Nearly everywhere the strong have tended to use their strength as a way to ease their personal burdens by making the weak bear them as well as their own. The strong rise to the top of any pyramid, and the weak become their servants. In fact, the strong in most systems see taking advantage of their own strengths as a natural right. "Society," so the idea goes, "owes me certain rights and privileges because of my talents, my education, or my powerful connections." The oppression mentality stands at the heart of "normal" living.

But Paul tells us that the "normality" of a sinful world is not to prevail in the church. Christians who are truly Christians, he asserts in various places, live by the law of love rather than the law of the jungle (see Rom. 13:8-10; Gal. 5:14). Instead of living by the accepted standards of a sinful world in which "might makes right," Christians are to exhibit "transformed" lives through the renewal of their minds in the ways of God's kingdom. They are to become "living sacrifices" in God's service (Rom 12:1, 2).

That was one of the hardest lessons for Christ's disciples to learn. The strongest among them, such as Peter and John, contended for the supreme places. One of Christ's most forceful lessons was that they were not to copy the world's patterns in such matters. Rather, Jesus said, they were to let their self be crucified (Matt. 16:24). In the new model the strong would be servants of the weak (Matt. 20:26).

A Lesson on Strength

One thing that Christianity teaches us is that God does not give us our strengths and talents and gifts for self-aggrandizement, but that we might more efficiently help others. What a wonderful place the church would be if we each let God "baptize" our strengths for service.

Such is the law of the kingdom of God and of Christ. In Romans 15:1 Paul tells us that the strong, among whom he included himself, needed not merely to tolerate the misunderstandings and foibles of the weak, but also to help them carry their burdens. A person of great talents, the apostle gave his life to serving those less capable and less enlightened than himself. And God is calling each of us today to that same ministry.

The definitions of "weak" and "strong" in Romans 15:1, of course, we must interpret in the context beginning in 14:1 and running through 15:13. The weak in that scenario were those who were immature in their faith regarding certain Jewish lifestyle issues in relation to the core meaning of the gospel.

Whereas in Romans 15:1 Paul was speaking to the strong, in verse 2 he is addressing both the strong and the weak. It is the responsibility of each church member to seek to build up every other member. Paul has now moved beyond the negative advice with which he began his extended treatment in Romans 14:3, in which he told the strong not to look down their noses at the scruples of the weak and the weak not to condemn those who weren't as strict as they were.

The apostle has now shifted from the negative to the positive with the injunction that everybody must work in unity to build up both those who agree with them and those who disagree.

Paul notes that the various segments of the church should aim at helping others for their "good" (verse 2). The point he is making is that we as Christians constantly need to seek to do for others what is for *their* benefit rather than ours. The definition of "good" for Paul in verse 2 is related to building up or edifying. Each Christian has a ministry to strengthen every other person in Christ.

In the context of Romans 14:1-15:13 that mutual upbuilding does not mean that the weak (those with overly sensitive consciences) should control the church by seeking to get everyone to live according to their majoring-on-minor-issues scruples or that the strong (those who understand the core of the gospel in its relation to such lifestyle issues as those raised in Romans 14) should despise the weak for their positions. Paul is not writing in Romans 15:2 about control, but rather is setting forth a principle of tender concern. The strong are to respect the weak, and vice versa. Of course, in Paul's mind (remember, he has linked himself with the strong in verse 1) genuine concern for the weak (those with an immature faith) implies an attempt to strengthen them over time by leading them out of their ill-founded scruples so that they will also be strong. He spent much of his ministry building up those weak in their faith and understanding.

Romans 15:3 sets forth Christ as an example in how to treat other people. Think about it. He could have come to earth with the attitude that in His Christian liberty He had a right to do as He pleased. After all, He didn't have to put up with all the foolish weaknesses of Peter and the other disciples. Christ could have said, "I have a life to live. Why should I be burdened with your stupidity? After all, I have already given you sufficient instruction."

Yet He didn't take that course of action. Patiently and repeatedly He bore the weakness of others. "His way," F. F. Bruce observes, "is to consider others first, to consult their interests and help them in every possible way" (Bruce, p. 240). Thus Paul sets forth Christ in Romans not only as a Christian's Savior, but also their example. In the context the apostle is suggesting that, given the example of Jesus, the strong in the church will not push for their rights to do what they want in spite of the scruples of the weak. Nor will the weak condemn others. Both groups will work toward unity.

Romans 15:3 not only points toward service to other church members, but also service to God, a concept reflected in the quotation from Psalm 69:9. Christ came to do the Father's will, to serve the Father in spite of the insults that such service brought from both those inside the church and from those on the outside.

The use of that quotation led him in Romans 15:4 to state that those things written in the Hebrew Scriptures were for the instruction of the church that it might have hope in spite of difficulties. Thus "he believes, like his Jewish contemporaries, that" God's Word "remains relevant to new situations" (Keener, p. 444). That thought is important for at least two reasons. First, our faith is strengthened when we see how God faithfully led His people down through Jewish history. They didn't always follow Him, but He never gave up on them. I find that encouraging because I live in a church equally less than perfect and know that He is still leading in spite of some of our individual and corporate blunders. Paul's remark in verse 4 about the Old Testament's applicability to Christianity is also vital because he will soon present a whole battery of scriptural quotations on the Jewish/Gentile issue in verses 9-12.

Romans 15:5 moves on to a prayer thought in which Paul prays that their patient and encouraging God might give them the will to "think alike" or "live in . . . harmony with one another" (RSV). His ultimate aim for them is that they might "with unity of mind and with one voice" glorify God (verse 6).

We find a most interesting picture of the church in Romans 14 and 15. The various members obviously had differences that they believed to be quite serious. In times past those varying perspectives had led to divisions in the church, with each faction judging and condemning the other. They still had genuine disputes on several issues that some of them believed were important to their Christian faith. And while Paul didn't agree that everything some of them desired to have unity on was vital, yet he didn't want them to change unless they felt genuinely convicted to do so. Rather, he counseled mutual tolerance.

Why? So that they might with one mind and voice glorify God (15:6). The point is—and it is an important one—that they didn't need to agree in every detail of belief or on every one of the lifestyle issues that had been dividing them. They could by demonstrating Christian love and tolerance for each other still exist in harmony.

On the other hand, if they continued to beat each other up over their differences, they could hardly glorify God in their community. But if they could gracefully allow for individual perspectives on points not central to the Christian faith, they could demonstrate a genuine witness for God to others.

The real purpose of the harmony among believers that Paul has been calling for is that "the God and Father of our Lord Jesus Christ" might be glorified and honored (Rom. 15:6). Unfortunately, constant bickering among church members glorifies no one except the devil himself. Paul here makes a heartfelt call/prayer for Christians to put away those differences that aren't central to their faith and to begin to live as Christians should.

God wanted the Roman Christians to have the character of Christ, expressed in such fruit as love, joy, and peace. Yet they, in their desire to do everything "right" on the one hand and to live in Christian freedom on the other, presented a picture to non-Christians of anything but love, joy, and peace.

Romans 14 and 15 contain an important lesson for the twenty-first century church. We need to put our differences to one side so that our lives and our congregations might truly be a glory to God rather than warts in the kingdom.

57. Hope, Joy, and Peace for All— Both Jew and Gentile

Romans 15:7-13

[7]Therefore accept one another even as Christ accepted you, for the glory of God. [8]For I say that Christ became a servant to the circumcised on behalf of the truth of God to confirm the promises to the fathers, [9]and for the Gentiles to glorify God for His mercy. As it is written,

> *"Therefore I will praise You among the Gentiles,*
> *And I will sing praise to Your name."*

[10]And again he says,

> *"Rejoice, O Gentiles, with His people."*

[11]And again,

> *"Praise the Lord all the Gentiles,*
> *And let all the peoples praise Him."*
> [12]*And again Isaiah says,*
> *"The root of Jesse shall come,*
> *And the One who rises to rule the Gentiles,*
> *In Him shall the Gentiles hope."*
> [13]*Now may the God of hope fill you with all joy and peace in believ-*
> *ing, so that you may abound in hope by the power of the Holy Spirit.*

A ccept one another." With those words Paul returns to the beginning of his argument in Romans 14:1. In fact, he sandwiches the extended, closely reasoned discussion about the strong and the weak between two cries for acceptance: "Accept the one who is weak" (14:1) and "accept one another" (15:7). The apostle addresses both pleas to the whole congregation at Rome, even though the first urges the church to welcome the weaker brother and the second entreats all church members to accept each other.

John Stott points out that both pleas have firm roots in a theological rationale: "The weak brother is to be accepted *for God has accepted him* (14:3), and the members are to welcome each other *just as Christ accepted you* (7a)" (Stott, p. 371).

Paul has stopped dividing his readers into the strong and the weak. The apostle, we should note, intimately relates their acceptance of each other to justification by faith. Just as Christ has received other believers on the basis of their faith in Him, so are we as fellow believers to accept one another. Or, as Paul put it earlier in his argument: "God has accepted him. Who are you to judge another's servant?" (14:3, 4). When Christ has accepted someone, who am I to say that I will not take him or her as a Christian brother or sister on the basis of differences involving some marginal lifestyle issue?

Those are important questions. And they raise once again the spiritual arrogance of those who have assumed a throne and made themselves judges over their fellow church members. Have we forgotten that we were also unworthy and still are unworthy? Has it slipped from our minds that our own membership in the community is on the basis of grace rather than that of our accomplishments?

Our acceptance of others also rests upon the gospel of grace. Of course, some of "those people" are disgusting. But then, so are you and I! Christianity is not a religion of the big head. It leaves no room for spiritual pride.

No! Just as God has accepted me with all of my faults, so must I accept others on the same basis. Christianity is a religion of living the transformed life (Rom. 12:2), of demonstrating God's grace and love in daily practice. When we forget that truth, we have forgotten what the point of it all is.

With Romans 15:8, 9 Paul has picked up a theme that has run throughout the book from chapter 1—the issue of the tension between Jews and Gentiles. Please note that he has rather subtly shifted his discussion from the weak and the strong back to the Jews and Gentiles. "This suggests," Ernst Käsemann points out, "at least that the conflict depicted earlier [chapter 14] has something to do with the diverse composition of the church at Rome, or, more precisely, that it involves the relationship between a Jewish-Christian minority and the Gentile-Christian majority," the weak and the strong, respectively (Käsemann, p. 384).

Thus the lines of separation that ran through the Christian community in Rome did not merely involve theological and lifestyle differences, but also racial, ethnic, and cultural ones. All of that seems rather modern. We need Paul's counsel to the Romans just as much today as when he first wrote it. The faces, names, and nationalities of the people involved might change, but the problems of individuals and groups remain basically the same across time and space. So it is also with the Bible's solution to those fundamental difficulties. For that reason the Bible is able to speak across the millennia and across cultures.

The good news Paul trumpets in Romans 15: 8, 9 is that salvation is open to both Jews and Gentiles. That truth was self-evident to the Jews in regard to themselves since they had "the promises to the fathers" (verse 8), but it needed to be demonstrated that those promises also included the Gentiles. Thus in order to substantiate the fact that Paul "derives his understanding of the mission of the Messiah from Scripture," he "follows his explanation in 15:8-9a with a lengthy chain citation" from the Hebrew Bible in verses 9b-12 (Beale, p. 688). That chain builds on verse 4, in which the apostle told his readers that God inspired the Old Testament Scriptures so that future generations would have hope. Verses 9-12 present four hope-filled quotations, at least one from each major division of the Jewish Bible—one from the Law, one from the Prophets, and two from the Writings. Through them Paul asserts that all the recognized divisions of Scripture witness to the fact that the Gentiles have their place in God's "mercy" (9a) or salvation.

There appears to be a definite progression as the apostle moves through his four quotations. The first quotation (9b) is one in which the psalmist praises God among the Gentiles. While it is natural to find a Hebrew singer praising God, Paul selected Psalm 18:49 because it demonstrates that such praising will take place in the presence of the Gentiles.

The second quotation (Rom. 15:10), taken from Deuteronomy 32:43, calls on the Gentiles to rejoice with Israel. One author has pointed out that "God has brought the blessings of salvation to both, and it is well accordingly that they rejoice together" (Morris, *Romans*, p. 505).

Paul's third quotation (verse 11), from Psalm 117:1, finds the Gentiles praising God independently of Israel. The fourth quotation (verse 12), from Isaiah 11:10, goes back to the foundation of salvation for both Jews and Gentiles. It speaks of "the root of Jesse," the only One in whom sinners can hope. The name of Jesse pointed Paul's readers back to the great king David. He belonged to the lineage of Jesse, and the Messiah or Christ was to come through that same line. The significance of Isaiah 11:10 for Paul is that it explicitly stated that the Messiah would be not only for the salvation of the Jews but also of the Gentiles, thereby reinforcing the conclusion of Romans 11:32 that God has mercy upon "all."

> "'Hope' in the NT does not mean 'wishful thinking,'" but "'a confident expectation'" (Harrison, p. 216).

With Romans 15:13 Paul has reached the end of the massive argument that he began in Romans 1:18. For 15 intense chapters he has hammered home what it means to be a Christian.

Now he is ready to stop. But how should he conclude? Given the power and logic of his argument he could have ended with a triumphalistic "I'm right and you're wrong" or "Now you have the real truth, so quit arguing."

But the apostle is out to win souls, not arguments. Thus he concludes the most influential presentation of salvation in the history of Christianity with a prayer.

He begins with the pregnant phrase "the God of hope." Hope expresses a central part of what the gospel is all about. A Christian is one who has hope. On what basis? "The God of hope." Everett Harrison points out that it is God who both "inspires hope and imparts it to his children" (Harrison, p. 216). Because God is faithful we can trust Him to fulfill His promises.

Paul prays that "the God of hope" will fill his Roman readers (and us) with joy and peace as they trust in Him. Here we have three more of his favorite words. Paul uses "joy" more than any other New Testament writer. And the church of every age needs to grasp that emphasis. Too many congregations remind me of a visit to the city morgue rather than a place of rejoicing. From the apostle's perspective the saved have plenty to rejoice about. Paul wants not only joy for believers, but also "peace," which they have because of their reconciliation to God (Rom. 5:1). His prayer connects Christian joy and peace to "believing," which is appropriate since all of a Christian's blessings are related to trust in the One who is hope Himself.

Paul closes his short prayer with the wish that those who trust in God will "abound in hope" or "overflow with hope" (NIV) through "the power of the Holy Spirit." Here we find the third mention of hope in two verses. The apostle knew that the world of his day was hopeless without Christ. More than anything else people needed hope. Things haven't changed. The world still longs for hope. That is why the gospel is so important. It is a message of hope, joy, and peace for those who through the Spirit learn to trust in the "God of hope."

We need to join Paul in his prayer. In addition, we must pray for both ourselves and others, that we might have the confirmed hope of salvation and the joy and peace that flow out of that hope. Amen!

Part VII

Saying Goodbye

Romans 15:14-16:27

58. A Tactful Introduction to Mission

Romans 15:14-21

> *[14]And I myself am confident my brothers concerning you that you your-selves are full of goodness, filled with all knowledge and able to admonish one another. [15]But I have written boldly to you in part so as to remind you again, because of the grace given to me from God [16]to be a minister of Christ Jesus to the Gentiles, ministering as a priest the good news of God, so that the offering of the Gentiles may be acceptable, sanctified by the Holy Spirit. [17]Therefore in Christ Jesus I have reason to boast in those things pertain-ing to God. [18]For I will not dare to speak of anything except what Christ has accomplished through me that has resulted in the obedience of the Gentiles, by word and deed, [19]in the power of signs and wonders, in the power of the Spirit; so that from Jerusalem and around to Illyricum I have fully proclaimed the good news of Christ. [20]And thus I aspired to preach the good news, not where Christ has already been named, so that I might not build on another's foundation; [21]but as it is written,*
>
> > *"Those to whom He had not been proclaimed will see,*
> > *And those who have not heard will understand."*

Paul has taken us a long way in his letter to the Romans, providing us with a tour de force on the plan of salvation. After introducing him-self to the Romans (Rom. 1:1-17) he immediately directed his readers to the basic problem of all humanity—sin (Rom. 1:18-3:20). It is that prob-lem that sets the stage for the rest of his Epistle.

The third step on Paul's journey took his readers through the wonders of justification by grace through faith in the sacrifice of Christ (3:21-5:21). They discovered that justification by faith is for Paul the basic platform on which everything else in a Christian life rests. And, he was careful to indicate, that just as every person is a sinner, so the only hope for every person is God's gracious gift in Jesus.

From justification Paul moved on to a guided tour of godliness, or what we might call living the sanctified life (6:1-8:39). From there he went on to point out that salvation is for everyone—both Jews and Gentiles (9:1-11:36). And finally he presented a word picture of what it means to live God's love in the real world of personal, civic, and church life (12:1-15:13). For Paul, getting saved was not an esoteric experience related to some private realm of the religious. To the contrary, the saved person lives as a saved person. It affects every aspect of existence.

With Romans 15:14 Paul is ready for the final step. He has finished his presentation of salvation. Now he is about to say goodbye. But in the process in Romans 15:14-16:27 he provides some reasons for writing his letter (15:14-21), outlines his future travel plans (15:22-33), and sends greetings to the people he knows in Rome (16:1-27).

In Romans 15:14 we find the apostle at his tactful best. In harmony with his statement in Romans 1:8 that their faith was well known, he writes that he is fully aware of their knowledge of the gospel and their ability to instruct one another. "But," he asserts in verse 15, he has written them some very strong (bold) things because of his apostolic commission. In this paragraph he does not explain the nature of his strong counsel but it was undoubtedly the great truth of the gospel that he had set forth in the first 15 chapters of Romans, and especially the issues related to the harmony between Jews and Gentiles that at one level form the backdrop of the letter. In the process, of course, Paul had undoubtedly provided them with inspired insights into the gospel that they had not realized before, an ongoing function of Romans throughout the centuries.

Meanwhile, verses 14 and 15 present us with a glimpse of a balanced ministry that provides a pastoral ideal worthy of emulation by all of us. Thus a genuine Christian not only can fearlessly rebuke sin and error, but he or she has a tact softened by love and care for those who are the object of ministry. Both boldness and tact need to blend in those who work for Christ as either laypeople or clergy. Unfortunately, some have boldness but lack tact. Such individuals know how to scourge people but are unable to win their love and confidence. On the other hand, others are so tactful that they never get to the point. A study of Paul's characteristics in Romans 15:14, 15 is of great value because he exemplified the needed balance between tact and boldness.

The apostle proceeds in verse 16 to the purpose of the grace that God had given him (verse 15), namely that he was "to be a minister of Christ Jesus to the Gentiles, ministering as a priest" to them the gospel message. His use of the priestly function of ministry here is unique in the New Testament, which sets forth Christ as the Christian's priest (Heb. 4:14-5:10), but it lines up with the idea of his Gentile converts being offerings presented to God.

Apparently Paul is taking his readers back to Romans 12:1, in which he urged the Romans to "offer" their "bodies as a living sacrifice." Thus he preached the gospel to the Gentiles so that they might offer themselves to God as an act of "spiritual worship" (12:1). That entire sequence, Leon Morris points out, "points to the thoroughgoing commitment which Paul demanded of his Gentile converts" (Morris, *Romans*, p. 511).

The success of his work among the Gentiles, Paul tells us in Romans 15:17, provides him a reason to "boast in those things pertaining to God." Here is a man who has had a great deal to say against boasting in Romans (see 3:27; 4:2; 2:17), yet here is boasting himself. But there is a crucial nuance here. He is not glorying in himself as he did in his pre-Christian days (see Phil. 3:4-6), but in what God has been able to do through him in bringing men and women to Jesus for salvation.

Paul highlights that thought in verse 18, in which the apostle asserts that he wouldn't "dare to speak of anything except what Christ has accomplished through me that has resulted in the obedience of the Gentiles" in both how they live and how they speak.

"Obedience" is an important word in Romans 15:18. While many people read Romans as if it were somehow for faith and against works, the book itself teaches just the opposite. In fact, Paul brackets it with the phrase "the obedience of faith" (1:5; 16:26). While he is dead set against the idea that good works are effective in achieving salvation (Rom. 3:20), he is just as emphatic that faith results in obedience or good works. That is a lesson reflected in the very structure of Romans, which first gets people justified (3:21-5:21) and then moves on to their subsequent obedience (6:1-8:39; 12:1-15:13). And just as obedience in Romans 15:18 signifies that the Gentiles "had left their former way of life and committed themselves to the service of Christ" (Morris, *Romans*, p. 513), so it means exactly the same for each believer in the twenty-first century.

Romans 15:19 tells us two things about Paul's ministry. First, that it was accomplished through the power of the Holy Spirit. And, second, that he preached "from Jerusalem and around to Illyricum." One interesting thing about that verse is that he never had a mission to the Gentiles in Jerusalem. Nor did he ever preach in Illyricum (today's Albania and the various divisions of the old Yugoslavia). Apparently what he meant was that he had evangelized from one to the other. It would be like people saying that they had traveled all over the United States from Canada to Mexico. Such a statement does not claim that they had visited either Canada or Mexico but that they had journeyed throughout the land in between. In a missionary ministry that took him to Turkey, Greece, and Macedonia, Paul's three missions, given the difficulty of travel in the first century, were a stupendous accomplishment. He is the missionary par excellence in the New Testament and a model for those to follow in the next two millennia.

That thought brings us to Paul's personal mission statement in Romans 15:20, 21. He wasn't merely a missionary, but a "pioneer missionary" whose task was to enter new territory to present the gospel message. He was well aware that not all Christians or even Christian missionaries had a pioneering role, that there were various kinds of functions in God's service. Thus he could write to the Corinthians that some plant and others water and that there are those who lay a foundation and those who build upon it (1 Cor. 3:6-14).

Yet while he appreciated the division of labor in the missionary enterprise, he firmly believed that his divine calling was to be that of a pioneer to that part of the world yet to be reached by the Christian message (Romans 15:20), reinforcing his position with a quotation from Isaiah 52:15 in verse 21.

If that is true, we need to ask, then why is he spending so much time and energy writing a letter to the Roman Christians, who belong to congregations that he had not founded or even visited (Rom. 1:13-15)? The answer becomes evident in Romans 15:22-33, in which Paul tells the Romans once again (see 1:8-15) of his plans to visit them as he turns his eyes toward pioneering work in Spain (15:24). It is to those plans that we now turn.

59. Missionary With a Plan

Romans 15:22-33

²²*For this reason I have often been hindered in coming to you. *²³*But now, no longer having a place in these regions, and having had a desire to come to you for several years *²⁴*whenever I travel to Spain, I hope to see you while passing through and to be sent onward by you from there, after I have been satisfied with your company for a while. *²⁵*But now I am going to Jerusalem to minister to the saints. *²⁶*For Macedonia and Achaia have been pleased to make a contribution for the poor among the saints in Jerusalem. *²⁷*They were pleased to do so because they are debtors to them. For if the Gentiles shared in their spiritual things, they ought also to minister to them in material things. *²⁸*Therefore, after I have completed this, and have put my seal on this fruit to them, I will go to you on my way to Spain. *²⁹*And I know that when I come to you, I will come in the fullness of the blessing of Christ.*

³⁰*Now I urge you, brothers, by our Lord Jesus Christ and through the love of the Spirit, to strive together with me in your prayers to God for me, *³¹*that I may be rescued from those who are disobedient in Judea, and that my service in Jerusalem might be acceptable to the saints; *³²*so that by God's will I may come to you in joy and be refreshed in your presence. *³³*Now the God of peace be with you all. Amen.*

Paul has come to another turning point in his letter. In verses 14-21 he laid out his basic reasons for writing to the Romans. Now he turns in the rest of chapter 15 to his future plans. He intends to begin pioneer missionary endeavors in Spain, and on the way he hopes to visit Rome. But before then he needs to bind off his labor in the east by traveling to Jerusalem with an offering from the Gentile Christians to their Jewish brothers and sisters in the faith. Unfortunately, we know from the book of Acts, that visit will lead to his arrest and his appeal to Caesar (Act 21:17-26:32). In the end he will reach Rome not as a pioneer missionary but as a prisoner of the Roman government.

Meanwhile, Romans 15:22-33 teaches us some important lessons about Paul. For one thing, he was a man with a plan (verses 22-26). He knew exactly what he desired to accomplish in life and precisely what steps he needed to take to fulfill his goals.

Of course, his plan in this case did not work out. And that frustrated scheme raises the question of planning in the believer's life. Some Christians act as if it is some sort of sin to figure out things beforehand—that God will lead them step by step without any direct involvement on their part. Here they are in disagreement with Paul, who had a plan, but who kept himself flexible so that he could adjust to changing circumstances as God opened and shut doors in his life. He planned, yet he also followed God's leading providence. Before leaving the concept of Paul as a man with a plan, we should note that he was persistent in seeking to carry it out. Thus it was that he had "often been hindered" in going to Rome, but that was still his intention. No matter how long it took, he kept plodding toward his goal. It is better to dream dreams and have them fail than to have no dreams at all. Without such dreamers of dreams progress will never take place.

> It is better to dream dreams and have them fail than to have no dreams at all. Without such dreamers of dreams progress will never take place.

A second thing we learn about Paul from Romans 15:22-33 is that he was a person who had his priorities straight. Even though he had completed his pioneering work in the eastern Mediterranean, had repeatedly desired to visit Rome for several years, and was eager to begin evangelizing Spain (verses 22-24), he believed that he had not quite finished his mission in the east. In particular, as the apostle to the Gentiles (Gal. 2:7, 8), a sector of the church that was beginning to overwhelm the Jewish Christian minority, he knew that he needed to make a major gesture of peace and healing in the east before moving on to new fields of missionary activity.

Thus he points out in Romans 15:25 that he must minister to the believers in Jerusalem. To that end he had spent a great deal of time and effort to raise money from the predominantly Gentile churches in Macedonia and Greece in a good-will gesture to help the Jewish Christians in the faith's Jerusalem birthplace (verse 26; cf. 2 Cor. 8:1-9:15).

Cut off from the usual sources of Jewish charity because of their new beliefs, the Christians in Jerusalem had experienced poverty from the earliest days of the church (Acts 6:1-7). Many who had had property sold it to alleviate the situation (Acts 4:34-37), but that was only a temporary solution. Once the money was gone, they had nothing to fall back on. It is into that void that Paul enters with his relief plan. But for the apostle the program was more than for just physical aid, it was to help build the unity of the church. Thus it was of crucial importance to the spiritual health of those on both sides of the racial divide.

As a result, when Paul says that the Gentiles made a "contribution" he uses *koin nia*, a word that primarily means "*fellowship, close relationship, . . . sign of fellowship, proof of brotherly unity*" (Bauer, pp. 552, 553). Thus Paul's ministry to Jerusalem was aimed at being an outward expression of the deep love that binds Christians into one body, the church.

And that unity was certainly needed in the church of Paul's day. After all, we have seen the tension between its Gentile and Jewish factions since the opening chapter of Romans. As a result, he has gone to great lengths to demonstrate that not only are both groups united in the problem of sin (Rom. 1:18-3:20), but that both are saved in exactly the same way (3:21-6:14). Thus, he concluded in Romans 11:32, God has mercy upon "all"— both Jew and Gentile (cf. 1:16, 17).

It is in that context that the apostle uses the concept of putting his "seal on this fruit to them" (verse 28). That strange expression probably had to do with the commercial practices of the times. We know, for example, that merchants placed seals on sacks of grain to assure the recipient that "the grain he received was the full amount that had been placed in the sack" (Newman, pp. 286, 287). The seal indicated that all was in order. With that understanding in mind, John Knox's explanation is helpful when he points out that when Paul has delivered the funds for relief to the Jewish Christians "and when it has been received . . . in the hoped for spirit, Paul will have ended his divinely appointed work in Asia Minor and Greece" and "the 'fruit' of his mission will have been 'sealed'" (Knox, p. 652). At that point he would be free to move on to new challenges and opportunities in the West. Paul was a man of priorities. It was his aim to complete one task before beginning the next.

A third thing we learn about Paul in verses 22-33 is that he had a complex understanding of God's blessings. He affirms in verse 29 that "I know that when I come to you, I will come in the fullness of the blessing of Christ." Far from certain of today's "gospel of health and wealth" television preachers who give the impression that you are short on faith if you are not both wealthy and healthy, the apostle's life trajectory took quite a different path. His obedience to Christ cost him dearly both financially and physically (see, e.g., 2 Cor. 11:23-27) and he would finally arrive in Rome a prisoner—*but still with God's blessing.*

Thus he could write during his imprisonment that "what has happened to me has really served to advance the gospel, so that it has become known throughout the whole praetorian guard [the body of soldiers who attended the emperor and his family—10 cohorts of 500 soldiers each] and to all the rest that my imprisonment is for Christ; and most of the brethren have been made confident in the Lord because of my imprisonment, and are much more bold to speak the word of God without fear" (Phil. 1:12-14, RSV). Apparently Paul believed his own words that God "works everything together for good" "to those who love" Him (Rom. 8:28). Perhaps some of us need to line up with him as we seek to identify God's true blessings in our lives.

A fourth thing we discover about Paul is that he was a man of prayer. He not only prayed himself, but he desired the prayers of the Romans church for him as he sought to carry out God's will in the struggles of life (Rom. 15:30). And struggles he would have. In particular, he wanted the church to pray that he might "be rescued from those who are disobedient in Judea" and that his "service in Jerusalem might be acceptable to the saints" (verse 31).

He would be facing two major obstacles in his mission of mercy to the Jewish capital. First, the unbelieving Jewish leaders viewed Paul as their number one troublemaker, a man at the forefront of spreading what they considered heresy throughout the empire. Nobody is more hated than a person who trades sides in the midst of a battle. And here is Paul, the one who had been at the forefront of those persecuting Christians (Acts 8:3; Gal. 1:13; Phil. 3:6), now the head of the religion's new missionary outreach. As the book of Acts demonstrates, some of the Jews would be willing to lose their own lives if they could get rid of this troublemaker. (Acts 23:12-15).

But Paul also anticipates possible problems among the Jewish Christians whom he is trying to help. In particular, some of the conservatives saw him as a dangerous apostate who in his work with the Gentiles had abandoned some of their cherished religious concepts and practices (see especially the book of Galatians) and had become a dangerous innovator. Such might consider taking his Gentile money as a bribe that would "buy a condonation of his breaches of the [ceremonial] law" (Morris, *Romans*, p. 524). Thus, by accepting his gift they would be endorsing his teachings among the Gentiles.

Paul, of course, realized that many Jewish Christians hadn't yet fully grasped the meaning of what Jesus had done on the cross in regard to the ceremonial system. He hoped in prayer and faith that his bringing of aid from the Gentiles would help them see that all Christians were indeed on the same side of the great struggle against the powers of darkness.

Lastly, we find in Romans 15:22-33 that Paul is a man of peace. He closes off the formal part of his letter with a blessing of "peace" for his Roman readers (verse 33). His introduction expressed the same wish of peace (1:7). Altogether he employs the word 11 times in Romans, and in addition uses "peaceably" once, when he admonishes his readers to "live peaceably with all" (Rom. 12:18, RSV). A lack of peace has characterized the world since the entrance of sin. And Paul knows that the only way people can find peace is through a relationship with Christ (5:1, 10).

And the good news is that Paul's God of peace not only wants to give us that gift, but he desires that we pass it on to those we live with, work with, and go to church with. In short, the apostle desires for us to find the same God and become peacemakers.

60. Lessons From a List of Names

Romans 16:1-16
> ¹*Now I commend to you our sister Phoebe, who is a deacon of the church in Cenchrea, ²that you may receive her in the Lord as befits the saints and may stand by her in whatever matter she may need of you, for she herself has been a helper of many including myself.*
>
> ³*Greet Prisca and Aquila, my coworkers in Christ Jesus, ⁴who risked their own necks for my life, to whom not only I give thanks but also all the churches of the Gentiles; ⁵also greet the church in their house. Greet my beloved Epaenetus, who is the first convert in Asia for Christ. ⁶Greet Mary, who has worked much for you. ⁷Greet Andronicus and Junias, my kinsmen and my fellow prisoners, who are outstanding among the apostles, who also were in Christ before me. ⁸Greet Ampliatus, my beloved in*

the Lord. [9]Greet Urbanus, our coworker in Christ, and Stachys my beloved. [10]Greet Apelles, who is approved in Christ. Greet those of the household of Aristobulus. [11]Greet Herodion, my kinsman. Greet those of the household of Narcissus, who are in the Lord. [12]Greet Tryphaena and Tryphosa, who are laboring in the Lord. Greet Persis the beloved, who has worked much in the Lord. [13]Greet Rufus, the chosen one in the Lord, and his mother and mine. [14]Greet Asyncritus, Phlegon, Hermes, Patrobas, Hermas, and the brothers with them. [15]Greet Philologus and Julia, Nereus and his sister, and Olympas, and all the saints with them. [16]Greet one another with a holy kiss. All the churches of Christ greet you.

Romans 16:1-16 falls into two paragraphs. The first is a letter of commendation. Such letters were common in the ancient world since travelers were often unknown and needed hospitality as they carried on their ministry or other business in an era before the rise of trustworthy hotels or other accommodations (see Acts 18:27; 2 Cor. 3:1; 4:2; 5:12; 3 John 9, 10). The reason Paul is commending Phoebe is that she was undoubtedly delivering his letter to the Roman Christians, and he wanted them to give her all the assistance she needed.

Paul describes her as a "deacon" of the church in Cenchrea, a port city for Corinth. What is fascinating about the commendation is that he calls her a "*diakonos,*" a Greek word meaning "servant" or "deacon." The Revised Standard Version's rendering of the word as "deaconess" is a sexually biased interpretation rather than a faithful translation. The New Revised Standard Version has corrected that problem.

But what we really need to ask is what Paul intended by *diakonos* in this passage. Did he mean a person who provides various types of service (thus a servant) or was he telling his readers that she held the office of deacon, one found in such verses as Philippians 1:1 and 1 Timothy 3:8, 12.

Opinion among New Testament scholars is divided, with John Murray, for example, concluding that "there is neither need nor warrant to suppose that she occupied or exercised what amounted to an ecclesiastical office comparable to that of the diaconate" (Murray, vol. 2, p. 226) and James D. G. Dunn asserting that "Phoebe is the first recorded 'deacon' in the history of Christianity" (Dunn, *Romans 9-16,* p. 887). Thomas Schreiner buttresses the latter position with several arguments:

1. "The designation 'deacon of the church in Cenchreae' suggests that

Phoebe served in this special capacity, for this is the only occasion in which the term [*diakonos*] is linked with a particular local church."

2. "The use of the masculine noun [*diakonos*] also suggests that the office is intended."

3. Beyond those points, Schreiner indicates that 1 Timothy 3:11 "probably identifies women as deacons." "Of course," he adds, "we need to beware of reading into early church offices the full-fledged development that was realized later" (Schreiner, p. 787).

Whatever Paul may have had in mind by his use of *diakonos* in Romans 16:1, 2, the most remarkable thing about those verses is that he depicted Phoebe as playing an influential part in the Christian community. Not only did she bring Paul's precious Epistle to Rome, but she had been "a helper of many" in the church.

But Phoebe was not the only female singled out for special mention in the New Testament. After all, it was Mary of Bethany who had heard Christ's prediction of His forthcoming death, whereas all of the disciples had been blinded by their prejudices. As a result, she anointed Him for death (Mark 14:8). Again, it was women who stood by Christ on the cross (Matt. 27:56) while the disciples largely distinguished themselves by their invisibility. Likewise, women became the first heralds of the good news that Christ had risen (Luke 24:10, 11).

The long list of greetings to people in Rome in Romans 16:3-16 is remarkable, given the fact that Paul had never been there. Part of that is due to the fact that many of the Jews and Jewish Christians exiled from Rome by the emperor Claudius about A.D. 49 (*Suetonius*, 25.4; Acts 18:2) had now returned, and part of it resulted from the ease of travel in the Mediterranean basin made possible by the *Pax Romana* (Roman peace).

His greeting tells us several things about the early church. One is, once again, that women must have been fairly active. Of the 27 individuals that the apostle greets, 9 of them are women—Priscilla, Mary, Junias, Tryphena, Tryphosa, Persis, the mother of Rufus, Julia, and the sister of Nerus. That is a remarkable proportion in a society dominated by males.

A second thing we can learn from this list is that it speaks of a house church (verse 5). When we in the twenty-first century think of churches, we envision large structures that hold an entire congregation. That wasn't so in the early church. The first church buildings of which we have knowledge do not appear until the third century. Early Christians worshipped on a regular basis in the homes of leading members. Such groups not only were intimate for the members but apparently represented nonthreatening environments in which to do evangelism. On the other hand, Paul writes as if the church in Rome was a unified congregation. Yet we have no information on how they may have maintained their unity or the nature of the "glue" that held them together. Of course, it was the weakness of that glue between the Gentile and Jewish segments of the Roman Christian community that is at the forefront of Paul's extended letter to them.

Christian history has seen many variations of the house church model as part of a larger congregation. Prominent in that genre are the Wesleyan "class meetings" of the eighteenth century and contemporary "cell groups" that help make Christian fellowship more vital and evangelism more effective.

Among the individuals Paul greets, probably the most recognizable to New Testament readers are Prisca (Priscilla) and Aquila (16:3), who were coworkers with Paul and are mentioned in such places as Acts 18:2, 18, 24-26; 1 Corinthians 16:19; 2 Timothy 4:19. But in many ways the most intriguing is Rufus (Rom. 16:13). That name takes our minds back to Mark 15, in which we find Roman soldiers compelling "a passer-by, Simon of Cyrene, who was coming in from the country, the father of Alexander and Rufus, to carry [Jesus'] cross" (Mark 15:21, RSV).

The Gospel writer obviously made his comment because his readers knew Rufus and Alexander. That suggestion is especially pertinent in regard to the list in Romans 16 since it is generally held that the Gospel of Mark was written primarily for the Christian community in Rome. Thus it is that the Rufus in Romans 16:13 just might be the same Rufus whom Mark calls the son of Simon of Cyrene.

That point cannot be proven, but what we can demonstrate by the two uses of the name of Rufus is that God knows each of His children personally. Thus we won't get lost in the cracks of a large church of innumerable other Christians. God remembers even Rufus, whose father had such an interesting part to play in Christ's crucifixion. He thinks even of Rufus in the church of Rome. Most significant is not the possibility that they were the same person, but that they were remembered at all.

As Jesus one time put it, God numbers even the hairs of our heads. We are personal to Him. He knows us by name. Each of us is significant to Him as individuals. Rufus, Paul tells us, was "the chosen one in the Lord" (16:13). That is true of every Christian, so since Paul highlighted it in Rufus's case, it must have meant that he had a special responsibility for God.

Paul also notes that Rufus's mother was his mother. I doubt that he and Rufus were blood brothers. Rather Paul is stating his closeness to her and the fact that all Christians belong to the family of God. Thus we have many brothers and sisters and mothers and fathers in the faith, as well as sons and daughters. And as in our earthly families, as Christians we have special responsibilities to our relatives in the faith.

The apostle closes off his long list of greetings with a command to "greet one another with a holy kiss" (16:16). The New Testament makes it plain that the holy kiss was a common form of greeting in the early church (see 1 Cor. 16:20; 1 Peter 5:14; 2 Cor. 13:12; 1 Thess. 5:26). Yet Christians don't practice that greeting in most parts of the world today. Why? Partly because the holy kiss tended often to become unholy. Thus it is that Clement of Alexandria (c. 150-c. 215) writes of people who "make the churches resound" with kissing. He then points out that "the shameless use of a kiss . . . occasions foul suspicions and evil reports" (Clement, *Youth's Instructor 3.11*). Beyond that, forms of greeting have altered across time. Today the handshake, the warm smile, and more recently a hug hold a similar place to the holy kiss of the early church.

But the most important thing is not the form of greeting but the greeting itself. People need and deserve a warm greeting when they attend church. One of the most unfortunate experiences is visiting a strange church and not being greeted warmly or even acknowledged at all. Such experiences raise the question of whether we are truly in the house of the God whom Scripture describes as caring.

61. A Disruptive Intermission

Romans 16:17-23

> [17]*Now I urge you, brothers, to watch out for those who cause divisions and obstacles in opposition to the teaching which you learned, and turn away from them.* [18]*For such persons do not serve our Lord Jesus Christ, but their own appetites, and through smooth speech and false eloquence deceive*

the hearts of the simple-minded. [19]For news of your obedience has reached to all people. Therefore I rejoice over you, but I desire you to be wise in what is good and innocent to the evil. [20]And the God of peace will crush Satan under your feet soon.

The grace of our Lord Jesus be with you.

[21]Timothy my coworker greets you; and also Lucius and Jason and Sosipater, my kinsmen.

[22]I, Tertius, the one who has written this letter, greet you in the Lord.

[23]Gaius, my host and that of the whole church, greets you. Erastus, the city treasurer, greets you, and Quartus, the brother.

[Verse 24 ("The grace of our Lord Jesus Christ be with you all. Amen.") is not in the most reliable Greek manuscripts.]

Romans 16:17-20 catches us by surprise. Here right in the middle of a series of cordial greetings (verses 1-16, 21-23) we find a strong warning against false teachers. Why?

Paul had just spoken in verse 16 about the holy kiss, signifying the church's unity. But based upon unfortunate experiences with dissidents in other congregations, he is well aware of what can take place in the Roman Christian community. Thus the impassioned warning that we find in verses 17-20.

That pastoral concern has influenced church leaders across the 20 centuries of Christian history. Pope Leo X, for example, issued a papal bull against Martin Luther in the early 1500s, complaining that a "wild boar" was ravishing God's "vineyard" (*Exsurge Domine*, in Bainton, p. 114). Luther, of course, was not doing that. To the contrary, he was more like an Old Testament prophet calling a wayward church back to its biblical roots.

But wild boars do ravish the church from time to time. That is what Paul warns about in verse 17. If that is so, we need to ask, how can we distinguish between "wild boars" destroying the unity of the church and prophetic voices calling the church back to the truth?

We find the answer in the second half of verse 17. Paul notes that those causing the problem are out of harmony with the doctrine that "you learned" from those faithful apostles who founded the church in Rome and other places. In that concept we have an insight similar to that of Jude 3, which reads: "Contend for the faith which was once for all delivered to the saints" (RSV). The apostolic warning is to always go back to the "beginning" or the teaching of the apostles themselves (see 1 John 2:7, 24; 3:11).

Here is an important test that we can apply to all so-called reformers. Do their teachings agree with the doctrines of Christ and the apostles as reflected in their instruction preserved in the New Testament?

False teachers tend to stress ideas not emphasized in the Bible, or flatly contradict its teachings. Many of them produce a fistful of texts and quotations and declare the church apostate. But when we carefully and unemotionally compare their claims with the main themes of Scripture, they stand exposed as wild boars rather than true prophets. Things haven't changed all that much in 2,000 years. Paul's warning in Romans 16:17 is still important today. So is his solution.

He does not specify the precise difficulties being presented by those who might cause divisions in the Roman church, but from the tenor and content of the letter it probably had something to do with the fracture line that ran between the Jewish and Gentile sectors of the community.

Romans 16:18 reveals the motivation of those who might cause trouble as being "their own appetites." Such false teachers, he is saying, may seem to be sincere and caring, but their primary concern is not Christ or the church but self-interest and self-gratification. It makes no difference if their appetite is for fame, financial gain, or influence—at the bottom of it all is self-centeredness.

Some years ago one of America's most popular TV programs was *PTL*. The official name was *Praise the Lord*, but before the arrest of its "star pastor" many had begun to call it *Pass the Loot*. The program made constant appeals for more and more money as its leaders fed "their own appetites."

Paul speaks in verse 18 not only of the motivation of the false teachers he had in mind but their methodology. Surrounded by an aura of sophistication they deliberately set out to delude the unwary through "smooth speech and false eloquence."

The church, unfortunately, has never been short of the type of people Paul is talking about. They always want to "help," always have the "truth," and always tell us that everybody (including the church) is wrong except them. And they are slick and convincing. If we could only help them by supporting their ministry, they suggest, then the truth could get out, and Jesus could come. The result, as in Paul's day, is that sincere, "unsuspecting" believers lend their support and send in their money. But just as in Paul's day, Christians need to be wise.

Romans 16:19 finds the apostle switching tactics from warning about false teachers to commendation of the faithful. In a sentence that reflects his sentiments in Romans 1:8, he reiterates that Christians everywhere knew of the faithfulness of the believers in Rome.

Paul's Counsel on Handling Problems Before They Get out of Hand

1. Christians need to understand their Bibles and what they teach (16:17).
2. Christians must be discriminating rather than naïve in the face of those who would lead them astray (verse 18).
3. Christians should remember that prevention is nearly always better than a remedial cure (verses 17-19).
4. Christians need to commend God's people whenever they can truthfully do so (verse 19). Too many just tear down. God is looking for followers who can build up His church.

The apostle is obviously dealing with a church that is basically sound. True, they have some issues to settle, as his Epistle to them makes evident. But on the whole the church in Rome is a healthy congregation. They have faith, and that faith has led them into a walk with Christ that is obedient to God's will. Whatever problems the Roman church may have had, they hadn't as yet flared out into serious proportions.

It is that exact point that the apostle seems to be speaking to in Romans 16:17-20. Being a wise leader, Paul realizes that prevention is better than a cure, that it is better to head off a problem rather than to have to deal with its ugly complexities once it has invaded the church. All too often a congregation or even an entire church allows a bad situation to develop because no one has the courage to confront it. Often, "when the situation has fully developed, it is too late to deal with it. It is easy enough to extinguish a spark if steps to do so are taken at once, but it is almost impossible to extinguish a forest fire" (Barclay, *Romans*, p. 240). In Romans 16:17-20 Paul provides us with counsel for dealing with problems before they become all-consuming.

Romans 16:20 at first glance seems rather problematic. After all, there does seem to be a bit of a contradiction in the "God of peace" crushing Satan. It hardly sounds peaceful.

The idea behind the verse comes from Genesis 3:15. After Adam and Eve sinned in Eden, God promised them that eventually Satan would be defeated. As the passage itself puts it in a verse directed at Satan, God "will crush your head, and you will strike his heal" (NIV). The underlying meaning is that in the end the Lord would be victorious and that the results of Satan's attacks against Him would in the long run be inconsequential.

God will be victorious. That is good news. It is a part of the gospel. But how can we consider a Satan-crushing God as the Lord of peace? The answer to that question lies in the fact that His ultimate goal is the total destruction of those things that cause disruption, alienation, and death in our world. They all came in through the rebellion of Satan. Humanity will not have true peace until the results of Satan's work have been removed. Thus God in His desire for peace needs to move aggressively against Satan and the forces of evil. In the process of gaining ultimate peace in a world gone wrong, the God of peace must destroy those who disrupt that peace.

The first step in crushing Satan took place on Calvary's cross. When Jesus exclaimed, "It is finished" (John 19:30, RSV), He signified that the defeat of Satan had been ultimately sealed.

But even though the victory has been won, it hasn't been consummated. That will take place after the millennium, when God eradicates Satan and evil (Rev. 20:9-14). At that point the Lord will "make all things new (Rev. 21:5, KJV). He wipes "away all tears . . . ; and there shall be no more death, neither sorrow, nor crying, neither shall there be any more pain: for the former things are passed away" (Rev. 21:4, KJV). Finally, Satan will have been fully "crushed," and God can recreate this earth to represent the peace that stands at the very center of His character.

Paul's closing greetings in Romans 16:21-23 demonstrate two things. First that he did not work alone, but saw ministry as a team effort. Second, that as in his other letters, the apostle used a secretary or scribe who wrote the bulk of the letter as he received it from Paul. We see the easy going and collegial relationship between the scribe and Paul reflected in the fact that Tertius felt free to add his own greeting in verse 23. At that point,

F. F. Bruce suggests, "Tertius may have handed the pen to Paul. The sender of a letter in antiquity, after dictating most of it, frequently wrote the last few words in his own hand. Such an autograph . . . was Paul's authenticating mark in all his letters" (Bruce, p. 265). Thus we can think of Paul writing the rest of the letter himself, perhaps even in the "large letters" he used to complete his epistle to the Galatians (Gal. 6:11, RSV).

62. Praise to the One Who "Is Able"

Romans 16:25-27

[25]Now to the One who is able to establish you according to my gospel and the preaching of Jesus Christ, according to the revelation of the mystery which has been kept secret for long ages [26]but is now made clear, and through prophetic writings, according to a command of the eternal God, has been made known to all the nations, for the obedience of faith; [27]to the only wise God, through Jesus Christ, be glory forever. Amen.

God is able! That phrase is one of the most important in the entire book of Romans. Not merely is God willing to save and strengthen or establish us, but He is totally capable of doing so.

The proof of His ability is the resurrection of Christ. It was at His resurrection that Christ "was declared the Son of God in power" (Rom. 1:4). And through His resurrection Christ attained "the keys of Death and Hades" (Rev. 1:18, RSV). His resurrection is a guarantee not only of our resurrection, but of God's power to save us completely and fully.

God is able! And because He is able we who have accepted Christ can have assurance that the One in whom we have believed will fulfill every promise in the gospel. Paul began his letter to the Romans with statements regarding the gospel and God's power to save, and he ends it in this final doxology with the same thoughts. The Epistle's very first verse used the word "gospel," and that word provided Paul's theme throughout his letter (see Rom. 1:15-17). And now at the end Paul employs the word "gospel" for the last time. But just as he did in chapter 1, once again he ties it to the idea of power. God is able to do what He has promised to do. That is the best part of the good news.

But God isn't in the business of salvation by Himself. As in Romans 1:1, Romans 16:27 links God the Father and Christ in the gospel plan. Preaching Jesus, as Paul repeatedly asserts, is all-important because He died in our place on the cross. God is able because of Christ. Because of Christ's life and death God is in a position to give human beings His saving grace freely (see 3:21-26). "The wages of sin is death, but the free gift of God is eternal life in Christ Jesus our Lord" (6:23). That is the gospel.

The apostle refers to the gospel as a "mystery which has been kept secret for long ages but is now made clear . . . through prophetic writings" (16:26). When we encounter the word "mystery" in our day we usually think of something incomprehensible. The biblical concept is somewhat different. While it includes the idea of something "inaccessible to human reason," it moves beyond that limitation to the concept that that which has been previously hidden has been made known "primarily" by "the saving acts of God in Christ" (Balz, vol. 2, p. 447).

But, we need to ask, didn't Paul begin Romans with a statement that the "gospel of God" had been "promised beforehand through his prophets in the holy scriptures (1:1, 2, RSV)? And didn't the entire sanctuary service with its sacrificial system point to Christ's sacrifice? How can it be that the gospel has been hidden and "kept secret for long ages" (16:25) if the prophets had already revealed it?

The answer to such questions is that while the sacrificial service pointed to Christ, it was only a mere "shadow" of the real thing (Heb. 10:1). While the Israelites could learn much from the shadows of things to come, a great deal of how God would eventually fulfill His purpose still remained unknown.

But Christ cleared up those mysteries when He actually came to earth. As the book of Hebrews says: "In many and various ways God spoke of old to our fathers by the prophets; but in these last days he has spoken to us by a Son" (Heb. 1:1, 2, RSV). Christ is the fullest revelation of the gospel. Whereas the Old Testament could point with words at what the Lord would do, Christ hanging on the cross and crying out, "It is finished" (John 19:30), demonstrated in concrete action what God had done. The mystery hinted at and alluded to by the prophets was at that point in time fully revealed (Rom. 16:26). As Christians we stand in the full light of the cross.

The words "the obedience of faith" bring to mind the very first paragraph of the letter to the Romans, in which Paul noted that he had "received grace and apostleship to bring about the obedience of faith among all the nations on behalf of His name" (1:5).

It is significant that the phrase "the obedience of faith" appears in both the first and the last paragraphs of Romans. Paul had a good reason for his bracketing of the bulk of the letter. Some of his contemporaries saw red when he repeatedly emphasized grace. They got upset, assuming that he was doing away with law and obedience. Many people still see red on the topic today. If someone speaks of free grace, they mumble snide remarks about "cheap grace." Beyond that, just as in Paul's day, they often became aggressive toward the preachers of grace, treating them as if they have apostatized.

So what is new? Things haven't changed much since the time of the apostle, including misunderstandings of grace. But if we follow Paul we don't have much to worry about. After all, "free grace" is not the same as "cheap grace." Cheap grace is grace without response or cost, but God's free grace is the most costly thing in the world. It not only required the life of the Son of God on Calvary, but it demands the self-centered lives of those who accept it. Paul makes it clear in Romans 6 that accepting free grace means a total transformation of our whole being (cf. 12:1, 2)—a death to the old ways and a resurrection to a new way of life based on a new set of principles.

The apostle had it right. We don't earn salvation by works or lawkeeping (Rom. 3:20), but those who are saved through faith will obey. They will have the obedience of faith and will love God's law (1:5; 16:26).

It is no accident that Paul's great letter on salvation speaks of the "obedience of faith" at its beginning and ending. The concept remained one of his themes all through the Epistle. Obedience has no value outside of a faith relationship, but inside that relationship obedience is vital.

Paul concludes his letter with "to the only wise God, through Jesus Christ, be glory forever. Amen" (16:27). What a conclusion! The apostle understands that God Himself is the very epicenter of Christianity. His praise is everlastingly to God the Father and Christ Jesus the Son. It is to that God that Paul offers his final doxology. Giving glory to God is a fitting way to end a book. It is also a proper way to begin every day and every church service. When reading verse 27 it is difficult not to think of Fanny Crosby's familiar hymn "To God Be the Glory," which we should view as a review of the great salvific themes of Paul's letter to the Romans.

One of the most important things that we can say about Paul in the letter to the Romans and in his entire ministry is that he put God at the center. What the Lord had done for him personally in Christ was never far from his mind. He knew where the center was. While doctrine and how one lived were important to Paul, they were never the most important. Everything, he believed, stood in relationship to the grace of God, the sacrifice of Christ, and the ongoing work of the Holy Spirit.

Christianity for Paul was the extreme opposite of self-centeredness or those religious practices that lead people to focus on themselves and their achievements for God. For the apostle, God was all in all, and even human achievement reflected what He does in people. With God at the center, it is little wonder that Paul started his book by referring to himself as a slave to Christ (1:1) and concluded it with praise to God (16:27).

And that takes us to Paul's last "amen." He used the word five times in Romans (1:25; 9:5; 11:36; 15:33; 16:27), each time in connection with God and His salvational work in Christ. It is fitting that the apostle ends his letter with "Amen." The word means "truly" or "most certainly." As such, it is an affirmation of all that Paul has so beautifully stated about God and His salvational plan in Romans. By concluding with "Amen," Paul is saying that it is without question true and certain. We can all add our grateful amens to that.

> ## To God Be the Glory
>
> "To God be the glory, great
>   things He hath done;
> So loved He the world that He
>   gave us His Son,
> Who yielded His life an
>   atonement for sin,
> And opened the life gate that
>   all may go in.
> Praise the Lord, praise the
>   Lord, Let the earth hear
>   His voice;
> Praise the Lord, praise the
>   Lord, Let the people
>   rejoice;
> O come to the Father, through
>   Jesus the Son,
> And give Him the glory, great
>   things He hath done."
> —Fanny Crosby

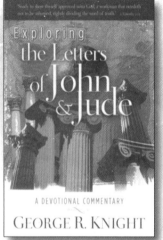
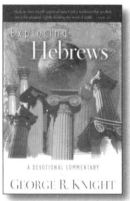
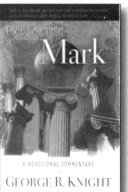
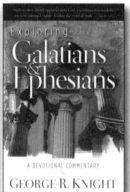
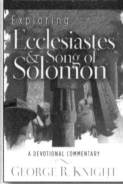